Our Sisters

The fight for justice for Christian women forced into marriage in Pakistan

Anna Townsend

Copyright © 2025 Anna Townsend

First published 2025 by Authentic Media Limited,
PO Box 6326, Bletchley, Milton Keynes, MK1 9GG.
authenticmedia.co.uk

The right of Anna Townsend to be identified as the Author of this Work
has been asserted in accordance with the
Copyright, Designs and Patents Act 1988.

All rights reserved.
No part of this publication may be reproduced, stored
in a retrieval system, or transmitted in any form or by any means,
electronic, mechanical, photocopying, recording or otherwise, without
the prior permission of the publisher or a licence permitting restricted
copying. In the UK such licences are issued by the Copyright Licensing
Agency, 5th Floor, Shackleton House, 4 Battle Bridge Lane, London SE1 2HX.

EU GPSR Authorised Representative
LOGOS EUROPE, 9 rue Nicolas Poussin, 17000, LA ROCHELLE, France
E-mail: contact@logoseurope.eu

British Library Cataloguing in Publication Data
A catalogue record for this book is available from the British Library.
ISBN: 978-1-78893-354-4
978-1-78893-355-1 (e-book)

Unless otherwise marked, Scripture quotations are taken from The Holy Bible,
New International Version Anglicised. Copyright © 1979, 1984, 2011 Biblica. Used
by permission of Hodder & Stoughton Ltd, an Hachette UK company. All rights
reserved. 'NIV' is a registered trademark of Biblica UK trademark number 1448790.

Scripture quotations marked CEV are from the Contemporary English Version
Copyright © 1991, 1992, 1995 by American Bible Society. Used by Permission.

Scripture quotations marked ESV are from The ESV® Bible (The Holy Bible, English
Standard Version®), published by HarperCollinsPublishers, © 2001 by Crossway. Used
by permission. All rights reserved.

Scripture quotations marked NCV taken from the New Century Version®.
Copyright © 2005 by Thomas Nelson. Used by permission. All rights reserved.

Scripture quotations marked NLT are taken from the Holy Bible, New Living
Translation, copyright ©1996, 2004, 2015 by Tyndale House Foundation. Used by
permission of Tyndale House Publishers, Carol Stream, Illinois 60188.
All rights reserved.

Cover design by Fresh Vision Design

Our Sisters is a deeply moving and courageous book. Anna Townsend sheds light on the painful reality of abduction, forced conversion and coerced marriages that Christian girls and women face in Pakistan. Yet she writes with compassion and hope, honouring the strength and resilience of these women. With careful research and personal storytelling, Townsend compels us to confront injustice and respond. This book is a call to action – one that urges us to stand for faith, freedom and dignity. A must-read for anyone who values human rights and the gospel's call to defend the vulnerable.

Nasir Saeed, founder and Director of the Centre for Legal Aid Assistance and Settlement UK

This is a powerful and important book. Through it we are introduced to the appalling treatment of Christian women and girls in Pakistan. The stories are harrowing, but need to be told and heard and Anna does a great job in making them accessible. Anna highlights appalling violence, as well as the corrupt and inadequate response of the justice system which leaves people with no redress or hope for change. Anna tells the stories of others, but also allows us to follow her own story including her learning, doubts and fears which enable all of us to set out on a similar journey, if we choose to do so.

In Chapter 13 Anna bravely brings the focus back to honour-based violence within Asian communities in the UK. Throughout the book there is an implicit question of what can we do? Anna does not let us off the hook, but gently suggests ways in which we can all get involved to make a difference.

Peter Grant, former International Director of DFID and Tearfund; co-founder of Restored

Forced marriage is a gross violation of human rights. It is a risk for persecuted women and girls in 42 of the 50 countries identified as most dangerous for Christians by Open Doors. The ensuing pain and trauma ricochet out to families, churches and communities. Anna's research into the abduction, forced conversion and marriage of young women and girls brings home the high cost of being a Christian in Pakistan. I am humbled by the bravery of these young women and girls to tell their stories and not be silenced. Their courage demands a response and, having heard, we must now ask the Lord how he is calling us to act.

Henrietta Blyth, CEO of Open Doors UK & Ireland

In *Our Sisters*, Anna Townsend embarks on an enlightening journey through time and across the world, guided by the Holy Spirit and a memory of a previous classmate's shocking disclosure, to collect the stories of courageous and resilient Pakistani Christian girls who have survived the harrowing atrocity of child marriage against all odds. She also looks at the men and women who put their lives and careers on the line to rescue victims and move mountains within the justice system. They strive towards a Pakistan which proudly displays its colourful social tapestry and empowers those who have been relegated to the frayed edges for far too long.

Ann Buwalda, Executive Director of Jubilee Campaign USA

Anna Townsend's powerful book sheds light on the harrowing realities faced by religious minority women and girls in Pakistan. Stories of abductions, forced conversions and forced marriages have too often been silenced.

Through a masterful blend of investigative journalism and compassionate storytelling, Townsend not only brings these stories to light but gives them the dignity of being heard. Drawing from firsthand accounts and rigorous field research, Townsend reveals the layers of trauma endured by victims – about young girls torn from their families, stripped of their faith and forced into lives of subjugation. The narrative is punctuated by moments of profound resilience: the whispered prayers of a mother fighting to reclaim her daughter, the quiet defiance of a young girl refusing to renounce her faith, and the unyielding courage of families seeking justice against all odds.

This book is more than an exposé; it is a call for global awareness and intervention. It urges policymakers, human rights advocates and global citizens to confront this crisis with the urgency it deserves. A profoundly important read, this book challenges our collective conscience and demands that we not only listen but act. Townsend has given a voice to the silenced, and it is incumbent upon us all to ensure that voice is heard.

Mervyn Thomas CMG, Founder President of CSW

I really think that Anna has done a great job with this book, and through writing it she has grown a deep awareness about the women who are being victimised on the basis of their beliefs and poor backgrounds. Being a reporter and human rights activist, I have reported on so many girls, children, who have been abducted and then forcibly married to Muslim men and compelled to live miserable lives after their forced conversions. No one can imagine the pain of these girls and their families who do not get justice after such persecution.

I hope the book *Our Sisters* will shed light on the cases of the victims, who are oppressed and facing multiple problems after their experiences. I salute Anna for her tireless efforts and courage in writing such a book. It shows the real face of this society where women are considered commodities and are still waiting for justice. I truly believe that this book will contribute to bringing about a positive change in society.

*Shafique Khokhar, human rights activist
and correspondent at AsiaNews*

Dedication

This book is dedicated to all the brave activists
and campaigners who selflessly stand up
for the vulnerable.

The Lord loves righteousness and justice;
the earth is full of his unfailing love.
Psalm 33:5

Contents

Acknowledgements		*xi*

Introduction – Two Inspiring Women and Two Starting Points — **1**

1	Heir – Cecil	12
2	Brave – Abhita	28
3	Lionheart – Joseph	44
4	Defiant – Mashaka	65
5	Girl Child – Nira	79
6	Word Wielder – Marcela	95
7	Speaker – Anna	112
8	Innocent – Shyla	117
9	Tide Turner – Saima	129
10	One of Us – Behien	145
11	Unexpected – Alam	156
12	Apple of His Eye – Emaan	176

13	Seeker – Anna	197
14	Magnifier – Becky	217

Conclusion   *237*
Bibliography   *247*
How to Help   *254*
Notes   *261*

Acknowledgements

Following the publication of my previous book, *Come with Me to Kathmandu*, I received heaps of support from friends and churches who helped organize the book's publication and gathered to celebrate. I'm hugely grateful to Heike, Carol, Rosie and Sue, who journeyed all the way to Belgium for the launch and to the talented team at IBC Jurbise, who constructed a TV-like studio at our church and helped me broadcast the launch on Facebook and YouTube.

My incredibly generous friends – Jenny, Tracy, and Jess – organized a simultaneous book-launch party in Huntsville, Alabama. Due to the time difference, it had to take place early in the morning, and I can't thank them enough, either.

Thanks to the support of good friends, I was invited to share about the book in many places. Special thanks go to everyone who helped organize these engagements and often hosted me in their homes as well: my parents Marilyn and John, Nic and his late wife Val, Jan, Kathy and Helen, Annie and Jack, Carol and the Dayspring faithful, Ali at Quench bookshop in Wokingham, Jane and her Soul Sisters, and *Holy Trinity's Woman's Hour*.

I am embarrassed to admit that I have never properly thanked the first person who encouraged me to write. She was my wonderful neighbour, Amanda Rooker, in Yorktown,

Virginia. Finding myself living next door to a bona fide book-writing coach was rather intimidating but has been an enormous blessing. I'm grateful for her patient encouragement with my first book, *Destination Transformation*, and I can track everything else I've written since then back to that springboard. Anyone can benefit from her wealth of book-writing wisdom by looking her up on LinkedIn under Split Seed Media; her posts are astute, insightful and vulnerable, and I eagerly look forward to reading each one.

Writing books about harrowing subjects can be isolating, but my community of Ko-fi followers has spurred me on with cups of coffee. Stuart has supported me for the longest time and invited me to talk about my work on his radio programme. Thank you.

Three women in Belgium have encouraged me to showcase my work more broadly. Thank you, Nicki, Nicola and Rosie, for shining a light for me. It has been a joy to pray regularly with local believers while living in Mons; I know our prayers have been heard, and I'm grateful for our unity.

My family has been supportive, as always, and I'm blessed to have Simon as my husband. He encourages me to be somewhat unconventional and spend a lot of time writing and reading. It's a privilege I don't take for granted, and I am so thankful.

This book has not been easy to write. I have had to rely on many people to connect with me and recommend me to others. First, Christian Solidarity Worldwide's Brussels office welcomed my research, and I appreciate the time Jonathan and Cecil gave me. Both Cecil and his sister Michelle in Lahore have been enormously helpful.

From the first time I met Joseph, I was enormously impressed with his passion. Although he has obligations all over the world, he has always made time to speak to me and opened up his wealth of contacts, including introducing me to his family. Thank you so much, and may God bless you in all your varied work. This book would be entirely different if I hadn't connected with Joseph at the European Prayer Breakfast, which I'm grateful to Carlton Deal for organizing and inviting me to.

The five young women I spoke to in Pakistan were courageous, and it was a privilege and honour to hear their stories. I hope they will each be safe and secure by the time this book is published, and they can look forward to the future with God-given hope. The picture I had of God placing them on a high rock far away from anyone trying to hurt them is still my prayer.

Marcela and Saima are incredibly bright and ambitious women. Thank you for sharing your stories. I pray you continue to shine a light on injustice and that you have the joy of knowing that action is taken thanks to your work.

Pastor Allam was so much more than I expected, and I'm delighted he was part of this book. May his work for God flourish, and I pray, too, that he remains safe.

The chance to include my friend Emaan's story was a wonderful experience. Thank you for being patient with me and explaining so much about Pakistan at the beginning of this process.

Finally, Becky was phenomenal. She is living an adventurous Christian life and seeing the lives of vulnerable women change in the process. Thank you for trusting me with your story.

It's all thanks to God that I have met these incredible people; he never lets me down. No matter where the British Army sends me and my husband, God is sovereign and always has a place prepared for us. Belgium was a rather unexpected house move, but it is immensely humbling to see how God has used our time here to connect me with people so I can continue to speak up for vulnerable women.

Introduction – Two Inspiring Women and Two Starting Points

Bonjour from Belgium. Only a couple of months ago, I found myself wondering why God had sent me to live in Belgium. Slowly it is becoming clear, and it appears that I am here because he wants me to write another book about women in Asia. I believe he wants me to raise awareness of how women are suffering there, and I hope you'll join me in my journey to discover how we can help. Let me explain.

I spent the last two years living in Nepal, where I run a Christian charity, Women Without Roofs – Nepal (WWR), that assists vulnerable women. While there, I was able to write my previous book, *Come with Me to Kathmandu*, yet now it is 2022 and I find myself an hour south of Brussels in a small city called Mons. Once again, I am here to accompany my British Army husband at his next posting. Belgium is a beautiful country that has seen enormous bloodshed over the last century, but life here is routine; there's a sense of justice and predictability. It's the complete opposite of the chaos and excitement of Kathmandu. Though I am back in Europe, my heart belongs to the women of Asia, many of whom suffer daily in difficult and degrading circumstances. I cannot forget them, and I hope to continue to act and write on their behalf here in Belgium.

One topic, in particular, has grabbed my attention: forced marriage. And in particular, forced marriage in Pakistan. Writing about this subject from within Pakistan would be dicey, so it's no wonder God has brought me to this haven in Belgium. As I am beginning to discover, numerous activists are also concerned about this issue, and many live nearby. It turns out I am in the perfect place to connect with and write about efforts to end forced marriage. Why did I ever question God's plans?

As soon as I consider forced marriage, which is both complex and upsetting, I immediately begin to ask God why. Why does he allow it? Why these women, and why does he appear to want me to write about it? It's an issue I have been thinking about for over a decade. Yet, apart from giving some money to a few charities working to stop it, I feel both ignorant about the intricacies of such an emotive issue and utterly powerless to prevent it.

My compassion for women abused by men and the communities who force them into marriage was first triggered in 2011. If you have read my book, *Come with Me to Kathmandu*, you may remember the story of Maria in Chapter 8. She grew up in a remote area of Nepal and came from an exceptionally impoverished and repressive community. When she was just 5 years old, her family began to send her on her own, for several months at a time, up a mountain to live with and care for a cow. It is a tradition that goes back centuries. While a teenager, she became a porter and carried cement and salt from the Nepali plains to mountain bazaars. By then, she was already married; like all the girls in her village, her parents gave her away in marriage before the onset of puberty.

Unsurprisingly Maria's first marriage failed; they had not chosen each other and were married to each other at such young ages. She eloped with a young man of her own choosing whom she loved dearly. They had children together, but calamity struck when he developed throat cancer. Having spent all their savings paying for various treatments to make him well, he died and left Maria as a bankrupt single mother. But further tragedy soon followed.

The village where Maria lived practised a folk version of Hinduism; there were no sacred texts since everyone was illiterate. Yet they all believed in evil spirits and, as a result, were highly superstitious. In particular, their world-view was shaped by belief in karma, the idea that one gets what one deserves. Consequently, the villagers believed Maria was to blame for her husband's death; therefore, she was bad luck and worthless. One man, in particular, began to harass her and eventually cornered her in a secluded paddy field, where he raped her.

Maria was raped by the same man more than once and, in the end, became pregnant. When Maria could no longer hide her baby bump, the village took action, and the elders met to discuss what should be done. To my profound astonishment and sadness their solution was to insist that the man take Maria into his home and marry her. Of course, Maria did not want this, and her enforced marriage only perpetuated his abuse of her. In the minds of the village elders, though, it was the only way this man could be made to take responsibility for Maria and her unborn child. And, in the eyes of everyone, she was ill-omened, and no one else would want to marry her anyhow.

When I first heard Maria's story, I was in shock. During one of my regular visits to Nepal, Esther, WWR's in-country manager, filled me in on Maria's background before I met her for the first time. Though I have explained the logic behind the villagers' actions above, in actual fact, it took me many years to understand why anyone would force a victim of rape to marry their attacker. I had never heard of such an occurrence in the West. It went against every sense of justice I possessed and all I understood about the value of human life. It was, to me, a colossal miscarriage of justice and a perversion of basic morals. When I met Maria, she was so gentle and kind. She had such a lovable and cheeky demeanour that my anger and perplexity only increased.

I began to ask God why and didn't get many answers. Passages such as Deuteronomy 22, in which God gave laws about the penalties for adultery and rape to the Israelites, also added to my confusion. Though in some versions it appears God might be condoning rape, other translations provided subtly different viewpoints. After wrestling with them, I felt that there was an underlying concern for consent; a couple found sleeping together would be treated differently depending on whether the woman had cried out for help to stop the man. If there was no one around to hear her screams, then she would not be punished.

I believed Maria did not deserve punishment, but I still wondered why God allowed such situations to occur. I felt confident that WWR existed to help women like her overcome their abuse and consequent marred identities. For a time, I pushed aside the why questions and focused on assisting in practical and relational ways. Often, it is far easier to deal with symptoms of injustice rather than tackle the underlying causes. I buried my head in the sand but couldn't forget Maria's story.

For many years my family has attended the New Wine summer church camps in the UK. For me, they are always times of refreshing and renewing my commitment to God and his purposes. At one conference in the early 2010s, I couldn't stop thinking about Maria's story. I wondered how many other women lived under repressive social norms and were forced to marry their rapists. I felt burdened for them and resolved to learn more and take action once I was home from the conference.

There was a lot to learn and discover. I trawled the internet for stories of rape and forced marriage, and collated my findings into a blog called 'QuiteCommon' (the blog still exists, although it is hopelessly out of date as I haven't been able to keep up with maintaining it). I called it 'QuiteCommon' since rape isn't so common as to be predictable, yet it isn't so rare as to be unnoteworthy.[1] As a result of these two factors, the issue is challenging to tackle, cropping up in myriad countries and contexts. Yet, unfortunately, it is never a significant enough problem to make headlines or draw all that much attention. I knew something had to be done but had no idea what that should be. So I signed up for various notifications and emails from non-government organizations (NGOs) and charities reporting on the issue and began receiving frequent news about cases of forced marriage. I also began to pray about the matter.

Pretty soon, it became apparent that rape and forced marriage happened more in Pakistan than anywhere else. Furthermore, I learned such abuse was used to persecute Christian and Hindu women and their families. Regularly, teenage girls were abducted from the street on their way to or from school, forcibly converted to Islam and then married to their assailant before being raped. It was hugely traumatic for them, and the families and communities to whom they belonged were also affected. Having witnessed such cruelty against their daughters and sisters, people feared that other girls would be targeted. In some cases, entire Christian families fled Pakistan.

The young Christian women of Pakistan remained on my mind. Although all my efforts at the time were directed towards helping women in Nepal, I could not forget them. It became clear that I might need to do more to help at some point, but I didn't know what that would be.

Maria was not the only woman to inspire me. In 2014, we moved to America and joined a church that provided aid to central Asia, including Pakistan. I went along to a prayer meeting for the region, and the leader asked about my interest and experience in the area. In my response, I didn't say a word about forced marriage and rape; at the time, these thoughts were just personal to me. Instead, the first thing that came to mind was to say that I had gone to school with many British Pakistanis, which was true.

Growing up in Reading, a large town forty miles west of London, I attended a diverse comprehensive in one of its suburbs. I remember a teacher telling me at the time that the school accurately reflected Britain's diversity, and I think he was right. The catchment area for the school included a new housing estate, an affluent area surrounding Reading University and many streets of terraced housing. A growing population of British Pakistanis had made their home there. Thanks to them, our school won numerous cricket trophies. More recently, the school has featured in Gareth Malone's *The Choir*, where it reached the final.[2]

As I responded to the question posed to me at the prayer meeting, a memory suddenly hit me. Have you ever seen a comedy routine with two clowns? One has a long beam of wood over his shoulder, and every time he looks around to find the second clown, the second clown bends down to do up a shoelace or pick up something. At any moment, it seems the first clown is about to clunk the second clown over the head with the beam, and the audience holds their breath with each near miss. This clown routine is a good analogy for what happened to me in that prayer meeting. It was as if I had been lacing up my shoes for twenty years, and I suddenly stood up. I was clunked over the head with a powerful memory and felt somewhat dazed for a moment.

I found myself telling the prayer group leader, a fantastic woman whom I later spent a lot of time with, about an incident that occurred around the time I turned 16 years old. School pupils in the UK take their GCSE exams at this age, and certain subjects are mandatory. One of these is English language, with a compulsory oral English element. Each pupil was required to come up with a discussion subject which they presented to a small group. After each presentation, we partook in discussions about the topics expounded by the other group members.

At my school, our English teacher placed everyone taking the English orals in random small groups drawn from other pupils in our year. It was a big school with over two hundred students in my cohort. Though I recognized some of the others in my oral exam group, I didn't know any of them well. One boy talked about football, and I presented something about how boys and girls were treated differently in academic classes at school – I hastily chose my subject and did not plan it well. There was one British-Pakistani in my group, and she raised the topic of forced marriage. She claimed that just a few weeks after our exams, she would fly to Pakistan and be made to marry one of her male relatives. She was outraged and described how her immediate family might murder her if she didn't follow their plan. It was the first time I had heard someone talk about 'honour' and the importance of maintaining it at all costs, and I didn't know what to make of her or her claims. I couldn't believe a girl's family members would kill their own sister, niece or daughter, and I wondered how a dishonourable act like that could be used to maintain honour. I was incredulous.

I am ashamed to say that following the discussion, I pretty much forgot about this girl. I was young and self-absorbed. After the summer, I went to a different school for my A-levels and never gave her much thought. At the root of it was my disbelief that her life was really in any danger; I suppose I concluded that she was exaggerating, though I wasn't conscious of thinking that. It's only in later life, as I have come to know more about what Pakistani women endure and have thought back to that incident, that I appreciate her bravery in telling us. We were a group of cossetted English teens with no one but ourselves, and perhaps our football teams, to worry about.

Yet, twenty years later, in America, the memory of what happened came to the forefront of my mind. I told the prayer leader about the situation that had occurred so many years before and experienced sudden and overwhelming sympathy for my schoolmate, a girl whose name I couldn't even remember. Was God trying to tell me something? Perhaps now was the time to do something to help my school-friend and girls like her.

As I think about forced marriage and the church's role in preventing it, I recall these two young women. Christian women in Pakistan are being abducted and forced into marriage as a form of persecution. Just like Maria, they have no voice, and their wider communities collaborate with the persecutors leading to multi-layered entrenched oppression. What should I, a Christian woman from the West, be doing to help? I'll start off exploring the answers to this question, and I invite you to join me in getting to know the activists who are trying to help, and the women and their families who are affected.

Then there are women from the UK and the wider western world who live in communities with churches and Christians, yet they are at risk of being sent to Pakistan for marriage. Like my classmate, they are at the mercy of their honour and shame traditions and in danger of their own families turning against them. Yet these girls are among us; we may see them daily, and they probably walk past our church buildings. Surely we can reach them and protect them. I am eager to discover the churches and social workers stepping into the breach to support them. I'll write about vulnerable young women at the end of this book, and my aim is to look for links between their suffering and the abuse of Christian women in Pakistan. More than anything, I would love to uncover what happened to my school-mate. Is she in Pakistan or the UK, and is she happy and safe?

Taking on such sensitive topics feels hugely daunting; most of the time, I don't feel qualified to write about such complex abuse. God has kept spurring me on, though.

Before I left Kathmandu, I got to know a large group of Pakistani Christian refugees who attended our international church. They had fled to Nepal when it became too unsafe for their families to remain in Pakistan. Each family could tell many harrowing stories of persecution. They had often been on the run within Pakistan for many months before taking the plunge and escaping to Kathmandu – hardly the top choice for anyone looking to relocate. Most were waiting to be processed by the United Nations High Commission for Refugees so that they could begin afresh in countries in the West. However, the average wait for relocation is fifteen years and, in the meantime, they were stuck in limbo in Kathmandu. Depression, post-traumatic stress disorder (PTSD) and other mental health challenges became their constant companions, although they were at least physically safe.

On one particular day, doubts about writing this book plagued me. Somehow I ended up sharing my ideas with a 30-something, single Pakistani refugee from church. Immediately she vehemently agreed that fear of abduction was a daily nightmare for Christian women in Pakistan. She showed me a picture of her two nieces; a girl of around 7 with black hair and deep brown eyes was holding her toddler sister. They looked so vulnerable, yet also so typical; the two girls were casually posing in front of the camera. My Pakistani friend told me how much her entire family feared for their safety and how, even though they were still young, they had to remain indoors most of the time so any potential abductors wouldn't spot them. She wept as she described how much she missed and worried about them. I knew then that writing this book was necessary. These girls matter to God, and anything I can do to protect them is worth pursuing. Having opened this book and read this far, I pray you also feel the same way.

I've also begun mentioning my interest in tracking down my school-friend to British female friends, many of whom are not Christian. They immediately recognized my desire to discover what happened since all of them (from different parts of the UK) remember rumours swirling at their schools of girls sent to Pakistan. I'm not alone in wanting to find out what happened to them.

Now I find myself in Belgium, and God is opening doors. To my surprise, last month, I found myself at the European Prayer Breakfast at the European Parliament, where I met with several activists campaigning to make life better for Pakistani women. I sat for breakfast in a large room with space for 600 people, and a Pakistani politician and his wife soon filled the empty chairs opposite me. I was gobsmacked at the way God orchestrated our meeting. Getting to know all these Christian campaigners is incredible, and I can't wait to tell you their stories. I want to learn from them what can be done to help women in Pakistan who are being forced into marriage, and I invite you to pray and act as well.

Isn't it astonishing that, as Christians, we are part of a family that extends right around the world into the darkest corners and most obscure places? Women in Pakistan are our sisters, and I invite you to join me as I learn more about them; together, we can champion their cause and help end forced marriage and the ensuing violence. I long for my sisters to flourish and for all of us to be empowered by the Spirit to work for justice. May this book be part of your calling to bring about the kingdom of God.

In my narrative, all the names of the victims of abuse have been changed to protect them. I have chosen aliases for them that are traditional Pakistani names. The women's family members are referred to without using names such as brother, sister, father, cousin, etc. I hope this doesn't become too irritating for the reader, and in each instance it is clear to whom I am referring. Each of the brave activists has given me permission to use their real name. Some place names have also been changed.

1

Heir – Cecil

Within a fortnight, I went from feeling as if our move to Belgium had been a divine faux pas to discovering a mountain of opportunities God had prepared for me. My head spun as I tried to keep up with the names of the people I was meeting and the overwhelming responsibility of knowing God was evidently calling me to write about women in Pakistan. My new contacts were all thanks to a Belgium-based missionary sent out by the same church in Virginia where the prayer meeting took place that I mentioned in the Introduction. The two of us met for brunch in a cosy restaurant in the Schaerbeek district of Brussels in November 2022, and he invited me to the European Prayer Breakfast, which he was organizing and which was due to take place in early December. The timing was impeccable.

Mons, where I live, is almost two hours by public transport from the European Parliament buildings, so I planned to stay overnight in central Brussels to make it in time for the early morning breakfast. Earlier in the year, I had noticed a small reference to an office in Brussels on the Christian Solidarity Worldwide (CSW) website, an organization that defends freedom of religion and belief. I emailed them to find out if their office was staffed and if anyone might be available to meet me the afternoon before the prayer breakfast. Since I would be in Brussels anyhow, I wanted to make the most of my time. I hoped to discuss forced marriage in Pakistan with someone and float my idea to write this book with an expert. To my delight, someone was willing to meet me.

Jonathan, CSW's Europe Liaison Officer, and I met in the lobby of the swanky Stanhope Hotel, not far from the Parliament buildings and some of Brussels' most exquisite palaces. At the elegant bar, I bought the most expensive water I have ever drunk. I couldn't help thinking that the entire experience differed vastly from the draughty shacks in Kathmandu, where I had interviewed women for my previous book.

Jonathan was immediately on board as I began to share my vision for this book and my desire to raise awareness of how forced marriage was being used to persecute Christian women and their families in Pakistan. He was well-spoken and, although reserved and modest, had definite enthusiasm for my work. He gave me a fascinating overview of his work with the European Parliament and other institutions of the European Union, where he lobbies decision-makers to highlight violations publicly and to use trade policy and diplomacy to uphold human rights. Pakistan, in particular, is desperate to maintain tariff-free trade with the European Union. CSW urges the EU to leverage this ambition so that freedom of religion and belief are guaranteed for all Pakistan's citizens, no matter their religious convictions.

Since he was not an expert on forced marriage and conversion, Jonathan suggested I should speak to Cecil, one of his colleagues, who is a Pakistani Christian and had been working for CSW for the previous eighteen months. He was based near London, so we decided to meet over Zoom.

Cecil immediately impressed me; he was articulate, passionate and knowledgeable. No matter what I asked him, he could provide in-depth answers to my questions and backed his experiences up with years, statute numbers and other data. We immediately bonded since we are both part of military families and, as he told me his story, I realized that Pakistan's history and his family's story were closely intertwined. Understanding Cecil's background was enlightening as I sought to better grasp the current situation for Christians in Pakistan.

The first Christian in Cecil's paternal family was his great-grandfather, who grew up in a village in Punjab. Punjab is one of Pakistan's four provinces, and nowadays it is the most populous. The Catholic Church had brought the gospel to the region by setting up schools and hospitals. When Cecil's great-grandfather was a child, the area was part of India and was ruled by the British. Protestant missionaries had also made their way to present-day Pakistan as they accompanied the British Raj. Both groups built enormous churches and cathedrals in Pakistan's major cities, many of which still stand today.

While a teenager, Cecil's great-grandfather had access to various religious books, including some provided by local Catholic missionaries. He was so moved by what he read that he decided to become a Christian. Unfortunately, his father disowned him when he converted, which meant he had to leave the land and village where his family had lived for generations. Having fled to a small town nearby, Cecil's great-grandfather found employment by working for Catholic missionaries. He became well-educated and eventually returned to his ancestral village to establish the Dalwal Mission High School, which remains a top-rated private school to this day. When Cecil's great-grandfather was principal, some pupils would travel for two hours by bullock cart to attend such a well-regarded school.

A generation later, Cecil's grandparents were raising their children in the same village. They were Christians, and any ill-will between the Muslim and Christian sides of the family had largely been reconciled. Although their family was at peace, politically everything was changing. There was mounting pressure on the British to leave India and, eventually, matters were resolved through Partition, a defining event for the Indian subcontinent.

Britain's rule of India had never been at the pleasure of its Indian subjects. Demands to hand the country back to democratically elected native rulers became louder and louder throughout the Second World War. Muhammed Ali Jinnah was the most vocal spokesperson for the country's Muslims. He joined activists such as Gandhi and Nehru in calling on successive British viceroys to allow the Indian subcontinent to rule itself. Initially, Jinnah wanted the Muslim states, such as Punjab, to have devolved autonomy within a single India. However, in 1940 he publicly called on Britain to resolve matters by allowing two nations to be formed once the British Raj withdrew. He stated that Islam and Hinduism were irreconcilably opposed and that each religious community required separate homelands on Indian soil.

In 1947, the demands of India's citizens were met, and control of their country was restored to them. Pakistan and India were created overnight on 14 August, and Cecil didn't miss a beat as he quoted the date to me. I imagine every Pakistani and Indian schoolchild can do the same; events on that day have defined their history ever since.

British officials hastily drew up borders between the two new nations. At that time, Pakistan consisted of two land masses, one to the west and another to the east of India. They were known then as West Pakistan and East Pakistan and today as Pakistan and Bangladesh. States such as Punjab were crudely divided into two, and some Punjabis found themselves in a Hindu-majority country and others in a Muslim homeland. The princely state of Jammu and Kashmir also found itself split up, and fighting over who controls that area continues to this day.

On paper, the new borders between India and Pakistan made little sense, but they were utterly illogical on the ground. Immediately, there was carnage and anarchy. Neighbours turned on each other, and Muslims left everything behind as they fled India to resettle in Pakistan. Similarly, Hindus who had been living in either East or West Pakistan bolted to present-day India. There was enormous bloodshed. Trains carrying displaced refugees were attacked, and carriage after carriage of dead bodies arrived on either side of the new borders. Attacks on women also took place, and rape was commonplace during those days of insanity. In all, around 14.5 million people migrated, and one million people were killed during Partition. When minorities in Britain complain that British people today are ignorant of Britain's bloody past, Partition is one of many events to which they are referring; it ought to be taught in our schools.

Many Sikhs, who are neither Hindu nor Muslim, lived in Punjab. In Cecil's ancestral village of Dalwal, Muslim rioters attempted to attack and kill a Sikh family. Cecil's grandmother gave the Sikh family shelter and stood in the mob's path. She courageously told them they would have to kill her first if they wanted to attack the Sikh family. Thankfully the gang turned on its heels, and Cecil's extended family arranged safe passage for the Sikh family to reach the Indian side of the border.

I was surprised to hear from Cecil that Pakistan had no state religion at its founding. Jinnah became the country's new governor general and was adamant that it should be a secular and liberal republic. Pakistan's new flag was even designed to reflect the presence of minorities. Although the Islamic crescent is the flag's main symbol, a broad white vertical stripe is also featured and represents people from all religious faiths.

It is hard to know precisely how many Hindus and other religious minorities ended up living in Pakistan immediately following Partition. There is a long-held belief that around a quarter of Pakistan's population in late 1947 was non-Muslim. However, the first census was not conducted until 1951, and it showed that just 14 per cent of people did not practise Islam. Had there been a significant decline in minorities as further migration occurred in the years after Partition, or had the estimates in 1947 been wrong? It is almost impossible to know, and the topic is still hotly debated as it has implications for the status of minority groups today.

From the outset, Jinnah's vision for Pakistan was based on a contradiction. For almost a decade before Partition, he had vehemently argued that Muslims and Hindus could not live together. He believed that the two religions, one monotheistic and the other polytheistic, were so at odds that neither faith could accommodate the other. Consequently, he was insistent that Muslims needed their own homeland, and that was one of the main reasons for Partition. Yet once Pakistan was formed, he believed the newly created country would have room for all religions and vowed to safeguard religious minorities, including Christians. Though his desire to be welcoming to all was commendable, it is easy to see the ambiguities in his vision, and he could not get the new country's leaders on board with his message.

The very name, Pakistan, means land of the pure; this was perhaps an early warning for Pakistan's Christians that they might not be safe in this newly created Muslim homeland. In Cecil's view, it took a couple of decades after the birth of Pakistan for anti-Christian sentiment to build. Regrettably, Jinnah died just one year after Partition, and Cecil was sorry to tell me that in 1956 conditions for Christians worsened when the country became an Islamic republic. Construction of a new capital city began, which was called Islamabad. The nation was evidently on the path to becoming an Islamic theocracy.

Meanwhile, in Dalwal, Cecil's grandparents were still living in precisely the same place as their family had lived for centuries. As one writer puts it, 'The . . . old inhabitants . . . had become accustomed to living in a land older than time . . . had been given a bad shock by independence, by being told to think of themselves, as well as the country itself as new.'[1] They had witnessed horrific events, and although their leaders told them to embrace the new possibilities that came with the birth of Pakistan, it must have been hard to get excited once the bloodletting at Partition was over and life went back to how it was before.

Cecil's father, also called Cecil (I will refer to him as Cecil Snr), was born in 1941 when Dalwal was still located in India. Cecil Snr experienced first-hand the trauma of Partition, and he grew up fiercely patriotic. While still a teenager, he joined the Pakistan Air Force (PAF) as an officer and met Cecil's mother during a posting to Karachi. She hailed from a Goan Catholic family that had migrated along the coast from Goa to Karachi throughout successive generations. Thomas, one of Jesus' disciples, is believed to have been the first Christian to reach Goa, so perhaps her faith goes back as far as him.

Shortly after Cecil's parents married, the 1965 war between Pakistan and India occurred. Cecil Snr was involved in the fighting and shot down three enemy planes for which he was awarded one of Pakistan's highest medals.

Then in 1971, fighting broke out again. To begin with, the violence was limited to skirmishes between East and West Pakistan; Rushdie describes the two nations as 'Wings without a body, sundered by the land-mass of its greatest foe [India]',[2] and united only by Allah. Bengali nationalists called for self-government and began a campaign that would eventually see East Pakistan secede and the creation of Bangladesh. Given that East and West Pakistan, separated by over 1,300 miles, did not share a common culture or language, it was perhaps inevitable that the two provinces would one day sever their ties.

The Bangladesh War of Independence began in March 1971; however, having observed the two sides fighting all through the monsoon, India joined the war to fight alongside Bangladesh on 3 December. Cecil Snr was among the pilots who bravely flew sorties into enemy territory and his plane was shot at. Fire engulfed the plane's right wing, but he had the wherewithal to point his aircraft in the direction of home. He glided towards safety for as long as possible but eventually had to eject.

As Cecil Snr descended, his parachute snagged on a tree. He was forced to cut himself free before running roughly 300 yards across no man's land to Pakistani soil. At the border, the guards yelled at him to identify himself and told him not to move. He had been sprinting across a minefield, and one wrong move could have blown him up. They yelled further directions to him and gradually guided him out of the minefield. Cecil Snr believed God performed multiple miracles to save his life that day, and he shared this story of miraculous deliverance throughout his life.

Following these exploits, Cecil Snr was awarded further medals, and a leading newspaper describes him as one of Pakistan's most beloved war heroes.[3] Fantastic videos of his achievements are available on YouTube;[4] he is ever so dashing and looks like a real-life Top Gun. A year later, Cecil was born, and a few years after that, Cecil Snr's name would appear in textbooks that described him as both a war hero and a Christian.

Although West Pakistan lost the war against East Pakistan and its ally, India, the Chaudhrys emerged from the war with status and acclaim. Cecil Snr was offered the post of air attaché at the Pakistani Embassy in London. Despite his blatant patriotism, General Zia-al-Huq himself switched the offer. Since Cecil Snr was a Christian, the general believed he might become too sympathetic to the British and spy for them. To avoid suspicion, Cecil Snr was appointed as the air attaché in Baghdad, Iraq, instead. Cecil believes many Christians miss out on similar high-profile promotions to this day.

The Chaudhrys found themselves in a beautiful apartment building along the banks of the Tigris, the main river that flows through Baghdad. While in Pakistan, most of Cecil Snr's postings had been to relatively small towns or remote air bases where there were no churches and few Pakistani Christians with whom they could fellowship. However, in Baghdad, the family attended a large international Catholic church, and it was here that Cecil took his first Holy Communion.

After four years, the family returned to Lahore, Pakistan, where Cecil began attending a secular private school; he was the only Christian pupil there. At the time, he was unaware of any violence or persecution directed towards Christians, although there was undoubtedly some discrimination. It was only after he had left school that he discovered some boys had been unwilling to sit with him; however, it did not matter much as he had plenty of friends who liked him and made him welcome. He believes Christian pupils at secular schools face much more ostracism today.

One day he was delighted when his teacher told the class they would be studying the war of 1965. The government-approved textbook listed Cecil Snr as a war hero, and Cecil felt enormous pride. His teacher informed the rest of the class that Cecil Snr's son was actually sitting with them. However, a classmate quickly turned to him and asked, 'How can your father be a war hero when all your lot [Christians] are good for is cleaning toilets?' Cecil gave back as good as he got and retorted immediately with a smart comment (I'm in awe of anyone that can do that), but I won't repeat what he said; more on that later.

I asked Cecil which emotion won the day; his pride in his father for featuring in a textbook and his teacher's approval, or shame and frustration due to his classmate's taunt? Thankfully, he said it was pride, and shortly afterwards this classmate became a close friend. Cecil's mother's sandwiches were known to be the most delicious, and for many years she sent Cecil to school with two; one for him and one for this friend.

The inclusion of Christian war heroes and patriots in government-approved textbooks was not to last. By 1990, Cecil Snr's name was no longer included, and only Muslim champions were celebrated. Later on, his family tried to appeal this decision and were told that educators no longer wanted to glorify war heroes; however, why were Muslim fighters still included if that were the case? Cecil explained that Pakistan's political and religious leaders actively fostered an Islamic identity for the nation. Sadly, Cecil believes that the Islamization of education in Pakistan is directly causing more ostracism and persecution of minorities, including Christians. He longs to see his father and other Christians celebrated for their patriotism. He believes that persecution will decline if children are taught from a young age that Christians have played a positive role in Pakistan's history.

Once Cecil completed his schooling, he went to college in Lahore. In the 1970s, all colleges in Pakistan had been nationalized, so he attended the government-run FC college. The FC stood for Forman Christian, and it was one of thousands of schools and colleges up and down the country that referred to Christianity in their names in recognition of their missionary origins. The Federal Ministry of Education also took over the school that Cecil's great-grandfather had established in Dalwal. I am surprised that the schools could reference their Christian origins at all and weren't entirely renamed, with all references to Christianity removed. Thankfully, in the early 2000s, many missionary schools and colleges were handed back to their church boards for oversight, so Cecil's college became a Presbyterian school again. In Dalwal, the Catholics resumed responsibility. Cecil regrets not benefitting from these changes as he had already graduated.

In 1986 Cecil Snr retired from the Pakistan Air Force. Despite his exemplary career, he had been passed over for promotion too many times and took the hint that Christians weren't welcome above his rank. He decided to put his time and reputation to good use by joining the board of the National Commission for Justice and Peace.

In 1986 the commission was just a year old, having been established by the Conference of Catholic Bishops in Pakistan to promote human rights and, in particular, to safeguard minorities. Cecil Snr began by joining the commission's campaign to end bonded labour in brick-kilns[5] and successfully recruited other human rights institutions to work alongside them. In 1992, they were rewarded for their efforts when a law was introduced to ban bonded labour in brick-kilns. Sadly, since then powerful landowners and factory owners have successfully bribed the police and other authorities to turn a blind eye to abuses. Most efforts to implement the new laws have been unsuccessful, so tragically, exploitation continues.

Throughout the 1990s and early 2000s, Cecil Snr was dedicated to advocating on these issues and many more. As he aged, he gradually stepped back from his responsibilities, and his children took the reins instead. In April 2012, while battling lung cancer, he slipped into a coma and passed away a few days later. His loss was keenly felt by both his family and the PAF. Although Cecil ensured his father was surrounded by family before his death, the PAF took charge of his body and all the funeral arrangements as soon as he died.

Cecil Snr's death was marked with full military honours. An air-vice-marshal took charge of all the arrangements, and there was a fourteen-gun salute at his funeral in Lahore. In addition, an honour guard flew from Islamabad to pay tribute to him. Punjab Province's chief minister, together with the serving chief of the PAF and four former chiefs, also attended the funeral. Wonderfully, the PAF was pleased to comply with the family's wishes for a Christian funeral. Cecil Snr's coffin was draped with the Pakistani flag, and medals were placed upon it before it was buried in a Christian cemetery.

Once the mourning period was complete, Cecil was approached by the National Commission for Justice and Peace and asked to continue his father's work by becoming their executive director; he gladly accepted. His father had spent many years campaigning against Pakistan's notorious blasphemy laws. By taking on his father's mantle, Cecil willingly involved himself in one of the most distressing and intractable issues facing Christians anywhere in the world.

Anyone with even a passing interest in ending religious persecution will undoubtedly have heard how Pakistan's blasphemy laws are being used to intimidate Christians and other minorities. Until I spoke with Cecil, though, I had no idea that the British introduced these rules over a century ago. In 1860, the first blasphemy laws were introduced as the imperialists tried to keep the peace between Muslims, Hindus and those of other faiths in their newly conquered territories. In the beginning, the regulations made sense and protected people of all faiths from being abused on the basis of religion, and their holy sites from desecration. Punishments were also relatively mild, and pardons were possible if one party apologized to the other. Following Partition, Cecil described a period of relative tolerance until the mid-1980s. From 1947 until 1984, there were just a handful of blasphemy cases;[6] then, in 1984, the laws were changed to provide greater protection for Muslims and Islam, and there have been thousands of charges and convictions since then.

Broadly speaking, three offences count as blasphemy today in Pakistan. They are: speaking against any prophet, disrespecting Islam and the Koran, and disparaging the Prophet Muhammad. The sentences for these offences vary from seven years in prison for the first, life imprisonment for the second and the death sentence if convicted of the last. Regrettably, little proof is required to convict someone, and court cases often come down to 'he said, she said' arguments on which the onus tends to fall on the accused to prove themselves innocent rather than the other way around. I chose not to share Cecil's smart-alec comment above, which he spoke in response to the school-friend who taunted him about his Christian faith, just in case someone might read it and consider the comment offensive to Muslims. The blasphemy laws are also misused, and Cecil outlined how they might be applied for economic gain. For instance, someone might accuse their neighbour of blasphemy, knowing they would end up in prison and their accuser could grab their land.

Tragically, the blasphemy laws have such great potency in Pakistan because they have been exploited for power and influence. Radical Muslim mullahs have convinced the general populace that they are divine rules ordained by Allah. Consequently, the laws are enormously popular among ordinary Muslims (plenty of Muslims oppose them, especially if they live outside of Pakistan), and popular sentiment is in favour of increasing the penalties for blasphemy rather than reducing them. Mobs regularly carry out summary justice themselves and set upon those suspected of blasphemy, often injuring them and sometimes killing the accused.

The fight to end the fear and intimidation that the blasphemy laws invoke in Pakistan's minorities continues to this day. One of the Christian refugees I got to know in Kathmandu fled Rawalpindi after he took down a poster from his front wall that included verses from the Koran. I also discovered that during religious festivals in Karachi, designated trash bins are placed in the street.[7] Anyone can dispose of pamphlets with religious texts by using these bins and thus avoid any accusation of blasphemy. Immediately after my interview with Cecil, I checked my emails, and there was an update from an NGO asking me to pray. The Pakistan Government was extending the definition of blasphemy to include disparaging the Prophet's wives, and the penalty for doing so would increase from seven to ten years. Then, just a few days later, I read that Pakistan was to ban Wikipedia because they believed the content was blasphemous. If an internationally known website cannot protect itself from censure, what hope do Pakistan's poor and marginalized Christians have?

Thankfully Cecil and his family are doing everything they can to fight for and protect Pakistan's Christians. Following her father's death, Cecil's sister, Michelle Chaudhry, set up the Cecil & Iris Chaudhry Foundation to assist impoverished and disempowered Christians. Cecil himself is now in the UK and using his expert knowledge as part of CSW's (Christian Solidarity Worldwide) South Asia team. Not every Pakistani Christian family can boast of a war hero and an executive director; however, I hope that by reading Cecil's story, you have gained a better and deeper understanding of the situation for Christians in Pakistan. Like many other families, they have gone through Partition and held on to ancestral ties despite neither of the newly created countries welcoming their faith. In the face of discrimination, they have remained loyal to their homeland and resolutely patriotic. They have experienced discrimination and limited career progression, as countless others have, and they are now seeking to help others, just as many Pakistani Christians are. I hope you will join me in praying for them, and I trust that Cecil's story will help contextualize the other stories in this book as we dive deeper into the specific issues facing Pakistani women, our sisters. Speaking to Cecil was just my introduction to the violence and abuse that can be directed towards Christians in Pakistan. Now I needed to go deeper and talk to some of the victims themselves.

2

Brave – Abhita

In mid-August 2023, torn and desecrated (meaning they had been written or scribbled on) pages from the Koran were found on the ground in a Christian enclave in Punjab. The pages were outside the home of Raja Masih, an illiterate man, so it was clear from the outset that he had not been responsible for writing on the sheets. However, angry mobs soon appeared to mete out summary justice, and frenzied crowds of Muslim men gathered in the enclave. Loudspeakers, more often used to call worshippers to prayer at local mosques, were instead used to summon angry rioters. The response to these calls was so ardent that some men brought a crane and wrecking ball with them, and others brought tractors.

The mobs attacked twenty-one churches and wreaked havoc on hundreds of houses. Christians living in the area fled for their lives and, as I write this, many are still unable to return to their homes, either because they were destroyed or because of fear that violence will resume. However, many Christians had no other place to go and crept back to their houses under cover of darkness in the days and weeks afterwards.

Given the enormous scale of the destruction, the speed at which it took place, and Raja Masih's apparent inability to write on the pages, Christian activists were convinced that the violence had been planned, although I could tell that it pained those I spoke to, to think this.

Of course, Muslim clerics quickly condemned the violence and claimed that these actions did not reflect true Islam, but these high-standing men did little to help identify the perpetrators nor bring them to justice. Christian NGOs were right to point out that actions must accompany their words; otherwise, hatred and violence directed at Christians (and other minorities) will continue in Pakistan.

In response to the coordinated attacks on Christians in Jaranwala, many Christian groups from around the world organized a humanitarian response to meet the immediate needs of those who had lost their homes and livelihoods. At the forefront of these responses was the Cecil & Iris Chaudhry Foundation. Lahore – where Michelle Chaudhry, Cecil's sister, runs CICF – is less than sixty miles from Jaranwala, and so the organization was quick to respond, rushing cooking products and hygiene packs to the scene.

In the wake of the disaster, I received news updates and photos from CSW and CICF detailing the work they were doing to rebuild lives. Michelle was pictured in many of these photos and had a striking appearance. With long grey hair and bright clothes, she was often surrounded by families reaching out to hug her and claim the items they desperately needed. She appeared to be a huge comfort to many and also someone who would suffer no nonsense. Looking at her, I felt that if I faced a crisis, I would love to have her with me, too.

Michelle and I exchanged a few voice messages via WhatsApp to set up my interview with Abhita, a young woman who had been abducted and forcibly converted and raped. In these messages, Michelle's voice was lyrical yet clipped. She sounded upper-class and spoke English with just a hint of an Asian accent. I couldn't wait to meet her online.

When we connected over Microsoft Teams in late September, Michelle and Abhita were sitting behind Michelle's desk at CICF. It looked as if they were having a great chat before I dialled in to join them. Abhita was radiant and beautiful; she had a graceful face illuminated by a shy smile, and Michelle was laughing with her. I could see a brilliant rapport between them, and it was obvious that Michelle was going to be a superb translator. Michelle was evidently as interested in Abhita's story as I was, and Abhita trusted her. The two of them often looked at each other, and Abhita made eye contact with both of us; I didn't sense that she felt any shame about what she had undergone. There was a gentle fieriness about Abhita and, in many ways, I wished we could go out for lunch together; they would both be brilliant company. However, we had tricky subjects to discuss, and though putting them off might be more pleasant, we were meeting online for a reason.

As usual, I wanted to begin the interview in prayer. I invited Michelle to pray in Urdu so Abhita would understand what was happening. I was both surprised and thrilled when Abhita jumped in and offered to pray for the interview herself. I loved her tenacity and faith, and my hopes for our discussion were further heightened. After Abhita had voiced her articulate prayer, Michelle translated and told me that Abhita had prayed for God to help her speak and that the memories and flashbacks to her traumatic experiences wouldn't be too painful. Abhita wanted to tell her story, and I was again honoured to hear it then and tell it in this book.

Abhita is 19 years old and is the third of seven children. She has two older brothers, so she is the eldest daughter.

Consequently, she was expected to help around the house and care for her younger siblings. Abhita was born and brought up near Faisalabad in Punjab, though she is now living closer to Lahore as she has had to flee her home town. While growing up, her father worked in another city as a driver, so her mother, who didn't need to work when Abhita was young, was alone most of the time and ran their household while bringing up Abhita and her six siblings.

As I am discovering is the case with many Pakistani Christian families, Abhita does not know when her family became Christian, so she could not tell me from whom her faith stemmed. Her family were officially members of the Catholic Church of Pakistan, but their nearest church was in the centre of Faisalabad, which was quite far from them. As a result, they attended non-denominational church gatherings nearby, which took place outside on spare plots of land. Typically, these congregations would attract between fifty and sixty people, and it was while attending these churches that her faith developed. In particular, Abhita remembers celebrating Christmas with her church family each year and how much fun that was.

At the government school that Abhita attended, there was a small minority of Christians who stuck together and tried to stay out of the way of the Muslim majority. Abhita was already several years behind before starting her classes. Given that her parents were illiterate, she did her best to keep up with her peers. Despite being older than her classmates, Abhita loved school and especially enjoyed sports; cricket was her favourite, and she also loved jump rope. Her teachers encouraged her, and she would speak to them about her dreams for the future. I get the impression that she was a well-liked and bright pupil, which makes sense given her sunny disposition.

Unfortunately, when Abhita was in fourth grade and her classmates were 10 years old, her father had an accident and was diagnosed with heart problems. He returned to the family home from the city where he had been working. Her mother had to go out to work instead and began carrying out domestic work in other people's homes, which did not pay well. Their household income decreased considerably, so Abhita was forced to drop out of school when she was just fourteen. Even though tuition at the government school was free, her family could no longer afford to pay for the required uniform and books.

Abhita accompanied her mother when she went to work, and the two of them would carry out the domestic tasks together. The family needed every penny they could earn since her father's heart problems necessitated expensive medical treatment, and the family had taken out loans to cover the cost, which needed to be repaid.

There wasn't much time or money for fun activities, and the family didn't have many friends, but one aunt in particular was good to them. Regrettably, she partially caused what happened to Abhita and has subsequently ended all contact with them. Abhita has also been unable to reconnect with her church congregation and misses all the fun she had in her earlier life before the traumatic events unfolded.

Abhita continued her story. In 2018, when she was 14, and her family was going through financial difficulties following her father's accident, they were doing everything they could to save money. This included going to the Tuesday and Sunday bazaars, which in Pakistan are traditionally cheaper than markets on other days of the week. The market closest to them, with the best bargains, was next to Abhita's aunt's house, a twenty-five-minute walk away. So early one Tuesday morning,

Abhita set off on her own to her aunt's place so they could visit the market together.

It was only 9:30 a.m. when Abhita reached her aunt's house, yet she discovered all the doors and windows locked. There was no one home. The woman next door, who was nominally a Christian, told Abhita that someone had died, and so everyone in her aunt's family had left in a hurry. This neighbour persuaded Abhita to come and wait in her house while assuring her that someone from her aunt's family would return soon. Sensibly, Abhita called her mother and father to let them know about her aunt and to ask permission to visit the neighbour's house. They consented; given the circumstances, there seemed no reason to suspect anything untoward would happen.

Once inside the neighbour's house, Abhita waited patiently. It was a warm day, and the walk from her home to her aunt's had made her hot. It was natural then to accept a cup of tea from this friendly neighbour, but it was a huge mistake.

Abhita woke up many hours later in a dark room; there were no windows, only gaps around the door, and she could tell it was night-time. Her body was cold; she had been lying on a concrete floor with no cover and was parched and hungry. Gut-wrenching panic took hold of her; where was she, and what had happened to her?

Describing the situation now, Abhita says she felt at that moment as if she was in a horror film. With the benefit of hindsight, she explained that her aunt's neighbour had poisoned the tea, and she had passed out immediately. Somehow, she had been bundled out of the house and driven to another location, which she now knows was an hour away from Faisalabad. This is where she found herself, having been locked in the room while the poison wore off.

As Abhita described these terrifying circumstances to me, I could see her biting her lip. The radiance that had been on her face earlier was gone, and she looked scared and fragile. I hoped going over these events wasn't too traumatic, and Michelle took a moment to touch her arm in sympathy. We both told Abhita how brave she was, and she seemed willing to keep telling her story, consoled by the knowledge that she was being noticed and listened to. Her words and her story mattered.

Returning to her narrative, Abhita explained how, as she lay on the cold floor and began to stir, her movements must have been heard by someone outside the door. An older woman came in, and Abhita saw that many more men and women were beyond the door. She began to cry and pleaded to go home. The woman told her that this was her home now because she had been purchased and now belonged to them.

Abhita screamed more loudly and wailed in horror at what was happening to her. This brought out the wrath of the woman, who began beating her. She slapped Abhita and told her to be quiet. The woman's advice to Abhita was that she should forget about her home and family. Abhita heard the lock clunk as the woman left her, and she was once again left alone in the cold and dark.

Abhita spent the night crying. Although she was famished by now, when breakfast was delivered to her in the morning, she refused to eat it. I'm not surprised, given that the last thing she had consumed had contained poison, I would have avoided anything provided by this family, too. However, the family were undeterred, and when Abhita began causing a racket and screaming to go home, they came back into the room and injected her in the arm with a drug that caused her to pass out again.

It is almost impossible for Abhita to recall the precise order of events and to describe what happened. She was barely conscious for many weeks due to the repeated use of drugs and poison. Now that she is free, she relies on her family to help her work out the timeline and believes she was locked up, beaten and drugged for around a month.

At some point, a Muslim cleric came to the house. She was told to accept Islam, and when she refused, the cleric slapped her. He and the older woman, whom she was instructed to call 'Auntie', continued to beat her until she had no choice but to recite the Muslim Shahada prayer, a mark of conversion. She was also forced to state some of the additional Kalima statements, which are rather like the Apostles' Creed for Christians and express core religious beliefs.

Once Abhita had been converted to Islam, Auntie returned to the room with a young man she said was her son. He was not much older than Abhita. Then, the cleric performed a half-hearted Nikah ceremony and pronounced the young man and Abhita to be husband and wife. I asked her if she thought Auntie had also forced her son into the marriage or whether he was willing to go through with the sham. Abhita told me that though he didn't appear keen to marry her, he was 'not unwilling'. I wonder what would have happened if he had stood up to his mother and refused to participate in Abhita's abduction, forced conversion, and marriage. Could he have ended her abuse if he had tried?

That night, Abhita was sent to her new husband's bedroom. As is the case in many Pakistani households, he was not sleeping alone, and all the men of the family were resting in the room with him. Understandably, Abhita screamed and yelled and refused to enter the bedroom. She would not stop kicking and shrieking, and her new husband, fearing that he would appear weak and humiliated in front of the other menfolk if he didn't manage to sleep with her, sent her back to her room. Auntie continued to implore her to consummate the marriage.

Abhita's new husband came to her room and tried to force himself on her, but she still wouldn't give in to him. So Auntie resorted to her usual solution and plied Abhita with more drugs. In her dazed state, her husband forced her to perform various sexual acts. She was too doped up to stand or stop him, but thankfully she does not remember being raped. Michelle stopped translating at this point, though, and turned to me directly. Having read the medical reports, Michelle confirmed that these indicated that Abhita had indeed been raped. I suppose it is better that she doesn't actually remember the act, but it must also be frightening not to know what was done to you.

Over the next few weeks, her torture continued. She was locked in the same room all the time and was repeatedly beaten, drugged and made to carry out sexual acts, not only for her husband but for other men as well. At the time, she was unaware that she had fallen into the hands of a gang made up of an extended family whose ultimate aim was to prostitute her. They had absolutely no interest in her other than breaking her spirit so she could earn money for them. The intention was to sell her to another gang or brothel once they had destroyed what hope she had left, and she stopped fighting back. In the end, she felt that their abuse of her became routine.

Back in Faisalabad, unsurprisingly, Abhita's parents were distraught over their lost daughter. They reported her missing to the local police, who thankfully did at least record the First Information Report (FIR) and appeared willing to undertake some sort of investigation. The police at least knew where to start their inquiries, thanks to Abhita's courteous call to her parents. On that fateful day when she was abducted, she had first requested permission to wait for her aunt in the neighbour's house. The police started asking their questions there.

The neighbour pretty quickly identified the cleric (who forcibly converted and performed Abhita's faux marriage ceremony) as orchestrating much of the plot, so the police tracked him down. As a respected religious leader, his opinion was at first believed. He confirmed that Abhita was known to him but lied by informing the police that she had been unhappy as a Christian. According to him, she had chosen to run away and had willingly converted and married a Muslim man. The cleric further claimed that Abhita was now happy and did not want to see her parents.

Simultaneously, the cleric contacted the gang imprisoning Abhita and advised them to submit the conversion and marriage certificates to the court. By doing this, they hoped to pre-empt any arrest warrants that might be issued.

Of course, Abhita's parents didn't believe any of the cleric's testimony and persuaded the police to issue a presentation order. This required Abhita to come to court so she could testify whether she had willingly converted and married.

Abhita made it to court but, before she appeared, her husband and his family told her precisely what to do. She was advised to sign whatever documents the magistrate gave her and to confirm that her marriage and conversion were her own choices. When the gang gave her these instructions, they pointed guns at her and threatened to kill her family if she didn't follow their plan. They accompanied her to the courthouse later that day, and they made sure Abhita knew their guns were with them, even though they had to be hidden.

Unfortunately for Abhita, her family were not at the courthouse when she was presented, so she did not see them and gain some comfort. She had no choice but to go along with the lies and pretend her conversion and marriage were genuine.

Once again, Abhita's family refused to accept the news that Abhita had willingly run away to marry. Abhita's father travelled to Lahore to bring Abhita's case to the attention of Saleem Iqbal,[1] a Pakistani Christian journalist. Saleem has spent over twenty-five years highlighting the plight of minorities in Pakistan and, due to his activism, he has received countless death threats. Bravely, he has continued his work, but in 2012 he sent his family to live abroad, where it would be safer for them.

With Saleem's help, Abhita's family convinced the police that the cleric was manipulating the situation and likely profiting from it, so he became a suspect. In a bold move by the police, the cleric was arrested, but before he was detained he had time to warn the gang who had kidnapped Abhita. He told them the police were closing in and they should run away.

I could tell that Abhita had something exciting to divulge; she leaned forward and explained what happened next. One day, she woke up to find that the gang that had been imprisoning her had vanished. They had heeded the cleric's warning and gone on the run, afraid that the police would arrest them next. They did not tell Abhita they were leaving, but the house was quiet, and no one came to her room to beat her up or provide her with food. She was still groggy from the cocktail of drugs they had regularly been pumping into her but, as she came to, she realized that this might be her only chance of escape.

She noticed that her husband had left a phone on a ledge; it was plugged in and still charging. Abhita could barely move, but she dragged herself across the room and shakily pressed herself up the wall to reach the phone. She discovered that the phone was an old model, and at one time, it had had an actual keypad (i.e. not a smartphone where the keyboard appears on the screen). However, the keypad on her husband's phone was missing; there was just a series of holes, and the microcircuit board was exposed.

For a moment, she simply stared at the phone, wondering what to do. It was obviously in working order because why else would her husband bother to charge it? She needed something to slide into the holes on the front panel to press the numbers. Then she noticed a broom on the other side of the room. She managed to pull one of the wiry bristles out of the broom and inserted the strand into the holes to call her father. Within minutes, she was speaking to him! Listening to her, I was astonished at her ingenuity. Praise the Lord that even in her drugged state, she knew her father's number, and thanks be to God for providing the phone and the broom!

At the very moment when Abhita's father answered her call, he was with Saleem Iqbal in Lahore. The activist could immediately give Abhita advice, and she was simultaneously relieved to hear her father's voice. Saleem told her to keep the phone switched on so it could be traced. It wasn't long before they knew exactly where she was. Of course, they couldn't trace the phone themselves; they had to contact the police to help them.

Saleem had dealt with enough cases before to know that if the police reached Abhita first, they would take her into custody, and if her husband came to claim her, they would side with him and release her back to him. Someone they trusted needed to be the first to reach her. Unfortunately, Abhita's father was in Lahore, so he couldn't rush to her. Instead, they called her mother, who courageously went with her brother and eldest son (Abhita's brother) to locate her. What a brave group of heroes!

Upon reaching the house, Abhita's saviours found it locked and apparently empty. Abhita was in a room upstairs but was still reeling from the effects of the drugs and hadn't eaten or drunk anything that day. Having made contact with her father, she might also have collapsed with relief, knowing help was finally coming. Despite banging on the door, her mother received no reply, but they decided to persist and broke the lock. They found Abhita passed out on the floor upstairs and swiftly got her away from the area. When the police turned up later, they found an empty building.

I was absolutely riveted by Abhita's story and noticed that Michelle was absorbed in it, too. Both of us were in admiration of her family's heroism and felt enormous relief that she was rescued. Of course, we knew there was a happy ending because Abhita was sitting with us, but we were on a rollercoaster of emotions as we listened to her.

Following her rescue, it was not safe for Abhita to return to their home town, so the family went straight from the crime scene by public bus to Lahore, a journey that lasted many hours. What a difficult journey that must have been. Abhita was barely conscious and needed urgent medical attention. However, the most pressing need was to get her somewhere safe and away from the gang and their cronies. I'm sure Abhita's mother must have had a million questions, but Abhita wasn't capable of answering them, and it was dangerous to discuss them in a public place.

Thanks to the determination of Saleem, Abhita's case went to court almost immediately. Her husband was ordered to present himself to the magistrate at the same time as she did. Looking at her and hearing what she could barely explain, the magistrate told her family to take her straight to the hospital. Her health was so poor by then that she remained in hospital for three months after that.

Abhita's aunt's neighbour, who instigated the tragedy by poisoning and selling Abhita, was arrested based on Abhita's testimony. However, this woman spent only a few days in prison before being released. She is now free to carry out this kind of violence again and remains living next door to Abhita's aunt.

Although Abhita's husband appeared in court, and it was apparent to everyone that she had experienced terrible abuse, he was not arrested. He walked free that day and, following his release, Abhita and her family received many threats. Thankfully, Saleen Iqbal runs a shelter in Lahore and Abhita and her family were invited to live there.

Despite Saleem's help, the cost of Abhita's court cases, hospital treatment and travel to Lahore were mounting. Having received so many threats, Abhita's family could not return to their home anyway, so they sold it. They bought a new, smaller place near Faisalabad and went to live there many months later when it seemed safe and the threats had died down. Sadly, more families needed shelter in Saleem's safe house, so they made room for them.

Michelle explained that abductions of Christian and Hindu girls are like a pandemic in Pakistan and that she feels overwhelmed and unable to keep up with the number of cases since there are so many. She knows of a mother in Sindh who told her that having beautiful girls felt like a sin. This woman shaves her daughters' heads to make them less attractive to men who may prey on them.

Now that Abhita's family is even further impoverished, she has to earn money to help keep them afloat. She found a job in a garment factory and works there for twelve hours each day. Her father is still unwell and cannot earn anything, and her mother is once again a domestic worker. If any of them becomes ill, their wages stop, so they constantly fear falling into deeper poverty. Ideally, Abhita would like to do a beautician course and, on hearing this, Michelle offered for CICF to help cover the cost. However, Abhita's eyes really light up when she mentions that, before her traumatic experiences, she wanted to be an engineer and earn good money to support her parents. Sadly, that is out of the question now.

In the area where Abhita's family now lives, they are stigmatized and have very few friends. Her two older brothers are having difficulty accepting what happened to her and, although they all live in the same house, they do not speak to her. As she told me this, a tear rolled down her cheek, and I could see this caused her a lot of pain. Her brothers have even told her she should be dead. Sadly, many girls who return from these situations do go on to commit suicide, particularly if they return pregnant. Even Abhita's father, who so bravely defended her, now treats her differently, which makes her especially sad. He has told her that she is the cause of their family's disgrace, which must be incredibly hurtful to hear. If only he would show her love and forgiveness, perhaps her brothers would follow suit.

Yet I had already witnessed Abhita's strong faith when she prayed at the start of our conversation. I asked her what helped her maintain her belief in God despite everything that had happened. Although she cannot read well, she listens to the psalms being sung and finds particular consolation in

Psalms 20 and 121. Please take a moment to look them up because they contain words of breathtaking confidence in God's promises. In Psalm 20:7 (NLT), the psalmist declares that he will 'boast in the name of the Lord our God'. Abhita had undoubtedly done that with me today.

At several points in our conversation, I noticed that Michelle was using a vape. I suppose it is unusual for me to see a Christian vaping, but I chastised myself for being taken aback. Given all the stress of her job and the pressure on her to help so many needy Christians who fear for their lives, it is unsurprising that she might take up a habit to help with stress. My own weakness is chocolate, but I'm more secretive, which isn't good. I liked Michelle all the more for being open and transparent and, again, wished we could socialize. There was a bold confidence about her faith in God that was very attractive.

As I said goodbye to Michelle and Abhita and thanked them for their time and confidence in me, I so wished we could go out together and chat more. I liked them both enormously and felt inspired by their resilience to continue their lives despite such weighty opposition. Seeing women support each other as they did gave me hope. God has provided each of us with the most incredible Christian sisters, and highlighting their courage and telling their inspiring stories is what this book is about.

3

Lionheart – Joseph

Let's go back to December 2022 and return to the European Prayer Breakfast. Buoyed by my positive meeting with Jonathan, I already felt my trip to Brussels had been worth it. I woke up early the following morning and made my way to the Parliament buildings for the prayer gathering. I wasn't expecting much more from God; Jonathan had already provided me with a helpful contact. However, there was plenty more in store for me, and the day was full of surprises.

There was a long line for entrance to the Parliament buildings since around six hundred people were expected at the breakfast, and we each had to collect a name badge and have our bags scanned. I briefly chatted with a member of Senedd Cymru as I queued; he is responsible for organizing the Welsh Prayer Breakfast; I had no idea all these events took place.

As I mentioned in the Introduction, I chose a random place to sit at a breakfast table in the European Parliament's large canteen and found myself facing a Punjabi politician and his wife (more about them later). I was astonished that I was seated opposite the only Pakistani couple in the room. Over an unnoteworthy breakfast of pastries, yoghurt and fruit, we exchanged contact details, and I gathered a fair few business cards from other attendees sitting near me. Then I slowly made my way to the subsequent meeting. Although the event is called a 'breakfast' there are, in fact, various events to attend across several days. The corridors were jam-packed with networking delegates, and the venue was up a couple of escalators, along a corridor and then up a lift. There were numerous ushers to help us find our way, but it took nearly ten minutes to get there. I was also towing a small suitcase along, having had to check out of my overnight accommodation earlier.

The next meeting was a discussion of European values, and it was held in a large auditorium consisting of desks arranged in large semicircles. There were headsets at each desk, so when in regular use, participants could hear interpreters speak to them from behind glass-fronted booths that ran around the back of the auditorium; I realized I had seen this room on television. As soon as I sat down, I discovered the pamphlets and business cards I had just collected were missing. Surely I couldn't have left them in the room where we had eaten breakfast? It was one of those moments when you feel so angry with yourself; God had just provided me with the most amazing contacts, and I had squandered them. There was no other option but to go back for them.

Having left my bags and suitcase behind, I put my head down, my elbows out and made a beeline to the canteen. I ducked under arms, detoured around coatracks and was back where I had just been in around three minutes this time. Although stewards were already clearing the room, the table where I had sat had, thankfully, not been touched. My neat pile of handouts and contact numbers was just where I had senselessly left it. Praise God!

Still chastising myself, I returned to the auditorium, carefully clutching my stack of business cards. As I entered the lift for the third time, I was joined by a group also on their way to the discussion. Among them was a Pakistani man describing a recent trip to his home country. The meeting was about to start, and I was pretty flustered by this point, so I thrust my notebook at him and told him I was hoping to write a book about Pakistan: would he mind giving me his contact details? He obliged, scribbling 'Joseph' and an email address on the paper before him. Then we both made our way into the auditorium.

For the next hour or so, there were various speeches from a panel consisting of a Croatian member of the European Parliament, a Belgian human-rights lawyer, a Slovakian former EU commissioner, a former Bulgarian MP, the Romanian founder of an anti-human-trafficking organization and an Estonian politician. Here's the lengthy blurb for the event: 'The roots and future of European values with attention to critical current socio-political concerns and a special focus on leadership development according to the principles of Jesus in the European context'. Although hearing from the people on stage was a privilege, like all politicians, they didn't make their points quickly, and the meeting dragged.

Eventually, there was time for Q&A. The Pakistani man I had just met was the third person to stand up and ask a question. Joseph immediately launched into a tirade against the EU and questioned why they allowed free trade with Pakistan when the forced conversion, marriage and rape of Pakistani Christian women continued. I turned to look at him and felt as if I had stepped into *The Matrix*; time stood still, and the room whirled around me. Although the panellists were each involved and committed to freedom of religion and belief, until then, they hadn't really mentioned it. Joseph's question had come out of the blue, and it was also a complete change of tone; his passion was evident. Of all the countries and issues in the world, here was a man I had just met talking vehemently about the problem I hoped to write about. When I think about the scores of countries where Christians are persecuted, any of their representatives could have been present and spoken up. Even on behalf of Pakistan, Joseph might have chosen to talk about the blasphemy laws. But no. Here he was, with me in Brussels, highlighting forced marriage. All the signs were there; I had to write about this issue. I was a little shaky for the rest of the day and on the train home that evening as I sensed God had carefully orchestrated events.

At the end of the discussion, a small group gathered around Joseph, eager to follow up on his challenge and presumably to obtain his contact details. However, thanks to my earlier forgetfulness, I had already collared him and had his email address. I caught up with him later in the day at a discussion on ending human trafficking[1] and was able to explain more about my plans for this book. I discovered he lived in Germany and was married to a Dutch woman. There and then, he emailed me a report he had been involved in writing that had been published a month earlier. It is entitled 'Conversion without Consent: A Report on the Abductions, Forced Conversions, and Forced Marriages of Christian Girls and Women in Pakistan' and contains the case details for one hundred Christian girls who were forcibly converted and married between January 2019 and October 2022. In short, it was the best resource I could have found to help me write.

I contacted Joseph again in February to ask if I could interview him and, hopefully, his Dutch wife. He agreed and inquired if I would also like to put questions to his sister and her husband. I was astounded to discover that Joseph's sister is Shagufta Kausar, one of Pakistan's most famous victims of their notorious blasphemy laws. She and her husband, Shafqat Emmanuel, had been imprisoned in separate jails for eight years and now live in Germany. What an honour to meet them; of course, I said yes.

Two weeks later, I caught the early morning train to Brussels before catching another to Bergheim in Germany, where the family now lives. Bergheim is a striking historical city situated along the Erft River. An intriguing hill called Glessener Höhe looms high above the surrounding countryside. In the Middle Ages, Bergheim grew rapidly and was granted city status; as it became wealthier, it needed to defend itself. Since then, the town has benefited from being situated on the Rhenish coalfield and its proximity to Cologne; many beautiful, elaborate and defensive buildings line its streets.

Before writing this book, I tried to get my theology in order and sought God about what he wanted to say through me about women forced into marriage in Pakistan. The picture he gave me for them is from Psalm 27:5 (NCV):

> During danger, he will keep me safe in his shelter.
>   He will hide me in his Holy Tent,
>   or he will keep me safe on a high mountain.

My hope is for God to use my writing to help women from Pakistan achieve safety, rather like setting them high on a mountain out of harm's way. I can think of no other city near Belgium – which is, after all, part of the 'low-country' – that better represents this verse. Glessener Höhe, near Bergheim, is essentially an enormous spoil heap from local mines, which is so striking because it is such a contrast to the flat plain around it; on its summit is a cross. The presence of the hill demonstrates to me that God can create a safe place anywhere. It was encouraging to know that Joseph and his family lived in this symbolic area after everything they had endured.

Joseph met me at the tram-stop, and we walked just a few yards to his sister's apartment. She shyly poked her head out of the kitchen to say hello, and I loved her smile. I warmed to her immediately. In the living-room sat Joseph's father; apparently, he and Joseph's mother live nearby, and during our interview, countless family members came to sit on the sofa next to us to say hello. The apartment was small, but it seemed to have Tardis qualities – there were relatives everywhere.

The family has been Christian for as long as any of them could remember. While Joseph's father knew he had been born and raised a Catholic, his mother had attended an army church in the village where she grew up and thought it might have been Protestant. Their families had lived in Punjab for generations and hailed from small rural villages that Joseph struggled to find on Google Maps for me. During the partition of India, they remained where they were, and only their grandfather's brother was 'lost' to India. Since he had married a Punjabi woman from the Indian side of the new border, he migrated there so he wouldn't lose touch with his wife's family. The family hadn't seen him since then, and he has now passed away.

Once Joseph's mother and father had married, they settled in Mian Channu, a small town where agriculture remains the primary industry. Joseph has fond memories of his family home, which was made of packed mud rather than bricks, and he remembers the cows, sheep, goats and chickens they raised and sold in the town's market. His eyes momentarily glazed over as he spoke longingly of the parrots and parakeets that perched in the trees; in his mind, he seemed to be listening to their squawks for a moment. Shagufta and Joseph have four brothers and sisters and, although they all attended school, they did not spend long in education; to this day, the sisters, in particular, are barely literate.

At this point, Joseph's wife, a tall and slender Dutch woman, joined us. She had been busy around the house trying to get a German electrician to fix the family's wiring. She had also been attending to their young daughter, who was around 3 years old and devoted to her grandfather. Joseph's father beamed as he was led on circuits around the living-room by his striking granddaughter. The two of them obviously adored each other.

By now, I was curious to know how Joseph had become so articulate and well-connected, given that his sister, who was only a few years older, appeared uneducated. After all, I had first encountered Joseph at the European Parliament, so the difference in their experiences and education seemed immense. Joseph's wife jokingly explained that he was 'the gifted one' though, in fact, it was a bout of ill health that had caused their vastly different life experiences.

Shagufta had married her mother's Christian cousin while still a teenager and had gone with him to live with their uncle, a protestant bishop. This uncle presided over a church in Gojra, just a few hours' drive from Mian Channu. The church had an attached compound containing houses where Christians lived. Shagufta took a job as a cleaner at the church, and Shafqat did manual work.

Back in Mian Channu, Joseph struggled with various illnesses and was diagnosed with an appendix problem. Having tried multiple treatments in nearby towns, he and his mother eventually travelled to Karachi to find a cure, where they stayed with another uncle. Karachi is Pakistan's most populous city and plays a role in Pakistan similar to those performed by New York and Sydney in their respective countries. Though none of these cities is a capital, each is a cultural hub, and their bustling ports have allowed the exchange of people and ideas. Before Partition, Karachi was home to just four hundred thousand people, yet it now houses over fourteen million people. No wonder it is dubbed an instant city, and Steve Inskeep aptly describes it as having 'appeared in a blink'.[2]

During what should have been a temporary stay in Karachi, Joseph encountered many new people and experiences. He and his mother began worshipping at an international Pentecostal church, and his faith grew along with his mastery of English. He started making friends with other young Christians, and they would spend whole nights praying together. The youth group experienced miracles, not least Joseph's healing, and the Holy Spirit seemed to be on the move. The church also provided him with connections to Christians overseas, and slowly, his world-view expanded; he loved the vibrancy of life in Karachi. As a result, he and his mother suggested that the entire family relocate to the vibrant port city. Of course, this didn't include his sister, who was already married.

At this point in our conversation, Joseph's wife had to leave. I believe she said she was heading to their home to sort out their recycling, which seemed like a stereotypically Dutch activity! In her place, Joseph's sister sat down with us; until then, she had been busy in the kitchen. She wore a traditional salwar kameez (the traditional three-part outfit worn by women in Pakistan), and the scarf over her shoulders looked a little greasy, as she had probably been wiping her hands on it as she cooked. Her face was kind, although somewhat withdrawn; I recognized her as someone who had experienced trauma and immediately felt drawn to her, and I hoped she did to me. Being with her, I felt transported back to all the women I had recently left behind in Nepal whom I love and miss so much.

While Joseph was in Karachi and on an upward trajectory, Shagufta and her husband were suffering more and more. First, Shafqat was accidentally shot by a gun while at work. Consequently, he became paralysed and was confined to a wheelchair. Though this meant he was no longer the breadwinner, the couple could make ends meet and continued to live in the Christian compound next to the church. They had four children together, three sons and a daughter. As we sat and chatted, her husband glided across the parquet floor in his wheelchair to say hello to me, two teenage sons turned up, and their 16-year-old daughter appeared out of one of the bedrooms – there really were people everywhere!

In 2013 their nightmare began when a Muslim mob turned up at the compound and accused them of blasphemy. According to the group, a local Muslim man had received text messages that insulted the Prophet Muhammad from a sim card registered to Shagufta's husband. Neither Shagufta nor Shafqat was literate, and the text messages were written in English, so there was no way they could have sent them but, nevertheless, the crowd accused them of blasphemy and bayed for blood. There was panic throughout the compound, and Shagufta's then-young children screamed and cried. When the police turned up, they arrested the entire family and took them to the local police station.

While in police custody, Shagufta and her husband were interrogated and tortured. Their children were held in an adjacent cell and heard everything. It must have been horrific for them. The police told Shagufta she would be stripped and taken naked to the street if she didn't comply with their demands, so eventually, they forced a false confession out of her. They were at the police station for just twenty-four hours, but it must have felt so much longer – they experienced pain and torment every moment.

Once the police had extracted their 'confessions', Shagufta and her husband were separated and sent to different prisons. Their children were collected by family members and taken to a secret location. Everyone feared the mob would come after their children next.

I'm sure many of you reading this will have heard of Asia Bibi; she was accused of blasphemy in Pakistan in 2009 and became the first woman whom Pakistan's courts sentenced to death under the controversial blasphemy laws. Her case divided and polarized Pakistan, ultimately causing the death of many others as mobs took to the street calling for her execution. Two renowned politicians who stood up for her were murdered, and her situation triggered international condemnation. Together with French journalist Anne-Isabelle Tollet, Asia Bibi has written her own story in a book entitled *Free at Last*,[3] and I can't recommend it highly enough. It is so essential and relevant to Shagufta's experiences that I suggest you stop reading this book and read theirs before returning here.

Let me briefly summarize Asia Bibi's experiences anyway; I hope I can do her story justice. In 2009, on a scorching day when the temperature was around 40 °C, in Asia's village, she drank from a cup at a well that Muslim women used. Since Asia was a Christian, the women accused her of purposefully defiling them and then escalated their allegation over the following days by accusing her of blasphemy. The police arrested Asia and isolated her for around a year before her case finally came to court. It was then, based on false accusations that the police had been complicit in fabricating, that she was found guilty and sentenced to death. She continued to be held in isolation in prison for fear that the other prisoners would lynch her; there is such widespread hatred for anyone accused of blasphemy in Pakistan. Even the guards assigned to look after her tortured and mistreated her.

At one point, the Pope spoke up for Asia, which only worsened matters, and turned what Pakistan viewed as a domestic court case into an international battle between Islam and Christianity. Pakistan's Muslims were infuriated that another religious leader would dare to interfere. This is a cautionary reminder to us, as Christians, that we need to be very sensitive about how we advocate for freedom of belief.

The Governor of Punjab tried to obtain justice for Asia, which so outraged his own bodyguard that the bodyguard killed the governor. Again, there were more protests and violence. When the bodyguard was sentenced to death for his boss's murder, mobs took to the streets once more. Even the governor's 20-year-old son was abducted and tortured by the Taliban; he has since written a book about the five years he spent in captivity.[4] Following these tragic events, the government minister for minorities stood up for Asia Bibi. He was a Christian, and he, too, was assassinated. There seemed to be no stopping the cycle of violence and hostility.

Asia's case was so well-known and controversial that everyone in Pakistan knew about her and had vehement opinions about what should happen to her. Yet Christians worldwide were praying for her, and eventually, a brave Muslim lawyer called Saiful Malook obtained justice for her in 2018. He and the judges that acquitted her had to go into hiding, such was the outrage sparked by their decision. Jan Figel, the EU special correspondent for religious freedom, also played a pivotal role; he was the former EU commissioner I mentioned above in this chapter, who had been present at the panel discussion at the European Parliament. As I heard his name, the dots began to connect for me. Though Asia was formally exonerated, she spent another year in hiding before finally reaching Canada, where she lives with her husband and children to this day.

Asia Bibi has written about Shagufta in her book, so I'll quote her words to explain the links between them:

> Shortly after I was freed, my cell became home to a new Christian woman sentenced to death for blasphemy. Shagufta Kausar, a mother of four children ages five to thirteen, and her husband, Shafqat Masih, were sentenced by a Pakistani court for having sent blasphemous text messages . . . My lawyer, Saiful Malook, who returned to Pakistan after I was freed, is defending them. Despite threats, he wants to help the victims of the blasphemy law, which is exceptionally brave of him . . . I pray every day for Shagufta Kausar and Shafqat Masih.[5]

Now, here I was in Germany, with Shagufta before me. What a privilege to be with her and to ask her more about conditions in prison, where she spent eight years. Like Asia Bibi, she too was held in isolation for fear of what the other prisoners might do to someone accused of blasphemy. During the first two years of her ordeal, she saw no one other than the guards assigned to her. After that, visitors, including her children and a lawyer, showed up around once a week. It wasn't easy to apply for visitation rights, which put many people off from coming to see her. During her entire captivity, she received only a couple of letters from her husband.

Given that she couldn't mix with other prisoners, her cell had its own small bathroom with running dirty water. There was a single wooden bed but no mattress. A net across the window ensured the guards and prisoners could not see her; as a result, the room was dark all day long. In the women's prison, most meals consisted of potatoes in watery vegetable gruel; occasionally, she had chapatis (flat bread) to eat, and once a month, there was rice. Her husband interjected here to relate that conditions in the men's prison were slightly better because he had rice to eat once a week.

Since she was on death row, she wore a different uniform from the other prisoners. This was a constant reminder that the crime she had been accused of was considered worse than many. Unsurprisingly, the isolation and her looming execution caused considerable mental anguish, and she described remaining sane as her biggest challenge. Every moment she felt as if she was falling and getting up again in faith. She could only pray and hope in Jesus, and in her eyes, I could see that she had yielded control of her life to him; there was a deep resignation in them, but also hope that, during eternity, there would be enough time for justice.

Since Shagufta spent her nights praying, the other prisoners and guards called her mad; they could hear her yet could not approach her, which meant she remained out of harm's way. She began to experience Jesus' tangible presence and credits him with giving her the gift of foreseeing events. She would know if a family member were sick before anyone could visit to tell her.

On one occasion, she felt as though she was dying and knew she was seriously ill. As she lay prostrate on the floor, she prayed for the chance to live to see her children and mother again. As she remained on the ground, the sky opened above her, and she saw Jesus on a cross; she immediately felt as though she had new life. Simultaneously the woman in the cell next to her collapsed, and the prison superintendent was called. He ordered health checks for all the prisoners, which resulted in Shagufta seeing a doctor for her sickness. She thanks God for this miracle and the opportunity for her health to improve.

Eventually, Saiful Malook, the lawyer who had secured Asia Bibi's release, was able to take on Shagufta and Shafqat's case. After much wrangling, the courts overturned their death sentences. Now that the two of them live in Germany, they feel free and are delighted that their parents, and Joseph and his wife, are nearby. Their four children are with them and attend local schools and colleges. Why the mob ever accused them of sending the text messages remains a mystery, but Shagufta no longer asks God why these things happened to her and instead takes her feelings of bitterness to God, who promises justice. Now that she is safe and reunited with her family, she is willing to leave everything else to him.

Shagufta stood up and returned to the galley kitchen with her daughter, leaving Joseph and me to catch up with what had happened to him while his sister was imprisoned. Shortly after the police took her family into custody, Joseph received a phone call in Karachi; the caller told him he would soon be targeted and accused of blasphemy. He immediately switched off his phone and sought help from a priest he was friendly with. Together they arranged for Joseph to flee to Spain, where Joseph ended up at the Refugee Reception Centre in

Valencia. While there, he appealed directly to the Archbishop of Valencia for help, and thankfully, Joseph's story moved the archbishop. Joseph was offered a home at the Salesian house and given work helping several clerics.

During the succeeding years, Joseph was invited to speak at various events on behalf of his sister and became a well-known activist. In 2015 he was involved in a demonstration against Pakistan's blasphemy laws outside the European Parliament. During the event, he spoke with a Dutch activist who worked for the Jubilee Campaign; they began to correspond about his sister and eventually began meeting. After a short while, they fell in love and were married in 2019. Now they are settled in Germany, and the Dutch activist is Joseph's wife, whom I had been speaking with an hour or so before. She is still campaigning for freedom of religion and belief.

There had been so much family history to catch up with, but Joseph and I now found time to discuss the collated accounts of forced marriage and conversion that he had helped produce. It was this report, after all, that had led me to speak with him. In my view, the report is a masterpiece as it represents months of hard work and scrutiny in exceptionally trying conditions. It contains both statistical data and firsthand accounts. Joseph and a team of activists and lawyers in Pakistan followed up with every Christian woman and family who registered a First Information Report (FIR) between January 2019 and October 2022 relating to forced conversion, abduction and forced marriage. Initially, the team expected their task would take a few months; however, as new cases continued to arise and verifying details proved difficult, it took almost two years before the report was ready for publication.

I questioned Joseph about why he chose to compile the cases and take a stand against forced marriage and conversion, given that until 2019 his focus had been on seeking justice for those accused of blasphemy. He told me that while watching a video message from a family whose daughter had been taken, he empathized with their powerlessness and that her case was extremely sad. I wonder, too, whether subconsciously, the birth of his daughter, shortly before then, had softened his heart towards female victims of rape, although he didn't mention this. He certainly wouldn't be the first to view the world differently after becoming a parent. In the case that caused him to act, the girl's name was Arzoo, and she was only 13 years old when a 44-year-old man abducted her. Mercifully, the crime was committed in Sindh province, the only region of Pakistan where there is a law against child marriage. A court nullified the union and ordered Arzoo to remain in a shelter home before permitting her to return home.

Joseph prepared a twelve-page report about Arzoo and, with the help of the Jubilee Campaign,[6] was able to present it to the Pakistani Ambassador to the Netherlands.[7] According to Joseph, Arzoo's testimony produced a lot of hype, and pretty soon, Christian activists in Pakistan regularly reported instances of forced marriage and conversion to him. Finding and collating the cases was not hard, but verifying the details was much more of a challenge.

Of course, not every Christian family feels bold enough to go to the police and register an FIR when an incident occurs. Given the terrible history of false blasphemy accusations detailed above and the powerlessness many Christians feel in Pakistan, scores of cases go unreported. Joseph believes the one hundred examples in his report are just the tip of the iceberg.

Not only did the actual abductions and forcible conversions shock Joseph, but he became increasingly outraged by the shoddy work done by the police and judges. Their actions frequently exacerbated cases and worsened the situations for the women and their families. As he examined each occurrence in more detail, the specifics appalled him. The girl and her abductor were often held in the same police cell, endangering the woman's safety and making her vulnerable to coercion. Judges were repeatedly blind to the evidence before them, ignoring birth certificates and pretending the girls were older than they were and could therefore consent to sex, marriage and conversion. Joseph was adamant that the abductors were guilty of lewd sex crimes, including paedophilia, and were using religious laws as a cover for their acts. Whether complicit or not, the police and judges frequently failed to see past the lies.

Not all cases were black and white, though. Being a female Christian teenager in Pakistan is tough and, every day, society tells them to feel ashamed of their minority status. It would be tempting to think that converting to Islam would make life much easier. Unable to talk with Muslim men, nominally Christian girls may start 'making eyes' at them, hoping to be whisked away. Yet if they successfully arrange to elope with these men and willingly convert to Islam, they are soon woken up to reality. In almost all circumstances, the men prohibit contact with the girl's Christian parents and imprison her at home. Now that she is theirs, they don't want her to run off or be drawn back to Christianity.

I had discussed the issue of whether the girls were genuine Christians or not with everyone I had met so far. Jonathan, Cecil and Joseph each felt strongly that whether a girl has an authentic faith of her own or not (and who can know her heart except God), protecting her freedom of belief and association is essential. No woman should be denied access to her birth family, and conversion to or from Islam and Christianity should be free and of the girl's own volition. Joseph was keen to point out that, in many cases, the girls showed astonishing bravery and were prepared to die rather than leave Christianity. He found them inspiring.

Joseph and I discussed at length the case of Nira from Rawalpindi, Punjab. During the financial crisis caused by the Covid pandemic, her Christian family kindly took one of their son's (Nira's brother) co-workers into their home. Regrettably, they outstayed their welcome and began taking too much interest in Nira, who was only 12 years old. The family asked them to leave, but they refused and reminded the family that since they were Muslim and the family were Christian, they could do what they liked. They implicitly threatened to accuse them of blasphemy.

Nira was kidnapped and spent six months being abused by the co-worker and his wife, and was raped daily. Her family lodged an FIR when she first disappeared, so the case went to court. Her 'marriage' and 'conversion' were deemed genuine at the hearing, even though her birth certificate clearly indicated she was only 12 years old. The magistrate sent her back to live with her abusers. Finally, she managed to escape again and this time, with the help of activists, she was reunited with her family (see Chapter 5 for a fuller account of Nira's experiences).

In Sindh province, a law prohibits marriage under the age of 18 (as mentioned above), but no such law exists in Punjab. It would be enormously helpful if this law could be implemented in Pakistan's other regions to protect more girls.

Joseph believed that nearly every case of abduction is committed by a man who is already married. The federal law in Pakistan currently permits a man to have up to four wives if his existing wives consent to him remarrying. I imagine that if your husband is the type of man who wants another wife, telling him no would probably be very difficult.

I wondered aloud if perhaps more Christian police might help bring about justice more swiftly, and Joseph agreed they could, but at present, their numbers were too small to count. As Cecil had also stated, Christians were often overlooked for promotion, so their impact on changing institutions was limited. I had recently listened to a podcast[8] about a female-only police department in Islamabad. The hope was that women would feel more confident about registering cases of domestic violence or sexual assault if they knew they could speak with female officers. The unit had been successful, but Joseph quickly pointed out that Christian women are usually abducted from remote and rural villages. The police unit in Islamabad was well-intentioned, but it would not do much to help women outside the capital. Of course, it is only a start, and if other police forces duplicated the unit elsewhere, that would be a great help.

When it came to lawyers and judges, Joseph strongly believed that Muslim lawyers were better able to defend Christians. He explained that lawyers needed to have exceptional knowledge of Islam and the Koran to make their arguments and would be respected more in court if they were Muslim. Given that defending Christians can lead to death threats and assassination, only a few Muslim lawyers were willing to take the risk.

In his collated report, Joseph had included the testimony of many girls who were drugged by their abductors before they were snatched. Sadly, Joseph confirmed what I already suspected: obtaining medicines without a prescription was easy. Thankfully, many of the girls had been rescued and restored to their families, which is why they could tell their stories, but I wondered how many were still held captive. I also wanted to know if those who were freed received any counselling for the trauma they had gone through. Joseph thought that, in some cases, they might receive some form of psychotherapy at the government-run shelter homes or perhaps more informal counselling from a pastor's wife. It seemed to me that there was an opportunity here to better help the survivors of abduction and forced conversion by providing therapy. I wonder if the girls look forward to their lives now; will anyone be willing to marry them if they choose that path?

Joseph was well aware of the risks of being a Christian leader in Pakistan and spoke compassionately about the brave yet necessarily timid church leaders that remain there. He felt these leaders were impotent; if they stand up to the bullying Muslim clerics who want to rid Pakistan of Christians, they might lose their life, but they could not go anywhere else. Pastors were desperately needed to guide their vulnerable Christian flocks but could not do anything to protect them. In his view, two actions remained possible: prayer and demonstrating love towards their Muslim brothers. However, I sensed Joseph was a man of action, and sometimes prayer didn't seem enough. It's so hard to love people who are persecuting your family and friends too.

In my view, God has placed Joseph in Europe because he is a righteous troublemaker; it's no accident that he's here. If he had continued to live in Pakistan, I am confident he would have continued to upset Muslim leaders and politicians because of his outspoken views. The threats he received in 2013 would likely have continued and, sadly, it would have been easy for him to end up in prison or worse. Social media keeps him well-informed about events and incidents of persecution and forced conversion in his homeland. In Germany, he can safely draw attention to them and work for change. In this, he is like a lion, roaring for justice,[9] hence the title I have chosen for this chapter. To me, Joseph personifies the words of Proverbs 28:1, which encourage the righteous to be as bold as a lion. When they roar, lions also invite others to join them in battle, and I hope that, having read about him, you'll want to support Joseph in his work with Voice (or perhaps Roar) for Justice.[10]

Shagufta returned to the room and brought steaming piles of rice, chapatis and spicy dal with her. We ate silently, and I reflected on everything I had heard that day. Joseph had promised to put me in touch with more victims of abduction, forced marriage and conversion in Pakistan, and I nervously anticipated finding out more.

4

Defiant – Mashaka

I was beginning to worry; I hadn't heard from my Pakistani contacts, and I was desperate to interview another girl in order to keep my promise to write this book. Unfortunately, events in Pakistan over the summer of 2023 had overwhelmed my intermediaries: there had been widespread violence and an explosion of aggression towards Christians; my friends were busy assisting the Christian community in the aftermath.

Thankfully, towards the end of September, Joseph got back in contact with me. He too was reeling from the events in Jaranwala that I described in Chapter 2. Just the day before our chat, he had been made aware of a 17-year-old girl, Mashaka, who was currently in hiding. His associates in Pakistan had only just taken a statement from her and were in the process of providing her and her family with legal assistance. Joseph was convinced that her case was genuine and needed to be told to a wider audience, so he invited me to talk with her the following week over Zoom; he would be our interpreter.

A few days after our phone conversation, I received a news article from Joseph concerning Mashaka, the girl I would interview. Accompanying the story was a photo of her; she stood in front of a block concrete wall and looked very young and skinny. She was the same age as my daughter – 16 years – and

I would be hearing about how she had been raped multiple times. My stomach lurched. As I looked at her standing by the wall of the compound that was protecting but also imprisoning her, I considered her situation and realized how privileged I was to hear her story. I wondered if I would be capable of interviewing someone so young who was still experiencing trauma. I didn't want to upset her with my questions, and I wanted to be sure she was willing to talk and was not being coerced. I would need to take things slowly, and when we met each other over Zoom, I assured her she could stop the interview at any time.

When the interview day came, despite my precautions, I quickly got the impression that Mashaka wanted to talk. She knew what had happened to her was dreadfully wrong, and she was determined to defy her rapists. Hence, I have chosen to name her as 'Defiant' in the title of this chapter.

Mashaka and her father appeared to be sitting beside each other on the end of a bed in a dark brick-built room when my call went through to them. They kept looking over the screen to talk to other people, and there appeared to be many members of a large family wandering about. Mashaka's father, whom she called Papa, looked gaunt and exhausted; I am sure that being on the run from his daughter's abductors must have been a terrifying experience, and it showed on his face and in his posture. For an Asian man, his hair was long and untidy, and my first impression was to write him off as unimportant to the events that unfolded. He didn't appear capable of much action. Yet I was wrong; he is a hero in this story and, as a church pastor, has demonstrated iron-clad faith in God. His bedraggled state was probably the result of many sleepless nights over the two years since the family's ordeal had begun.

Before our conversation started, I invited Joseph to open in prayer for us. Mashaka immediately grabbed her dupatta, the scarf part of her salwar kameez, and placed it over her head. Like many Asian Christian women, she held the conventional belief that women should cover their heads when praying. Thankfully, I happened to be wearing a scarf, too, and so I lifted mine over my head as well. I wanted to respect her commitment to submission in God's presence, which she was visibly demonstrating by the use of her scarf. Once we had asked God to guide our conversation, we continued talking.

Mashaka was born in Lahore but grew up in a small village in Okara, around 100 kilometres away, where they were the only Christian family among the area's approximately 10,000 inhabitants. They lived on their ancestral land, and it had been many generations since the first Christian convert in their family. As a result, they did not know how Christianity had reached them. Mashaka's father attended seminary as a young man, and it was while there that his faith came alive. Now 56 years old, he had been a full-time pastor all his adult life, and he balanced this with cultivating some crops and keeping some animals on his small plot, as most land-owning Pakistanis do. The church that Mashaka's father pastors did not have a building and instead met in members' homes. Since there were no other Christians in their village, they travelled to surrounding settlements for meetings and, all told, there were about fifty people in their church.

Mashaka's family were especially vulnerable since they were outnumbered so heavily in their village. Although it wasn't large, the land they owned was productive, and it caught the attention of a nearby Muslim family who resented the presence of a Christian family in their village. This Muslim family decided to intimidate the pastor and his family and hoped to cause trouble for them so they would leave their land. Once gone, the Muslim family hoped to claim it for themselves. In October 2021, they broke into Mashaka's home, stole some items and defaced the house by scrawling graffiti across the front.

Mashaka's father bravely reported what had happened at his home to the local police, and they turned up at their property to take statements and see for themselves what had happened. Despite Mashaka's family being Christians, the police appeared to take the matter seriously, and one particular inspector was very diligent. The case was registered, and a First Information Report number was issued. This alone is unusual, as very often the police refuse to allow Christians to lodge official cases against Muslims.

Mashaka was outnumbered at school, where she and her older brother were the only Christians. She said this was difficult for her as her Muslim friends sometimes tried to convert her, and she would end up arguing with them. Her favourite subject was English, and she had ambitions to be a doctor. When I interviewed her, it had already been a year since she last attended school, and she seemed frustrated and sad as she told me about her past life, but I sensed that none of it mattered to her any more; her life had been violently interrupted, and what was the point of thinking about those things now?

Wanting to change the subject, Mashaka offered to give me a tour of the compound where she was temporarily hiding. I saw the family's cow and goat, and there were people everywhere, primarily engaged in preparing food. I noticed a low charpoy, an Asian bedstead, used indoors and out, and felt a pang of familiarity. The charpoy evoked strong memories of India and Nepal; the simplest things can trigger such wistfulness.

Joseph explained that the home belonged to a Christian family who were his distant relatives; they had five daughters, meaning they were somewhat socially outcast. He had been helping to support them and had learned of Mashaka and her plight through them. Just one week before my interview with her, Mashaka's family and his relatives had attended the same Christian funeral. When Joseph's relatives heard Mashaka needed help, they offered to hide her and her father for a few weeks. They also advised them to contact Joseph and Voice for Justice, who were now engaged in trying to advocate for them.

Given that the compound was so busy, Joseph encouraged Mashaka to find somewhere quieter where we could talk about what had happened to her privately. She entered a different dark room and lowered her voice.

Mashaka explained that in early 2022, following the robberies and damage to their house, their complaint went before a magistrate and court proceedings were initiated. Her father appeared at the local magistrate's court to give evidence, and the police arrested the perpetrators, all of whom came from one large family that I will call the Sattars. Regrettably, the case was suddenly dropped, and Mashaka's father was forced to withdraw his complaints. We can confidently assume that the Sattars paid a bribe (or perhaps several), and everything they had done was conveniently brushed under the carpet.

Although there was no justice for Mashaka and her family, they thought their difficult times were over and were reasonably content to move on with their lives. They had made more progress with the court cases than hoped and wanted to put the incident behind them. The Sattars, however, were not content with how things had turned out. They felt aggrieved about the trouble they had been put through with the local judiciary and were enraged that they had been forced to pay a bribe. Unbeknown to Mashaka, the Sattars began to plot their revenge.

In October 2022, a year after the first break-in, Mashaka was getting ready for school when several men broke into their home. They carried an aerosol can and, when they had sprayed it in her father's face, she watched him fall to the floor unconscious. Then they came for her and partially knocked her out with the drug in the can, too. Then they grabbed her and bundled her into the back of a waiting car.

This was the beginning of the most harrowing day of Mashaka's life. She was driven from place to place, and since she was nearly unconscious, she couldn't be sure where she went. The group switched cars several times, and during these swaps, which took place in remote places, she was beaten and raped by all four of the men who had snatched her. They took turns with her body and ripped her clothes. It was impossible to stop them because of the toxic aerosol fumes; and each man carried a gun, so she feared for her life. Just hours after leaving her house, she was covered in bruises, and her face was red raw from the slaps they lashed on her.

Everything happened while Mashaka was in a drug-induced haze, and I'm grateful she can't fully remember all the gruesome details of what happened to her. The third or fourth place the group came to was a madrassa, an Islamic school next to a mosque. In her dishevelled and bloody state, she was hauled before a cleric and told to convert to Islam. Initially, she was defiant and unwilling to do so, so the men continued to hit her in front of the cleric and, when they threatened to kill her, she gave in. The men handed the cleric the sum of 50,000 PKR (approximately £150) for a certificate of conversion, and she was given a new name. This name was never used by the men who took her there, though; instead, they chose to call her all kinds of slurs but, officially, her Muslim name was now Zara Fatimah.

From there, the group left the madrassa, and her abductors gave her a change of clothes. They took her to a lawyer's office in Okara, and she deduced that she wasn't all that far from home; they had been driving in circles. At this office, she was again forced to comply with the group's wishes and had to press her thumbprint to a certificate of marriage. When she dared to ask why she was being forced to do this, they slapped her in front of the lawyer and told her they would kill her older brother and family if she didn't obey. According to Joseph, lawyers are respectable members of Pakistani society, but all this one did was watch Mashaka being abused and said nothing to stop it.

Mashaka was now married to Abdul Sattar, who was just 23 years old at the time. Although he had been one of the men who abducted and raped her, she believes he, too, was forced to take part in the Sattar family's plot for revenge. Abdul was by no means innocent, and there is no excuse for his actions, but under pressure from his family he participated in the abuse against her. If he had stood up to his family and refused to take part, they would no doubt have found another man to take the leading role.

At the end of this horrific day, Mashaka was taken to a remote area and locked inside a shed usually used to keep animals. Over the following fortnight, several more men visited her to rape her. Some of these men were married, some were old, and others were young and single. It was a free-for-all, and she felt as if she was barely alive. They repeatedly told her how much they hated Christians, especially her father. Very often, the men forgot to feed her or give her water and, if she did receive some sustenance, it was never more often than once a day.

After about two weeks, the abuse from the other men ended, and Mashaka was left to live as Abdul's wife. The whole situation was a sham, though, as he never took her to his home, and she didn't meet any women from his family, such as his mother. She continued to live in the animal barn, and Abdul would rape her. Sometimes, she tried to fight back, and on other occasions, she tried to steal his mobile phone to call her father. When Abdul caught her doing this, he would cut her with a knife or put the knife in a fire before burning her with it. Her arm is still covered in scars that testify to the horrific violence he inflicted upon her.

Mashaka's voice is small but strong as she tells us all this. She sounds like a child, but she is emboldened, and it is clear that she is glad to be telling her story and that we are listening. Joseph also adds some of his own thoughts at this point; he explains that after several months, many girls give up fighting or trying to escape. They convince themselves that this is their new life and that their own families would no longer accept them even if they did return. Mashaka was different, though, and she did not give up. Although she began to pretend to be nice to Abdul to reduce the abuse he inflicted on her, she was still looking for a way to escape.

In the meantime, Mashaka's father was also refusing to give up. When he came round from the toxin he had been exposed to from the spray can, he immediately called the police.

They arrived at his house, and he told them everything. Despite his horrendous ordeal and the identifying details he gave them, the local police refused to register the case or do anything to help. Mashaka's father suspects that the Sattar family had already tipped the police off and had bribed them to take no action, therefore wasting his time.

Over the next few weeks, Mashaka's father appealed to as many other police officers as possible and wrote to them about his daughter's disappearance. Eventually, he made contact with a high-ranking officer who finally took action and registered the case. This resulted in a court summons; Abdul Sattar was asked to present his 'wife' before a magistrate.

Before Mashaka arrived at the courthouse, Abdul and his family told her precisely what to do. The magistrate would ask if her conversion and marriage were consensual, and if she disagreed in court, Abdul and his brothers would kill her. The Sattars threatened to finish off her family, too. Mashaka had no choice; she would have to lie to the magistrate to protect her family, which she did. What I find most sad and frustrating is that the magistrate believed the word of a teenage girl; he did not ask for her birth certificate or proof of age before accepting her false testimony. It should have been evident to him that she was under duress and not acting of her own free will. Joseph and Voice for Justice also feel strongly about the lack of checks made to verify the age of witnesses and are vehemently campaigning for proof of age to be made mandatory in cases such as this.

Mashaka's father was also at the courthouse, hoping to take her home if the magistrate nullified her conversion and marriage. They saw each other in an external corridor, but it was too late. By then, Mashaka had already made her false confession, and she was whisked away from her father by the Sattars. I am sure at that moment, he must have felt utterly defeated and heartbroken; I can't imagine how he kept going.

Back at the animal barn, Mashaka was made a prisoner again. However, her new tactic of being nice to Abdul began to pay off, and he started to trust her. He dropped his guard a little, making him less careful than he should have been. On one occasion, he went away and mistakenly left his phone behind. Mashaka seized the opportunity and immediately called her father, who borrowed a motorbike scooter from a friend and bravely came to get her. Finally, they were reunited.

Unable to return to their family home because the Sattars would know where they were, the family went into hiding. They travelled to another city where they lived with various Christian families. Since Mashaka's father was a 'wanted man', he had to remain indoors most of the time, and he was therefore unable to work to pay their way. Their host families would put them up for a few weeks before asking them to move on. Everyone feared the Sattars, who were well-connected and who they knew would be trying to track them down. The best option was to keep moving from place to place, even though this was exhausting and they barely had the means.

As mentioned above, Mashaka's father had repeatedly tried to obtain justice for his property and daughter through the judiciary. Not all the cases had been resolved, and he was summoned to court again to tie up some bureaucratic loose ends. The Sattar family sent some lackeys to the courthouse to identify and tail him. These men followed her father back to their stopgap safe house and told Abdul Sattar where Mashaka was hiding.

Just days later, Mashaka was abducted again. I can't imagine the terror she experienced this time around and the flashbacks she would have had of her earlier experiences. Every alarm bell in her head must have been clanging. She was taken to a different animal shed and locked in, and a few days later, she met Abdul's mother for the first time. I suppose his mother must have discovered what Abdul had done when it became public at the court. Unsurprisingly, given that she was part of such a cruel family, Abdul's mother was no kinder to Mashaka than he was. All three of them were forced to live together as they knew the police would be looking for Mashaka. They couldn't return to the former animal shed as Mashaka's father knew where it was, and they couldn't remain at home because the police knew where it was. Mother and son continued to lock Mashaka in an animal room. He would rape her, and his mother screamed obscenities about Christians at her.

From time to time, Abdul tried to be kinder and told Mashaka that they were married and she should just get used to it. He told her he liked her and wanted her to remain his wife. She employed the same tactic as before and tried to be friendly, knowing he would be less likely to beat her if she complied with his wishes. Abdul was 'not the sharpest tool in the shed' and began to trust her again. Two months after her second abduction, he once again left his mobile phone in the room with her. When the place was quiet, she rang her father, who came immediately to rescue her. What a hero!

Since he so bravely collected her, Mashaka's father has continued to receive death and abduction threats on his phone. Mashaka tells him he should change the number, but since she has so evidently memorized his current number, I can see that he might be reluctant to switch it. The two of them have been on the run for the last five months, and I am speaking to them while they still have no permanent home or refuge. Their story has not ended.

Throughout my conversation with Mashaka, I wanted to be confident that she was sharing with me through choice rather than coercion. I repeatedly reminded her only to tell me what she wanted to. If memories were too painful, dredging them up was unnecessary. However, I got no sense from her that she was shy about what had happened; in fact, the opposite was true. She was well aware that these events were dreadful, and she wanted Christians around the world to know. In particular, Joseph stressed that her abductions had been planned; these were not crimes committed in the heat of passion but acts of evil perpetrated in cold blood.

I only sensed sadness from Mashaka when I asked about school; she had been out of school for a year since her abduction in October 2022 and mourned the opportunities she once looked forward to. She does not know what the future holds and told me her only desire is to live, nothing more. To hear a teenager speak so bluntly was hard. I wish she had higher expectations for her life and was hopeful, but how can she be?

As for her and her father's itinerant lifestyle, their relatives are gradually closing their doors to them. Understandably, their wider family, who live not far above the poverty line to begin with, don't want to risk becoming targets and making life even more challenging for themselves. The Sattar family is actively seeking after Mashaka and her father, and revenge will be violent if they are found. I can understand why their relatives fear sheltering them.

I stupidly asked how she and her father maintained their faith in God. Did they feel close to him, or did they sometimes feel abandoned? My clumsy words caused offence. I did not intend to suggest that God might have abandoned them, and I regretted my phrasing. Still, at the same time, I was desperately curious to know how they could maintain their Christian faith despite being targeted because of it. My faith feels so flimsy in comparison. They told me they had seen God perform so many miracles that they had to believe in him. On *one* occasion, Mashaka's father had prayed for a man who was mute to speak, and he did! I felt inspired by their faith and resolved to pray for more miracles so that my faith would not falter when hardships came my way. Their offence at my question also caused me to consider if I would be similarly offended if someone suggested God had abandoned me. I had a lot to learn from them.

My follow-up question was better; thankfully, I was learning. I asked how we should pray for her, and she gave me three requests. First, she wants the threats they are receiving to stop. Then, she wants to be safe. Finally, she hopes her father will continue his Christian ministry. I asked her about Pakistan; what does she want for her country? Her reply was focused on the Sattar family and groups like theirs who terrorize Christians. She sighed and thought momentarily before saying, 'May God forgive them', which I thought was an especially wise and careful answer. When I asked if she could forgive them, she said 'No', which is perfectly understandable given that the Sattars are still making threats towards her. She told me that her prayer right now is for justice, and I am grateful that 'God is just: He will pay back trouble to those who trouble you' (2 Thess. 1:6, NIV).

Joseph and Voice for Justice are helping Mashaka and her father, but their assistance is mostly legal aid. The support Voice for Justice can give depends on the time their in-country advocates have available to help Mashaka's family. Since the organization is run on a shoestring, there is sadly very little available to help with material needs, although Joseph wishes this were not the case.

I wish I could have sat with Mashaka for our interview so that I could have embraced her when it ended. Originally, I had thought I would like to visit Pakistan to conduct these interviews but, had I done that, I as a white British woman might have been spotted going to the village and compound where she's hiding. I might have unwittingly put their lives further at risk. It's far safer for her if I remain here in Belgium, and meeting and interviewing her over Zoom is an honour.

When my daughter who is the same age as Mashaka returned home late from school that evening after a football game, I held her tight. My daughter is not without worries; she is growing older and has to think about her future but, mostly, she is free to enjoy life and follow her passions. My daughter's presence was comforting after everything Mashaka had told me. I pray that Mashaka will one day be able to live a similarly worry-free life in which she has time to pursue her interests. As her father supports her through this impossibly difficult period, I hope they find comfort in each other and 'may the God of hope fill [them] with all joy and peace in believing, so that by the power of the Holy Spirit [they] may abound in hope' (Rom. 15:13, ESV).

5

Girl Child – Nira

Have you noticed that every day of the year is assigned multiple titles? For instance, I begin writing this chapter on 15 December 2023 and, according to Google, I have three reasons to celebrate. It is Bill of Rights Day in America, Cupcake Day, and International Tea Day. I am delighted to inform you that International Tea Day is being commemorated as I write this at the military base where I live. How very proper! For the entire month of December, we are also asked to enjoy exotic fruits and root vegetables. Tomorrow promises better treats than today, and I look forward to marking National Chocolate-covered Anything Day. Yippee!

Back in October, Joseph had invited me to observe a much more critical and non-food-related day. It was the United Nations Day of the Girl Child, and he would be addressing an online meeting to highlight the plight of persecuted Christian and Hindu girls in Pakistan. Incidentally, the UN refers to a 'girl child' rather than just 'girl' to make clear that they mean a female who is a minor. In modern parlance, the term 'girl' has lost the implication of youth it once carried.

Joseph and several other witnesses and activists would be presenting to a meeting with one of the longest names I have encountered. The event was titled, 'Hybrid UNGA78 3rd

Committee parallel event – Urgent call to action to protect the Girl Child: Combat slavery and stem kidnapping, trafficking, forced marriage and religious conversions of underage girls and women'. It further cemented my impression that the United Nations likes to clarify what it means precisely. I suppose working in an international environment with people from around the world, it is best to be as distinct as possible.

The meeting was broadcast from a wood-panelled conference room in the UN Plaza, New York. Just five people were in the room, sitting around an octagonal table; however, multiple cameras could focus alternately on different speakers. Some of these cameras were set to mirror the image before them, and others weren't, so overall, it was pretty disconcerting and challenging to gauge who people were addressing when they spoke. Most of the contributors and observers, like myself, were watching online.

The key person in the room was the Special Rapporteur on Contemporary Forms of Slavery, Professor Obokata from Japan. The woman who introduced him had an American accent, so she dropped her 't's when she said his name; it sounded to me as if she said his name was Professor Avocado. However, I'm not judging; I'm sure I couldn't say his name correctly, either! Professor Obokata was extraordinarily polite and organized, and when I looked him up online, I discovered that he had taught at Keele University and is now at York University (where my son studies). Before this, I wasn't aware that special rapporteurs had other jobs. I had hoped they would devote all their time to causes such as ending slavery, especially since his role encompassed researching slavery across the entire world. Perhaps his knowledge should be shared with the next generation of lawyers and activists at universities, but I can't help thinking he must have an enormous workload.

Professor Okobata began by explaining his job and that his role included documenting instances of trafficking; child marriage is included within the definition of trafficking (another indicator that he has an extensive remit; surely armies of full-time workers are needed to investigate these issues). Sadly, there had been an uptick in the number of under-age marriages during the Covid pandemic as families sought to palm off their daughters on other families, who would bear the responsibility of feeding and clothing them.

If the special rapporteur had reason for concern, he could contact governments and encourage them to act. He seemed like such a nice man but his role struck me as weak overall. If all he could do was 'encourage' governments to observe human rights and look after girls, then no one was really holding them to account. Maybe others in the UN had more power?

The panel discussion began with Caroline Doss – an Egyptian woman and President of Coptic Solidarity – who shared her experiences standing up for Coptic Christian girls. These girls could be snatched or deceived by Muslim men and would disappear. Thankfully, many girls had been successfully tracked down through the use of social media; however, she was frustrated that abductors were rarely arrested, and prosecutions were almost unheard of. The formal justice sector was completely letting these girls down and, even once the girls were reunited with their families, no help was given for coping with the repercussions of their trauma.

Although Caroline had become quite upset during her short and moving presentation, the discussion moved on quickly, and Joseph was next. His address was finely tuned to the audience's needs, and he highlighted several issues that affected girl children that could be addressed with international pressure. First, he articulated the need for the minimum age of marriage to be 18 years across both sexes and in all provinces in Pakistan. Currently, the age limit can be as low as 16 for girls in some areas and, often, birth certificates are ignored with no heed paid to the age of the girl. He then summarized his published report pertinently by stating that 86 per cent of the cases they had documented involved girls under 18. He finished by adding that Sharia laws must not take precedence over secular laws as, in general, these reduced the merit of women's testimony. Once again, I was impressed with Joseph's fierce passion to end this form of persecution, which was tempered effectively by his encyclopaedic knowledge of the subject. He came across exceptionally well, and I was silently cheering him on from behind my computer screen.

We moved to Nigeria next and to a woman whose own mother had been sold for marriage when she was a teenager. The special rapporteur was attentive to her moving story and her calls for politicians in Nigeria to set a better example by not marrying young girls themselves. Until Nigeria's elite changed their ways, she did not see the situation improving for the average girl.

The meeting continued apace, and two fascinating female activists were up next. The first, Marcela Szymanski, is Editor-in-chief at Aid to the Church in Need, a huge Catholic development agency working in 150 countries. She is responsible for producing their biennial Religious Freedom report and, in 2021, also compiled 'Hear Her Cries: The Kidnapping, Forced Conversion and Sexual Victimisation of Christian

Women and Girls'. Based in Brussels, I jotted down her name and hoped to arrange to meet her.

Then it was Sonja Dahlman's turn to speak, and she offered another perspective. As a journalist, she had covered the abuse of Yazidi women by the Islamic State. Her reflections on how their stories were reported in the media were enlightening and challenging. She was also a theologian, and this combination meant that her comments gave me much food for thought. More about her later, too.

All these topics were covered in just forty-five minutes. The special rapporteur spoke again and offered his assistance in holding governments accountable. He also offered to intervene in individual cases if the advocates could provide him with details. He had one further question for each activist and asked how they wanted to see awareness lead to action. It's a question I have also been pondering as I write this book.

Joseph gave a comprehensive answer and highlighted the need for existing laws in Pakistan to be implemented; the UN should demand that they are. He finished by inviting the special rapporteur to visit Pakistan with him so he could see for himself the pain caused to the girls, their families and their communities. It was an impactful conclusion.

A month or so later, I received a message from Joseph to tell me that Nira wanted to share her story with me. In my haste, I forgot to check with Joseph how old she was, so I found myself one Monday morning in December interviewing a 14-year-old over Zoom. I was a little annoyed; I had already turned down a couple of interviews Joseph had suggested because the girls were too young. Yet here I was. However, by the end of our talk, I had changed my mind. Nira was still in the middle of her crisis and wanted to talk to me because she needed all the support she could get without delay. I would have been wrong to deny her the opportunity to ask for help, so I listened.

Nira was shy and withdrawn. I knew she had been abducted and raped; her story is summarized in Chapter 2 about Joseph, and I found myself talking down to her. I did this because she is a child, and it seemed appropriate, yet the idea that she had been abused became more and more abhorrent to me. If she is young enough to be spoken to in softer tones than I would with an adult, then her abductor must have lost all his humanity. I could not get my knowledge of what she had endured to compute with meeting this young girl in front of me.

I began to ask her some questions about her childhood, but it was evident that she didn't want to be reminded of happier days. Her answers were monosyllabic; her father was a daily wage labourer, and her mother did domestic work. She was born and raised in Rawalpindi and did not know when her family had first converted to Christianity. Before her abduction, her family used to walk for fifteen minutes to a medium-sized church; about 100 people attended each week.

Nira had two older brothers. The eldest appeared on screen to say hello, and he was completely different from his sister. He exuded a gentle warmth and willingness to talk that his sister had none of. I hoped that Nira wasn't being forced to speak to me, and I thanked her again for being willing to share her story.

We tried to start the conversation again; Joseph was coaxing Nira to say more since I was an author and had to have longer answers so I could write about her. We learnt a little about her first school, how it was Muslim, but that was OK because there were always three or four Christians in each class, so she wasn't alone. A Christian school was nearby, but her parents couldn't afford to send her there. Although Catholic missionaries set up countless schools across Pakistan during the twentieth century, in most areas, they no longer benefit the country's Christians. Since these Catholic schools had become so successful and prestigious, only the most elite members of Pakistani society, who are almost all Muslim, could afford to attend them. Though many are no longer leading schools, they are still too expensive for most impoverished Pakistani Christians.

I tried to coax Nira to say more and asked if she had enjoyed anything at school. Her expression didn't change, but she stated that she did enjoy school and though her marks were good, there was not much else about school to be proud of. That was all she wanted to tell me about it.

Nira spoke as much through her eyes as with her words. When Joseph translated her words for me, she would look away. Though she didn't smile, her eyes would widen if she was telling me something happier. Thankfully, she was slightly more optimistic about her current school; her family had been forced to move after her abduction and recovery, so now there was a charitable Christian school close to them.[1] Her class was planning a Christmas function with a Christmas tree, manger and other activities. Listlessly, she told us that she would be in the choir and that there might be dancing. It would be her first school Christmas celebration, so I don't think she knew what to expect. I continued to smile at her as much as I could, and slowly, I think she began to trust Joseph and me.

When Nira seemed ready, I asked if she'd like to tell us about what had happened to her. She looked down, pursed her lips and said she was. She became relatively chattier then, perhaps seeing my other questions as a waste of time and wanting to get on with the central part of her story.

In October 2022, Nira felt unwell and was off school for the day; both her parents were at work. Two guests, a married couple, turned up at her home, and she telephoned her parents to let them know. These visitors were familiar to her, as they had spent several months living with her family. Her elder brother had worked with the husband, called Imran, and when Imran had fallen on hard times, her charitable brother had offered to put them up for a while. The couple had moved into Nira's home with their three young children.

While living with them, Nira's family had witnessed the man's violent moods. Imran was abusive to his wife and children, and his children behaved oddly; on occasion, they had eaten flakes of paint from the walls. After four or five months, Nira's family had to ask their guests to leave. I believe it had been by mutual agreement. Both families were tired of sharing the same home and were ready to part ways. However, just fifteen days later, the couple were back, and Nira was alone with them. She had never given much thought to Imran; she disliked and avoided him. She had no idea he was interested in her or even noticed her.

Once back inside her home, Imran immediately began lying to Nira. He told her that since Mother's Day was coming up, he had telephoned her parents, and they had agreed that she could go to the shops with them to buy a gift for her mother. Nira was suspicious immediately, as this seemed unlikely, but she couldn't say no to Imran; it would have been rude to do so, and she knew his temper.

Once in the car with them, supposedly on their way to a market, the couple offered Nira some juice, which she accepted. Appallingly, the juice contained a strong sedative, and she blacked out. Many hours passed, and she woke up in an unfamiliar, locked room. It was night by then, and unbeknown to her, Imran and his wife had brought her 200 kilometres from her home to another city entirely. They were now in Faisalabad.

Once again, Nira's eyes are talking to me. As she recalls the terrifying fear she experienced when she awoke in a strange room, she looks dazed again and withdraws. I don't ask her any further questions and instead allow her to tell me when she wants. She proffered short snippets of information that paint a picture of what happened next.

She screamed and shouted at Imran and his family and demanded to know where she was. He boldly told her he had kidnapped her and, since this was her new situation, she ought to get used to it. Then he beat her to shut her up.

There were hammers and steel. He hit her with those.

Some things occurred that she could not explain, and by this, I understood that they were sexual, and Nira perhaps didn't have the vocabulary to describe them.

He electrocuted her.

Nira had to perform all the tasks that an enslaved person would do. Imran lived in a brick-kiln community, and she had to carry out arduous tasks there. She also cooked, cleaned and cared for his children, who were 2, 5 and 8 years old. These young children witnessed her abuse, as did Imran's wife, mother and brother. On a few occasions, they tried to stop him but were not successful for long. It is likely that each of them was scared of him, as well. Nira had seen Imran beat his wife and suspected that his wife was secretly relieved that another girl was on the receiving end of his sadistic outbursts for a change.

In all, Imran held Nira captive for seven months and fifteen days. During all this time, Nira's parents knew where she was but were powerless to free her. Incredibly, Imran had sent her parents a text message on the day he abducted Nira to tell them he was taking her. He lacked all humanity.

Nira's older brother joined us on Zoom to explain what had happened. After reading Imran's text message, Nira's parents went to the local police station to lodge a First Information Report, but since it was a religious festival, only a skeleton staff was present at the police station, and they weren't interested in taking action to find Nira.

A few days later, the police asked for a bribe of 80,000 PKR (approximately £225) before they would do anything. Nira's brother took a week or so to raise this amount and handed it over to the police. So, after Nira had been held captive for two weeks, the police turned up and arrested both Imran and his wife and brought them, with Nira, to the police station. Nira's family had to pay yet another bribe so they could speak with her.

While in police custody, Imran was held in the men's section, but Nira and Imran's wife were detained in the same cell in the women's area. Imran's wife took out her anger and fear on Nira and berated her constantly. She told Nira that Imran would kill her parents and brothers if she tried to get away from him.

By the time of his arrest, Imran had already acquired documents stating that Nira had converted to Islam and that she was now married to him. The three of them appeared in front of a judge, but Nira could not speak the truth about her abduction and abuse since she was thoroughly scared of Imran and had taken the threats made by his wife to heart. Imran had also bribed the police and, since he had a little more money than Nira's family, he could afford a higher sum and thus the police gave evidence in his favour. The judge ignored Nira's birth certificate and other documents provided by her family, which clearly stated she was only 13 years old. Outrageously, he sent her back with Imran and his wife to their home, her prison.

Nira's captivity endured for another seven months. I can't imagine how desperate and defeated her family must have felt. Knowing your child is being abused is every parent's worst nightmare. In the meantime, all they could do was contact kind-hearted activists like Joseph and try to draw attention to her case. Various Pakistani Christian news outlets (these are mostly online) picked up her story, and her situation became reasonably well-known among the Christian community. According to Joseph, it was published just 'here and there' in the wider Pakistani media.

Imran was, in fact, a Muslim convert. He had grown up as a nominal Christian, and when he wanted to marry a Muslim woman, he converted to Islam. No doubt, he had also observed how life in Pakistan was easier for Muslims. Despite his conversion, Imran and his family still had their home among a Christian brick-kiln neighbourhood. Although Imran tried to keep Nira hidden and beat her to keep quiet, a Christian family living nearby noticed a young girl was being abused. They bravely tried to rescue her, and one day they got her into their house and concealed her from Imran. Mercifully, Nira was able to explain who she was and, thanks to the news coverage, this family could contact her brother, who came to collect her. It transpired that the two Christian families were distantly related.

As soon as Nira's brother saw her, he knew she needed immediate medical treatment. She was scarred all over from the electric shocks and beatings, and some of the wounds were still fresh. Nira was very weak and almost unrecognizable. Imran had cut her hair in a fit of jealousy, not wanting her to be recognized or any other man to look at her. Her brother took her straight to a hospital.

Once Nira was reunited with her family, they realized they could not stay where they had been living, nor could Nira return to her old school. So they upped sticks and moved to a new area and school where no one knew them. This move had taken place five months before my interview with Nira.

Fittingly, her mother returned home at this point in our conversation and appeared in the doorway behind Nira. She had been at the hospital with Nira's middle brother because she had an ongoing illness; I wondered if it might be stress-related. Nira's older brother, who had been speaking to us, had also been preparing dinner, but now his mother took over. Before she went to the stove, I asked if she wanted to tell me anything. She came to the phone immediately with an urgent message.

Nira's mother spoke to me with a vehemence neither her son nor daughter had yet used. She was desperate for justice and wanted Imran locked up. She explained that Imran had been spotted at Nira's new school twice in the last three weeks. Suddenly, the timing of my interview made sense. Nira and Joseph had reached out to me and wanted to tell her story because they needed immediate help. Nira was in danger again; Imran could snatch her at any time, and they were contacting everyone they thought could help, including me. I had been worried that I was making Nira relive painful memories by conducting my interview with her, but Imran himself was causing the distress. He believed Nira was legally his wife, and he wanted her back. No wonder the family were terrified.

All Nira's family could do was hope to reopen the case and that the police would take definitive and proper action this time. They had repeatedly tried to secure justice, going to various police departments and asking higher-ranking police officers for assistance. However, Imran kept coming up with more money than they could, and he would grease the palm of whoever he could to make rulings in his favour. Imran even sold off his ancestral land to afford the bribes, angering his extended family. The police would routinely turn up to interrogate everyone, and Nira's brother heard on the grapevine that Imran's family were deeply ashamed and exasperated with him.

Thankfully, Nira's family successfully managed to have her sham marriage annulled in the courts. However, Imran didn't recognize the annulment and, while Nira was free from him, he felt humiliated; only getting her back would appease him. Meanwhile, Nira's mother not only wanted him to leave them alone but also desired that he be punished. I can't blame her. His presence at Nira's school terrified all of them.

Nira came back on the phone, and we began to wrap up the interview. For the first time, she cried and told me that, unfortunately, each time she and her family approached the police or a court for help, she had to recount her story all over again. This was traumatizing for her, and she was sick of repeating the details. Each time she did so, it upset her more, and she felt everything she said was ignored anyway. If the police or judges believed her, why didn't they lock up Imran? I thanked her again for trusting me with her story, and she expressed relief that I had not pushed her for extra information. She smiled through her tears, and I hoped and prayed I had done the right thing by speaking with her.

I finished by asking her what her hopes for the future were. She aspired to become a doctor and was grateful no one at her new school knew what had happened to her. Hopefully, she will be left alone to study and work towards a happier future in peace. She mumbled a prayer, and I joined her in calling on God to prevent Imran from ever contacting her again. Before we ended our call, Nira thanked and admired Joseph for all he was doing to help.

As soon as our chat had ended, I felt awful. Was I right to have spoken to such a young victim? I, too, felt dread wash over me at the thought of Imran abducting her again. He had to be stopped, but I felt utterly powerless to do anything. That afternoon, I came down with a fever (probably Covid) and slept terribly. I tossed and turned in my bed all night as my temperature soared and everything Nira had shared with me raced through my feverish dreams. I awoke, still dreadfully unwell, but with the knowledge that simply writing a chapter about Nira that no one would read for another two years was not good enough. I needed to do something to help her immediately, but what?

As a published author and Christian writer, I now have a body of work in the public domain that anyone can view. It's a little scary and bizarre; sometimes, my good friends might call me out on something I am doing and remind me to take note of my own work, especially when I'm having a wobble about something! In this case, I felt God remind me of a YouVersion Bible plan I had written earlier in the year about the Good Samaritan.[2] On Day 5 of the plan, using Vincent van Gogh's painting of the parable as my inspiration, I suggested that the Good Samaritan might have asked one of the priests to help him lift the man onto his horse. The priest, who could have felt overwhelmed by all the injured man's needs, might have found it easier to help if someone asked him to perform a specific short-term task.

I decided to take my own advice and invite others to help Nira in a specific way. I had to wait a couple of days until I felt better, and then I sent a newsletter to my subscribers asking them to do three things. First, I asked them to pray for Imran to be arrested and detained. Second, I asked them to send me an 'Amen' or verse of encouragement that I could forward to Nira via Joseph. Finally, I suggested they invite other prayer warriors to pray too. I wanted to be clear and specific, not asking too much, and putting the onus on God to act. He was Nira's protector, not me, and I had faith that he could do something even though I felt powerless. Once again, I was reminded of the image I shared in Chapter 2; taking Psalm 27:5 as my inspiration, I called on God to metaphorically place Nira high on a rock and conceal her out of Imran's sight.

I had interviewed Nira on Monday and, as soon as I was well, I sent out my subscriber newsletter three days later, on Thursday. I received a few messages of support for Nira and forwarded these to her. (My subscriber list isn't all that big; thank you so very much if you were one of those who responded.[3]) Despite my supposed faith in God, I was astonished on Sunday when Joseph contacted me to say Imran had been arrested the day before, on Saturday. Of course, I shouldn't have been surprised; I know God answers prayers. But the speed and thoroughness of his answer took me by surprise. Oh, me of little faith!

Two weeks later, Imran was still in custody; it appeared that this time, he really had run out of money to bribe the police to let him go. Finally, justice was being done. The longer he remained in custody, the greater the chance he'd be deterred from stalking Nira in the future. Perhaps if he's incarcerated for a long time, his wife and children will be able to build a new life without him and they, too, will be able to live without fear of abuse. I pray that he will remain behind bars.

Of course, if you are reading these words in my published book, I wonder if you will also feel powerless since it will be at least two years after the events I have described. Can I encourage you to keep praying? Nira will still be a 'girl child' when this book is released; she won't turn 18 until 2027 and, of course, just because she is older doesn't mean she will feel any safer. Imran, whether free or in prison when you read this, will most likely still have sadistic tendencies and a violent temper. Please pray that he is unable to abuse anyone. Finally, I am sure I will still be in contact with Joseph, so why not send me a message to pass to him that will encourage him and the women and families he is helping at that time? I can be contacted on my website (www.DislocatedChristians.org).

At the start of this chapter, I wrote about the multitude of names we give to days and all the bizarre events we are meant to celebrate on each of them. I could give Imran many names, too; he could be labelled as a paedophile, a monster and an abuser. Yet, even he is made in the image of God, and it would be wrong of me to write him off. I hope you will join me in praying that he will rediscover his Christian faith, and experience deep and thorough forgiveness for his actions. I pray he will repent whole-heartedly; miracles can and do still happen.

Jesus told us, 'You have heard that it was said, "Love your neighbour and hate your enemy." But I tell you, love your enemies and pray for those who persecute you' (Matt. 5:43–4). This is my daily challenge.

6

Word Wielder – Marcela

Following the publication of my book about women in Kathmandu, I was interviewed by several British Christian radio stations. One of these was Hope FM, based in Bournemouth. The talk show was called, *My Story My Song* and was hosted by the amiable Stuart Anderson. The programme was formatted like a Christian *Desert Island Discs*, and I was asked to choose five meaningful songs and explain why they were important to me.[1] My third selection was a classical piece by Bach; I explained that whenever I write, I can't listen to music with words and prefer to type along to a Classical Focus playlist on Spotify that begins with one of Bach's cello suites. As I commence this chapter, there's no way I can listen to such placid music; it is not in keeping with the person I'm profiling in this chapter at all. Instead, I have discovered a playlist called Feisty Classical, which is much more apt.

I first encountered Marcela during the UN briefing on the Day of the Girl Child in 2023, which I had watched to support Joseph (see Chapter 5). Marcela was incredibly knowledgeable about her broad remit to document global cases of persecution and compile them into the well-regarded Religious Freedom report. This chronicle of injustice is sadly over 1,000 pages long and covers instances of oppression in 196 countries.

With her UK colleagues, she also authored a report in 2022 called 'Hear Her Cries', specifically about persecution against women, which included testimony from Pakistan.

When I heard her speak online, Marcela was persuasive, passionate and thoroughly professional. She did not exaggerate nor inflame her audience, yet she was unequivocal that terrible crimes against many people, including young women, were being committed, and action to stop them needed to be taken. As she spoke, she stressed that it was not only necessary but also possible to protect women, and I admired her pragmatic approach.

Since Marcela was based in Brussels, not far from my home in Mons, I was keen to meet her in person and interview her about the role of communicators in stopping atrocities against women. After reading about the women in the three previous chapters, I imagine my readers might feel overwhelmed and powerless; I hoped Marcela's story would inspire everyone to become involved in global efforts to end violence by using the power of their voices. I made contact but could not meet Marcela for a couple of months because she had plans to visit Washington, DC, where she would be presenting in front of the Congress's Foreign Affairs Committee. Of course, I would wait.

In the meantime, Marcela and I began a conversation by email, and she sent me a treasure trove of articles. Most challenging to me was one she had written, 'On the Misleading Use of the Terms "Forced Conversion" and "Forced Marriage" of Girls and Women'.[2] It made me stop and reflect on my own use of language; was I guilty of using misleading terms?

In essence, Marcela's article argues that the term 'marriage' is too gentle to describe what women forced into these situations in Pakistan (among other places) experience. Instead of highlighting the long-term and sustained physical and sexual torture they are subjected to, it makes their experiences appear civil and normal. In my own research, I had already encountered people who confused the idea of arranged marriage with forced marriage. There is a vast difference between them; a forced marriage means the woman is compelled into a situation whereby she is repeatedly raped and cannot get away from her abuser. This amounts not only to physical but also to psychological torture.

In Marcela's (currently) unpublished piece, she states that forced marriage would be better labelled as enslavement and that it is a severe violation of a woman's human rights. This is particularly important since, if a crime is labelled as slavery then, under international law, it gives a woman many more rights and potential paths to justice. In short, words matter and can mean the difference between freedom and captivity.

Once Marcela had returned from her high-status trip to the USA, I arranged to meet and interview her at her home near the famous battlefield of Waterloo. It seemed an appropriate place for someone who fought for the rights of others to live. However, a week before our meeting, I received a formal WhatsApp message from Joseph asking me if I might be willing to submit a prerecorded video for a parallel event to the sixty-eighth session of the United Nations Commission on the Status of Women. The Jubilee Campaign, the American organization that Joseph works closely with, was organizing the event, during which they hoped to shine a spotlight on gaps in social protection systems for minority women in four countries: Egypt, Syria, Iraq and Pakistan. Joseph was asking me to share my insights on the persecution faced by women and girls in Pakistan.

Having seen how these meetings worked in practice a couple of months earlier, I immediately said yes to Joseph. Though I didn't have any details about the event, I knew that I had more than enough material to talk for five minutes or so, and I wanted to highlight the injustices I had been hearing about in Pakistan. I also had nothing to lose; being an independent author gives me tremendous freedom.

Once I had said yes to Joseph, I began to seriously consider what I would say. The parallel event was less than two weeks away, and I wanted to represent Pakistan's Christian women well. I would no doubt be speaking to representatives at the UN who already knew about the issues, so what could I possibly add to the discussion that they hadn't heard before? The challenge posed by Marcela's article also swirled through my mind: what terms should I use to describe the circumstances of the girls I had interviewed?

Back in 2011, I learned a hard lesson about communicating the needs of others. The organization I run, Women Without Roofs – Nepal (WWR), had successfully applied to participate in a Christian charity version of *Dragon's Den* (known as *Shark Tank* in the USA) in the City of London. Wealthy Christian benefactors would gather in a conference room within the Square Mile and listen to pitches from five Christian charities before deciding, there and then, how much to donate to each of them. Each charity would have just five minutes to make their proposals. There were strict rules for the charity presentations; we were allowed to show only one photo and to utilize one speaker. As WWR's representative, I would put forward our case for funding. The donors had a further twenty minutes to make up their minds and write their cheques, which were presented before everyone returned home. At the event I attended, almost £50,000 was donated within the hour-long meeting, and my organization, WWR, received £14,000 (we received the second-highest amount).

About a week before the event, I had had a timed practice run in front of a women's group at a local church. I had told them what WWR did, how many women we helped, and I had also described our set-up in Nepal and the UK. My presentation had completely missed the mark; no one had been interested or impressed, and when I had finished speaking, there was silence. I went home and cried.

Though the reaction of my friends deeply hurt me, practising in front of them was pivotal for my future work. I realized that to successfully help people understand what happens in Nepal, I had to relate real-life accounts and engage my audience emotionally. This has shaped how I write and communicate today; I am telling my story and the life experiences of others now because I hope my readers will connect and identify with our emotions, motives and challenges. I endeavour to avoid exploiting the women I write about, though, and I try not to sensationalize their experiences; it can be hard to find the right balance.

Of course, tugging on people's heart-strings to get them to act or support a cause isn't always right. It can lead to the wrong priorities, and money might get channelled to those who cry loudest rather than to the greatest needs. By definition, the weakest and most vulnerable have no voice to make their needs heard. Much work has been done to remain objective and to counter the effects of emotional pleas. The ethicist Peter Singer[3] and the Bill and Melinda Gates Foundation, among others, champion a data-driven approach to aid and, famously, their research concluded that purchasing anti-malarial bed nets is one of the most effective ways to save lives. But, in a complex world where suffering can't always be counted, I believe telling the stories of individuals remains vital.

As I continued to ponder how best to communicate the needs of Pakistan at the UN Parallel Event, I received an invitation through my husband to attend a talk at the NATO base where he works. Although the event was open to all dependants as well as NATO staff, I think I was the only wife to turn up; everyone else was in uniform or office wear. Around one hundred personnel sat in the Montgomery Theatre on base to hear a highly decorated British police officer and former advisor to multiple British home secretaries talk about stopping human trafficking. He did this by telling the story of one vulnerable young man. Evidently, this policeman also believed in the power of stories. The case he described was about a victim called Darrell Simester, who was rescued in 2013 from a farm in South Wales where he had been enslaved for thirteen years.

What struck me most about Darrell's story was the role that different organizations had played in obtaining justice for him. Darrell's parents repeatedly asked the police to help them locate their vulnerable son. Yet it was only when they turned to social and local media, which emphasized the emotional impact of Darrell's disappearance, that action was taken. When Darrell was at long last found on the farm, and there was a tense stand-off between his family and his captors that was about to turn nasty, his family didn't call the police but rang up the local media, who turned up with a camera.

Once again, I was struck by the power of words and stories. The *Sun*, a tabloid newspaper in the UK, threw its best journalists and resources into uncovering everything Darrell had suffered. When the story broke, it triggered a public outcry.

This, in turn, led to political interest by representatives anxious to keep their constituents happy, and legislation was eventually changed to protect victims like Darrell in the future. Without the camera shots that were used as evidence and the widespread moral outrage that the *Sun*'s coverage unleashed, the police, on their own, might not have been able to change the law. Both hard police work and passionate reporting worked in tandem to improve the legal situation for victims of human trafficking. I wondered if similar could be done to improve the lives of Christian women in Pakistan.

I was excited to hear Marcela's opinion on the power of communication and as the day of our meeting arrived. I hoped I would find the right words for our interview. When I arrived at her home, her Dutch husband showed me in and found Marcela for me. Marcela is Mexican by birth and grew up speaking Spanish; she talked to her husband in Dutch and then turned to greet me in English. Already, I felt I was observing a superior communicator.

Marcela's surname is Szymanski, which, as I suspected, is a Polish name. Her great-grandfather went to Mexico in the early twentieth century to flee poverty and the wars that had overrun Europe then. He worked in security for Mexico's oilfields, and I suggested to Marcela that she was continuing her ancestor's vocation of protecting others. She laughed; I don't think she had seen it like this before.

Among her immediate family, Marcela was the second of five children. Since her father was often away, her mother was regularly overwhelmed with caring for their boisterous household. At the age of six, Marcela distinctly remembers trying to talk to her mother, who would not listen and kept talking over her. Her frustration with her mother left a lasting impression and, subsequently, Marcela discovered that when she wrote, she was respected and could make herself heard through her writing. A few years later, Marcela noticed that what she read in newspapers did not tally with reality. From that early age of her first communications frustration, she devoured many (in her view) age-inappropriate articles about the state of politics and crime in Mexico, and she determined she would become a journalist, to which her parents vehemently objected. By the time she applied to university, Marcela was set on her desire to uncover corruption and write the truth. I believe she is firmly committed to the idea of the media being a vital component of democracy and that it is necessary to hold governments accountable.

Marcela is a lifelong learner; her first degree was a BA in communications from Universidad Anáhuac in Mexico City. After this, she moved to Brussels, having been recruited as the EU correspondent for a Mexican television channel. She began reporting on relations between the Mexican Government and the EU, chiefly trade deals between them. Although the Mexican delegation to Brussels was usually cagey and tried to avoid journalists, she found the European negotiators far more transparent (particularly the friendly Finnish contingent!). She could easily approach them and ask where talks would take place. She built trust with the delegation's chauffeurs and asked them when they were due to take the Mexican commission to various hotels for discussions.

Once Marcela knew which hotels were hosting talks, she would enter them and ask to 'check' the conference rooms where negotiations were scheduled. On one occasion, she discovered a meeting room with cloth-covered tables set out in anticipation of talks later that day. She pushed one of the tables against the wall, pulled the tablecloth down to reach the floor and then hid herself underneath, where she took copious notes on everything discussed. During this period, her investigative journalist skills became finely honed, and she told me that she continues to utilize them as she uncovers human rights abuses today. This is necessary in Pakistan, where so much abuse of women happens behind closed doors, and sniffing out the real story is vital.

While Marcela was perfecting her journalistic skills, her future husband was working for the Council of the European Union in Brussels, and the two of them met at the city's Gilbert and Sullivan Society. They married, and when her husband relocated to Atlanta, USA, she accompanied him and decided to study for a master's degree in economics before completing a Ph.D. in international politics. She gave birth to a son, and then her family returned to Brussels, where they bought the house where they still live. I had already noticed stunning informal portraits of her family on the walls of her living-room. As a mother, Marcela felt she could no longer work the irregular hours that being a correspondent demanded, so she 'recycled herself' into an EU relations media specialist.

Marcela took a position with an independent global public affairs consultancy. As an advocate and lobbyist, Marcela's task was to represent countries to the EU so they could achieve policy objectives and obtain favourable trade deals. Among her first clients were the governments of Kazakhstan and Indonesia, and the EU Presidency by Greece, who sought the best possible agreements with the powerful EU. As we continued to talk, she name-dropped many more famous leaders; I was astounded.

In 2003, Marcela found herself at the heart of one of the biggest political maelstroms to rock the EU. Following Iraqi

President Saddam Hussein's refusal to disarm, the USA led the so-called 'coalition of the willing', made up of countries joining the USA in the war in Iraq. EU nations and their respective populations were deeply divided over whether to go to war; the evidence that Iraq had weapons of mass destruction was shaky, to say the least. Consequently, it seemed the EU might splinter as countries refused to ally with one another.

As Georges Papandreou, the EU President, travelled from country to country trying to hold it together, it was Marcela's job to ensure he was always prepared and never caught off guard by the media. As countries and populations protested and negotiated, her job was to keep him appraised of everything going on and to foresee and brief him on any problematic questions he might be asked when he arrived somewhere. I can tell she loved doing this and is also enormously proud that the EU held together and even expanded. Her firm helped to arrange a massive celebration in April 2003 at the Parthenon in Athens, where ten new countries were welcomed to the EU, and the Treaty of Accession was adopted.

As an aside, Marcela tells me she has time for only two politicians, whom she feels 'are what you see' and have integrity. These two are Georges Papandreou and the late former American President, Jimmy Carter. Unfortunately, there wasn't time to discuss how she knew him.

My interview with Marcela took place just after the news of Alexei Navalny's unwarranted death in an Arctic penal colony. He was an ardent critic of Vladimir Putin and had been imprisoned for decrying the Russian dictator. Marcela's next client in the 2000s was similarly detested by Vladimir Putin. At the time, Vladimir Putin regularly travelled outside Russia, and Marcela would turn up wherever he went to persuade journalists to ask him difficult questions and to remind him of her client's right to a fair trial. This client is still alive today, so I think Marcela can consider herself as having done a successful job for him. Unfortunately, she believes that now Vladimir Putin no longer travels outside of Russia (since invading Ukraine, he has been charged with war crimes and could be arrested), actions like hers can no longer be used to hold him accountable, and so no one could speak up for Navalny.

While working for a Scandinavian consultancy, Marcela first encountered Aid to the Church in Need (ACN), by whom she is now employed. This vast organization distributes aid from the Catholic Church and its lay members to beneficiaries supported by almost six thousand projects in one hundred and fifty countries. Applications for assistance are made through bishops and local Catholic dioceses, and the organization focuses on channelling aid to the suffering church so that it can continue helping others in distress. This suffering might be due to war or natural disasters, and its impact might be poverty or persecution; in many cases, it encompasses all of them. In total, ACN spent a staggering €148 million on its activities in 2022, and Pakistan is one of its largest recipients within Asia, hence my interest in its activities and Marcela's work.

Having formed a good working relationship with ACN, she decided to apply when the organization required a new editor-in-chief for its biblically proportioned Religious Freedom in the World report. It was an epic undertaking. The Religious Freedom report takes two years to produce and is almost one thousand pages long. It is translated into six languages and launched worldwide according to a strict media timetable.

When she took it on, expert authors and each of the national offices of ACN contributed information about religious freedom in their country for the report. They would send the evidence in a format that suited them and reflected the data they could find. Marcela standardized the entire process and information-gathering method. She required the same information from every country and provided clear definitions so that evidence from one country could be compared with another. She insisted that each entry in the report should have the same structure as the others so that users could easily find what they were looking for. Most importantly, she introduced a means of tracking laws so that it was easier to see when certain legal rights were granted to citizens of each country and which nations were lagging behind in terms of religious freedom. Every fragment of information had to be backed up with a source so the report was demonstrably reliable. All these changes were done with advocacy in mind. Marcela was adamant that the report would be helpful to anyone advocating for and on behalf of religious freedom.

Unsurprisingly, the first report was the hardest to compile. Marcela had to convince countless representatives in each country and many new authors that the new standardized format was important and necessary. In all, she was responsible for editing and publishing four editions of the report over ten years. Each subsequent edition became a little easier as the authors and editorial team got used to the format and could see its worth. Ultimately, the process was so efficient that the information-gathering exercise was akin to completing a form.

As each version of the report was compiled, Marcela noticed that women from countless countries were subjected to specific and higher levels of persecution than men. Regrettably, all of the world's major religions tend to place men above women. When one of these religions is dominant in a country, the religion can become completely male-centred (or even macho) in its external practice, and women suffer. This observation inspired her to amass evidence to compile the 'Hear Her Cries' report she spoke eloquently about at the previous UN event. Once again, she wanted the report to be functional and made sure the data was concrete and could be reliably used to brief the press. The ACN office in the UK added creativity to the publishing process, and the information was printed as a brochure. She was pleased that the team's innovations presented a persuasive argument for protecting vulnerable women.

Sadly, Marcela's final Religious Freedom in the World report was beset by difficulties as the Covid pandemic had a massive impact. Not only did ACN lose staff, which was upsetting and resulted in much loss of working knowledge, but also the data contained in the report was either impossible to obtain or reflected a tragic uptick in persecution. Covid was regrettably exacerbating friction between religious groups in some countries. The report's publication deadline, announced a year in advance and co-ordinated across continents, had to be pushed back several times, which caused Marcela considerable stress. She and several other ACN staff fell sick and, in her case, it took her a month to recover.

Upon returning to work with ACN, Marcela relinquished the editor-in-chief role and took up the mantle of Head of International Advocacy. Despite the pressures and deluge of appalling news she has to deal with, she says this is a far easier role for her and one she can do almost with her eyes closed. Most recently, her advocacy role took her to Washington, DC, which was why I had to wait before arranging my interview with her.

Currently, Marcela believes four countries require the most monitoring of their supposed commitment to freedom of religion and belief. They are Nigeria, India, Nicaragua and Pakistan, and each of them appears to be on a steep downward trajectory with regard to the tolerance of other faiths and the treatment of minorities. The current situation in Nigeria was the focus of her advocacy in America, and I am glad to report that she was successful.

Nigeria is a country of two halves. In the Muslim-majority north, Christians face enormous persecution. More believers are killed there each year than in all other countries combined.[4] This has led to massive internal migration as tens of thousands of Christians have been forced to leave their land and become refugees within their own borders, seeking refuge in the churches. Marcela pulled up a map on her phone to show me what was happening. Despite being within a day's drive of Nigeria's capital, Abuja, no one there, let alone anyone from the outside world, seemed to know or care about the enormous Internally Displaced People camps that were springing up and are continuing to grow. However, Catholic bishops and first responders collated evidence and submitted it to Marcela's team at ACN. Clearly, the situation needed surveilling, and Nigeria was no longer upholding its commitments to religious freedom.

It was a privilege to hear Marcela explain her advocacy strategy when faced with situations like that in Nigeria. Her response is based on the answers to four questions, the first of which is: What's killing people? In this case, although the Muslim tribes were carrying out the massacres, it was the Nigerian Government's nonchalance that allowed them to get away with it.

Having identified the main actor, the next question is: Who does the Nigerian Government fear? As with many countries, the US administration was high on that list.

Then she asked: What can the US administration 'threaten' the Nigerian Government with? This answer had multiple components but centred on less favourable trade with the USA and closer monitoring by them.

This led to the final question: Who could decide to take these measures? In this instance, it was Anthony Blinken, US Secretary of State, and the US House of Representatives. So, that's where she focused her advocacy efforts.

The result was House Resolution 82, which 'calls for the Department of State to designate Nigeria as a country of particular concern for egregious violations of religious freedom. It also states that the President should appoint a Special Envoy for Nigeria and the Lake Chad Region with the rank of Ambassador to monitor and combat atrocities there'.[5] Her visit to Washington DC had been a success.

Much of Marcela's advocacy relies upon disturbing evidence, and she receives photos and videos of atrocities from around the world almost as soon as they happen. She shared some of these with me, and I saw the lifeless bodies of a family in Nigeria piled up in the back of a van. The image made my stomach lurch, and I wondered if the constant barrage of terrible news she has to deal with makes her question her faith. She grew up Catholic, although none of her family went to church. Nowadays, she attends Mass regularly both in her local parish in Waterloo and wherever she travels. She says this is vital to her; without faith in God, coping with all the suffering she hears about would be impossible. There is too much pain, and she finds solace in knowing that one day she will have eternal life (hopefully on the 'good side', she added), and there will be no more crying or tears.

As I write this, I hope young Christians will sense a calling to advocacy and grasp Marcela's excitement for fighting battles with words and persuasion. Of course, I hope women in Pakistan will benefit from having more people speak out, but many other countries and people groups need advocates, too.

I learnt so much from Marcela; she is meticulous about what she says and writes but also stresses the importance of listening. She told me that too many lobbyists are 'on send' and spout all manner of information but do not think about who is listening. They waste their time complaining repeatedly to the wrong people, which amounts to 'no more than throwing pebbles in a lake'. Having an effective strategy is imperative. She also cautions against saying that these bad things 'happen all the time'; we should never accept atrocities as the status quo. I admire her ongoing outrage at the abuse of women. In her line of work, it is easy to become accustomed to hearing stories of persecution and violence, and it can be hard to remain compassionate. However, she remains feistily defiant.

In advocating for religious freedom, women, in particular, can find it hard to be heard. All of the world's main religions elevate male leaders above women and, time and again, Marcela finds herself in a room full of men. Very often, she is on the receiving end of mansplaining,[6] so she is savvy and doesn't waste her time with those who speak down to her. Women have a role to play here, too, and need to model how best to listen to others; sometimes, we are guilty of talking across each other. Furthermore, native English speakers are often guilty of monopolizing dialogue and not giving time for speakers of other languages to participate. English speakers must also learn to communicate in different languages so the voices of diverse people can participate in discussions. Marcela's final piece of advice was that the key to success in any negotiation is to get the decision-maker to repeat what you have just told them. If they think it is their own idea, even better.

As I absorb all this wisdom and return to thinking about my contribution on behalf of women in Pakistan to the UN Parallel Event, I feel overawed and thankful. I'm even more conscious of the power of words and the need to wield them well. I want to do justice to the stories I have heard from women in Pakistan; they face daily persecution, and I don't want to squander my opportunity to speak up for them. Marcela is an inspiring role model and I also want to follow her example. I pray too, for anyone reading this, that Marcela's story will inspire you. She has committed herself to professionalism and speaking truth; she believes anyone can do likewise. Her life is extraordinary, and the people she has met have been central to global events. This is precisely where Christians are called and need to be.

7

Speaker – Anna

On 20 March 2024, I participated by video in a parallel event at the sixty-eighth United Nations Commission on the Status of Women (CSW68). The programme was organized by the Jubilee Campaign and Coptic Solidarity. The text of my address is below or, if you would like a break from reading, you can view my contribution at https://youtu.be/BKhXiMp9Y2A

> Thank you so much for inviting me to speak to you today. I have been living and working on and off in Nepal for the last 20 years; however, for the last 2 years, I have been writing a book about women in Pakistan.
>
> My research began in Kathmandu, Nepal, where several hundred Pakistani Christians are living as refugees and asylum seekers, having escaped allegations of blasphemy in their homeland.
>
> Imagine for a moment a common scene in movies: a room criss-crossed with red laser beams. The slightest move will trigger alarm bells, and the protagonist will be caught.

Every Christian in Pakistan is similarly trapped by the blasphemy laws; the slightest infraction causes a popular outcry.

During my initial research, I found that the typical type of indiscretions that offend the Muslim community and provoke allegations of blasphemy are actions such as:

- Dropping a leaflet with verses from the Koran on it;
- Cleaning and painting a wall to remove a poster;
- Producing a church flyer;
- Drinking or eating from the wrong utensils or in the wrong place;
- Making a little more money than your neighbours; or
- Asking the wrong question in school.

These are everyday actions and, just like the red laser beams, it is easy to unknowingly cross an unseen line, cause offence and trigger an uproar

Until I began my research, I had no idea how wildly popular the blasphemy laws were. They have unwavering support among the general population in Pakistan, most of whom would like to see them strengthened rather than weakened, as I'd previously imagined.

It is in the context of these blasphemy rules that Christian families become targets for attack.

My inquiries have focused on speaking to girls affected by abduction, forced conversion and marriage. However, these girls are simply the weakest members of their families and often become targets because they are easiest to pick off.

When I began my interviews, I needed to speak to women over the age of 17 so they would be 18 by the time my book was published and, therefore, able to give legal permission for their stories to be included.

Distressingly, all the girls I have spoken to have been younger; typically, they are 14 years old when snatched; they are children. And their abductors should be identified as paedophiles and called out for torturing children.

When I ask the girls about their childhoods, before abduction, they are unable to speak of it; it has no meaning for them now. Remembering happier times appears to be impossible for them, and it is immensely sad to see them talk without hope.

By labelling the crime against them as forced 'marriage', it gives the impression that the girls are older and of marriageable age. They are not.

I have also read strong arguments for using the term 'enslavement' to describe the situation the girls find themselves in. This better emphasizes the ongoing abuse the girls are subjected to and also associates the crime with anti-slavery legislation. Internationally, a victim has more rights if she is recognized as a victim of human trafficking and slavery, rather than 'marriage'.

One particular girl had no confidence in the police. During her captivity, when the police had first intervened, she and the couple holding her had been taken to a police station. The girl had been locked up in the women's section, in the same cell as the wife of her abuser. This wife had been complicit in the girl's abduction and subsequent torture. In the police station, the wife continued to threaten her.

Another family told me that although they had no option but to rely on the police to arrest the abductor, when it came to the rescue, they had to take action themselves, which put them in enormous danger.

Their daughter was abandoned by her captor in an empty house but, by accident, a mobile phone had been left on a high window sill. Their daughter managed to telephone for help, but her family knew they had to reach her before the police. If the police took her into their custody, she would be returned to her abductor. They were confident this would happen since her abuser had obtained fake marriage and conversion certificates and, although the police knew these had been signed under duress, they would not go against them.

Every single survivor I have interviewed has been on the run from her abductor. All of them have had to leave their childhood homes and live, work and attend school elsewhere. The entire family has been uprooted, and they are rebuilding their lives in new cities.

Protection from the police and authorities after rescue is entirely absent. Unless the perpetrator is locked up, which in each case has never been for long, there is no plan to keep the girl safe. Her family has to use its own resources and contacts to flee and find refuge.

One girl I spoke to had moved elsewhere and started at a new school; in the week prior to my interview with her, her abductor had been spotted lurking outside her new classroom. She was petrified that he would snatch her again.

Any initiatives to provide victims with counselling and psychological support will have no effect until the girls feel safe. Furthermore, psychological support needs to extend to the entire family. Female survivors told me they now had distant relationships with their fathers and older brothers, and this caused them ongoing shame.

In summary, blasphemy legislation needs to be overhauled and much should be done to professionalize the police in Pakistan and help them prioritize the needs of victims. I believe laws are now in place that would protect girls, if they were adhered to, but there is an unwillingness by the police to put these laws into action on behalf of Christians. Once justice has been achieved, psychological counselling, so desperately needed by the girls and their families, will help them all to recover.

Thank you for your time.

8

Innocent – Shyla

It was time to interview another girl and, thankfully, Joseph was again keen to help. He suggested I speak with a girl whose father had been arrested for trying to secure her release. In Pakistan's upside-down justice system, he had been arrested for not releasing his 13-year-old daughter back to her abductor. The logic behind this seemed ridiculous, but I jumped at the opportunity to speak with them and suggested some possible dates. Only then did Joseph mention he was in Brazil and wouldn't return for a few days. However, even with jetlag, he was very happy to help me with an interview the day after his return. I was extremely grateful.

It turned out that Joseph had been in Brazil in 2024 for the G20 summit of global leaders. He had been boldly calling on decision-makers to pressurize countries to repeal blasphemy laws. He had also been demanding justice in the wake of the Jaranwala attacks in Pakistan, and for child marriage and sexual slavery to end. Photos that Voice for Justice posted on social media showed him standing among activists holding placards on the streets of Rio de Janeiro, where the summit took place. I have no idea if presidents and prime ministers pay heed to the cries of street protestors at these busy events, but I hope and pray that some of their entourage may see the rallies and take action. I love how Joseph continues to obey God's command in Isaiah to defend the oppressed:

Learn to do right; seek justice.
> Defend the oppressed.
Take up the cause of the fatherless;
> plead the case of the widow.
>> *Isaiah 1:17*

As usual, connecting with Shyla and her family in Pakistan wasn't easy. At the arranged time, they didn't call Joseph and so, after waiting a little while, he patiently contacted her Pakistani lawyer, who rang her father to chase them up. Joseph and I then conducted a bizarre interview through Zoom, with Joseph speaking to them via phone and translating. I could just about see Shyla on Joseph's phone as he held it up to his camera. She was young and innocent-looking; she had large eyes and was very shy. I felt sick to my stomach to know that she had been abused.

It wasn't late in Pakistan, but Shyla kept rubbing her eyes, and getting even a sentence from her was difficult. She was just so young and presumably unused to speaking with adults. However, she kept on smiling and seemed comfortable with us. I began by asking her about her childhood. Although she was born in a town called Khanewal, she now lives in Multan, which is the setting for Awais Khan's fictional novel, *No Honor*. He describes Multan as a city with village-like values. It is considered one of the most conservative cities in all of Pakistan, where women, even those who are Muslim, are particularly oppressed. This is evident from the city's population statistics, whereby men outnumber women by ten to nine, a sure sign of sex-selective abortion and the lesser worth given to women and girls.

Shyla lives with her two younger brothers, her father, who is a hotel cleaner, and her mother, who offers beauty treatments from home. They have moved several times within Multan, which is likely to indicate their poverty and the consequent instability. Despite this, they have been stable enough for Shyla to receive some education, and she reached the end of seventh grade at a school for both Muslims and Christians. I asked her if she had any hobbies or enjoyed sports, and Joseph, in an effort to encourage her to speak, asked if she liked football, cricket or basketball perhaps. She replied that it was none of these and, instead, she liked hide-and-seek; it was another blunt reminder of just how young she was.

Similarly, we asked her about their Christian faith, and she told us that her family attended church and that she liked Sunday school. In particular, she had enjoyed participating in the Christmas nativity, where she played the role of Joseph (which made Joseph smile). All the children who took part had been presented with a Bible, which she held up to the camera to show us. It was a beautiful book with gold embossed letters on the front. The text was in English, and she opened a page to highlight how small the font was. It was apparent that she was very proud of it.

As we asked these simple questions, Shyla responded to us exactly as a child would; she spoke and acted innocently and with the mannerisms of a youngster. This is important in light of decisions made by judges later in her story. In every respect, it was obvious that she was a child.

Having heard about Shyla's childhood, it felt awkward to move the conversation on to the difficult circumstances surrounding her abduction, but it was necessary. Shining a light on these atrocities is essential to prevent them, and colluding in their cover-up helps no one. I prayed that talking about these events wouldn't re-traumatize Shyla and, initially, she became more forthright as she described what had happened.

A family friend, whom they called 'Auntie', lived next door to them (the literal translation of the Urdu means they 'shared walls') and used to come to their home for Shyla's mother's beauty treatments. During these visits, Shyla would often help out her mum, and Auntie noticed how pretty and polite she was. Auntie began to tell Shyla that she should convert to Islam and that life would be easier if she did. Auntie also told Shyla about her nephew, who was in his twenties. Apparently, she also spoke to her nephew about Shyla, and he began to visit his aunt's house more regularly and would often snoop around looking for Shyla and trying to catch her attention.

Shyla's mother would occasionally visit her client's homes to provide beauty therapies. Auntie next door took advantage of these absences and invited herself into Shyla's home while she was alone. During these visits, Shyla tried to be polite, but Auntie continued to harass her and did all she could to persuade her to convert to Islam. Sometimes, both Auntie and her nephew would visit. They relentlessly badgered Shyla, and she could do nothing about it. Her parents couldn't say anything either in case their neighbours caused more trouble, which was entirely possible given that they were Muslim and had more sway within the community.

One day, when Shyla was alone in the house, three people turned up at the door. She opened the door and let them in, believing she had nothing to fear; after all, they had visited her home before. Auntie and her nephew were there, along with another man. Before Shyla could even think, let alone raise the alarm, they grabbed her, covered her mouth and carried her out of the house. Together, they placed her in a car and drove her to the outskirts of Multan, where there was an unremarkable village that she didn't recognize. As they drove, Auntie and the men told her to do as she was told; otherwise, her mother and father would be killed.

Waiting for them in one of the village houses was an imam who had already prepared documents for Shyla to sign. One was a marriage certificate, and the other was a new birth certificate that falsely showed she was 18 years old and named Zehra Bibi. Zehra is a popular Muslim name since Muhammad gave it to one of his daughters. Though Bibi is a term of respect since it means 'lady', her abductors showed Shyla absolutely no respect; her treatment at their hands was the opposite. With the papers before her, the small gang repeatedly told her that Islam is powerful; they were therefore powerful, and she must succumb to their power by signing the documents. She resisted for as long as she could, but eventually, the imam grabbed her hand and made her stamp the papers with her inked thumb.

Once the paperwork was out of the way, her kidnappers grabbed Shyla again and drove her to a new location where she was kept in a small room. She believes the house belonged to another 'Auntie', and it was here that the worst of her abuse began. Now that she was married to the nephew, he believed he had a right to rape her, and he would visit her daily to make her fulfil her 'wifely obligations'. He also allowed his brother to have sex with her on some occasions. Realizing that she could not stop them from abusing her, Shyla tried to be as compliant as possible and to win them over by being submissive. Her plan would eventually work.

I find it especially terrible that, as well as the nephews, at least two 'Aunties' were involved in Shyla's abuse. I can't help feeling that these women should have protected her. How could they have enabled their nephews' abuse of a young girl? Were they unable to see her humanity and vulnerability because she is a Christian?

Shyla has become quieter as we have been talking, and her mother, sitting beside her, has helpfully taken over telling most of the story. I was relieved by this because I wanted to spare Shyla from detailing her abuse to me. However, what happened next to Shyla can be explained only in light of events back at her home, so the phone was passed to her mother, who held it up to her face. There was a strong likeness, and Shyla's mother was also very beautiful. She continued to describe what it was like for her when she discovered her daughter was missing.

Shyla's mother returned home from her appointment at the client's house to discover an empty house. She knew something was wrong, but she waited until her husband came back from work soon afterwards before calling the police emergency line 15, which is similar to 999 in the UK. Although they were promised swift assistance, it took several calls before the police eventually turned up at their home to take statements from them and to find out what had happened. It was late at night by the time the police left, but they were in no rush and clearly had no intention of trying to track down the missing daughter. In fact, rather than investigating what had happened to Shyla, the police questioning had felt more like an interrogation.

Following more calls the following day, the police eventually registered a First Information Report and came back to their neighbourhood to arrest the abductor's brother, who lived next door. He was placed in a cell at the police station and was supposedly questioned by the police, but he continued to deny knowing anything about the abduction. After a week, he was released.

Shyla's father is also on the call with me and, despite a lengthy power outage, we continue talking once the connection is restored. He explained that when the brother was released, he realized the police weren't interested in the case as they had done nothing to actually track down his daughter. He had also received copies of Shyla's falsified birth and marriage certificates from an anonymous WhatsApp number, which the police also chose to ignore. Frustrated at the lack of police action, he felt it was time to contact a Christian lawyer, and this is how news of Shyla's abduction first reached Joseph.

With the help of a Pakistani lawyer and with Joseph's advice, the family filed a writ petition, which, in order to be heard, required Shyla's 'husband' to present her before a judge. For once, legal machinations moved quickly and, just a week later, the writ petition was heard at Multan's Supreme Court. Shyla and her 'new family' appeared before the judge, and her real family compiled evidence that she was a minor. A dossier containing her actual birth certificate and school reports clearly demonstrated her proper birth date and name. However, as I made clear above, just by looking at her and seeing her mannerisms, it is obvious to anyone that she is under the age of consent.

In court, Shyla was asked to state her name and age and confirm if she was Muslim and married. Since her abductors had threatened to kill her family if she told the truth, she was compelled to lie. She stated that she was Zehra Bibi, aged 18. When she said these words, her mother cried out to the judge, 'My lord, I am her mother.' Rather than showing any sympathy, the cowardly judge ordered her mother out of the courtroom and believed Shyla's blatant falsehoods. He ordered that she remain in the custody of her abductors, which naturally was heartbreaking for her parents to hear.

They did not give up, though. Over the next few weeks, their tenacious lawyer filed two more writ petitions to different judges at Multan's Supreme Court. Each time the case came up, though, the same thing happened. Despite all the evidence to the contrary, the spineless judges believed Shyla's words, and she was returned to her captors. As Joseph relays this information to me, I can tell he is thoroughly frustrated and angry with Punjab's judicial system. These judges should not have bowed to pressure from spurious Islamic groups to keep Shyla a prisoner and ought to have released her back to her family. The judges insisted on their own interpretation of Sharia law (which can also be called Mohammedan law) and decided that the falsified marriage certificate was akin to ownership papers. This narrow-minded reading was applied, even though anyone could see Shyla was only a child.

Despite the terrible decisions made by the judges in the courtrooms, the writ petitions were affecting Shyla and how her kidnappers treated her. Presumably, her abductors naively expected to take Shyla and keep her as their own without further interference from her family. However, the writ petitions and orders to present her in court meant they were under constant pressure to remain close to Multan and to treat her well so she didn't appear with visible injuries. In addition, with the help of local journalists, Joseph wrote about her situation on social media, and news outlets picked up her story. The multiple writ petitions and media coverage were putting ever more pressure on her kidnappers and ruining their plans.

As a result, Shyla's abductors came up with a new and more cruel strategy. They decided to sell her to someone in Saudi Arabia and began making pornographic videos of her. They also stripped her and took photos of her while naked. Apparently, they had already accepted a deposit for her from someone who wanted to buy her, and they flashed this money in front of Shyla to encourage her to go along with their sleazy film-making. A few weeks later, they took her to Lahore, around 320 kilometres away, where they planned to hand her over to the purchaser. All the while, she continued to comply with their demands as much as she could stomach, to avoid being beaten and abused.

Eventually, Shyla's compliance paid off. Her abductors dropped their guard, and her 'husband' left his phone in the room with her. She hastily grabbed it and called the one number she had memorized: her father's. She didn't know where she was, so she couldn't tell him how to find her, but she could at least tell him that she was alive. Her family were overjoyed to hear from her and attempted to have the call traced by the police officers assigned to their case. Unfortunately, the detectives could provide only a vague location for the source of the call; it was far too inaccurate to allow her to be found and rescued.

Then her family's lawyer filed another writ petition, which came just in time, and the gang had to leave Lahore and return to Multan. Once again, her abductor's plans were thwarted. Brilliantly, this coincided with a press release by the United

Nations. Joseph had been in contact with the UN Special Procedures Council, and they had put out a joint statement which included details about Shyla's case. It was a fantastic breakthrough and ultimately helped ensure her safety.

While in Multan for the final writ petition, with the press searchlight sweeping ever closer to the gang that held Shyla, she managed to escape. Her family suspects she was allowed to flee because of the trouble Joseph and the lawyers were causing. Once again, her 'husband' dropped his guard, and she quickly called her father to say she was on her way. She travelled across the city to her family home and, naturally, everyone was delighted to see her. However, they feared what would happen next. After all, her abductors lived next door.

Sadly, Shyla's church did not offer any support to her family during the period when she was missing. They were too afraid of what might happen to them if they got involved. However, Joseph and his brave lawyer friends did not shy away, and once Shyla was reunited with her family, they stepped up again and found a new place in another of Multan's districts for the family to stay; they even provided all the furniture the family would need. Joseph was in Pakistan when the move occurred, and he vividly remembers moving furniture in 40-degree heat at the height of summer.

Wanting to ensure Shyla's absolute safety, they tried sending her to a convent for a short while, but she was too homesick to remain there, so she returned to her family, which I am sure was the right decision. The family now lives in secret, and they do not even attend church, nor does Shyla go to school. Her abduction only occurred six months ago, and they remain far too fearful to let her out of their sight.

Shyla's family's troubles are sadly not over. Shortly after her family was rehomed, her 'husband' filed an FIR against her father, claiming that he had abducted his wife. It is absurd. The case went to court, and Shyla's father was sentenced to 'physical custody' for three days. Everyone in Pakistan knows that this means the judge gave the police permission to interrogate and torture him.

Unfortunately, the case remains open, and her father is still accused and uncertain of what will happen to him. However, he has not given up his fighting spirit and is currently arguing in the courts for his daughter's marriage to be annulled. Once again, her abductors are not happy with this as it makes them look bad and, instead, they are arguing for a divorce, which would legitimize the marriage in the first place. They are using the pornographic images they have of Shyla to try to blackmail the family and force them to back down. All these threats and counter-threats perpetuate a vicious legal cycle, with each side coming up with new ways to accuse and counter the other. Most recently, her abductors have invoked the notorious blasphemy laws, whose presence threatens the lives of every non-Muslim in Pakistan. I hope and pray that Shyla's abductors will soon run out of enthusiasm for further legal action and will drop all their accusations. Only then will she be able to live in peace.

As our conversation progressed, there were longer and more frequent power cuts; in the end, Joseph and I were left talking to each other. Sadly, I could not say a proper goodbye and thank you to Shyla and her family. Joseph and I ended our conversation by praying, though, and he told me about some projects he is considering that would bring the plight of girls like Shyla to a larger audience. Spreading the word about injustice is good, but the challenge for all of us who hear about the difficulties Christian women in Pakistan face is what we are going to do to improve their situation. I hope you'll start by joining us in prayer and will seek God for how he wants you to take action. It's no accident that you are reading this book.

9

Tide Turner – Saima

For all its faults, the online world is a place where people can express themselves however they like. Anyone can create a profile on social media or build a website; their humour, humanity and, unfortunately, any false beliefs can be disseminated for the entire world to view. Amid all the noise and clickbait, there are articles and videos online that tell the truth, and the people who post them courageously strive to raise awareness of vital issues.

Throughout the time I have been writing this book, I have been scouring the internet to discover people and sources of reliable information about violence against Christian women in Pakistan. Although many reputable Western NGOs report on these tragedies, it has proved tricky to find journalists from within Pakistan (who write in English) with much of an audience. However, they do exist, and they work hard to represent varied voices and experiences. Their role is perilous as they speak up for the very minorities they often represent, and the threat of a blasphemy allegation or physical persecution is never far away. I was keen to find and speak with one of these risk-takers and include their story in this book.

As I jumped from link to link on X (formerly known as Twitter) around the time of International Women's Day in

March 2024, I found myself on the White Post website. It did not describe itself as a Christian news platform but rather as a 'Digital Inclusive News Network'.[1] Its well-formatted news articles highlighted minority issues, and the YMCA of Lahore was a major advertiser. I paused; this appeared to be a source of the elusive voices I had been searching for. As I thought about it further, I realized that the name White Post itself was a reference to minorities and referred to the white vertical stripe in Pakistan's flag, which symbolizes that people of all faiths are part of the nation (see Chapter 1). I sent a direct message to the White Post's X profile, not knowing who would respond.

Thankfully, a forthcoming person welcomed my comments and started replying to me immediately. Initially, I didn't know who they were or whether they were male or female. We arranged to speak on WhatsApp a few days later when I could finally put a voice to the name. Kashif Nawab, a man, introduced himself as the founder of the Christian Journalists Association of Pakistan (CJAP). I had struck gold! Speaking to me was not just one reporter but someone who represented many others.

Initially, I assumed CJAP was a professional membership and lobbying organization, much like it would be in the UK. However, I was to be proved wrong. As Kashif explained, although it is concerned with those two functions, its remit was much broader and deeper. In 2019, when Kashif had already been running a relief organization called Social Action Transformation of Humanity for ten years, he had the idea to begin a group to support Christian journalists specifically. To be a Christian journalist in Pakistan is a precarious occupation. Carrying out their work requires reporters to have access to people and events but, all too often, Christians in

Pakistan face hindrances that prevent them from doing their job. Even enrolling on a training course might be problematic for non-Muslims. These barriers result in lost job opportunities and, consequently, income instability. Yet, thankfully, some Christians in Pakistan are determined to report the truth and want to follow God's calling on their lives to become journalists. It is these people whom Kashif wanted to unite, train, encourage and support. So, not only was CJAP a collective voice, but it also helped sustain journalists who found themselves struggling.

Although Kashif's plans for CJAP were only nascent in 2019, just a few months later, the Covid pandemic struck, and CJAP's members were out of work and in desperate need. At the suggestion of the Bishop of Peshawar, Kashif was able to organize food distributions to out-of-work reporters and their families. Then, as the country began to open up, he organized free-of-charge training sessions in multiple cities and offered subsidized travel to those living further afield. By taking CJAP across Pakistan, he has helped to build a network of journalists and their collective capacity.

As we continued to talk, Kashif told me that, at present, there are approximately one hundred and fifty members of CJAP, and most of these individuals work freelance for international news agencies. Their options for finding employment with Pakistani media outlets are limited due to their faith. Not only are employers reluctant to take on Christians, but many of these Christian reporters want to document minority issues and alleged blasphemy cases, which are allocated almost no space in the Pakistani media. Since the international media tends to employ and send its own native English speakers to report in Pakistan, any journalist from Pakistan who wants to work for the foreign press finds it easier to obtain work capturing images. Consequently, most beneficiaries of CJAP are photo-journalists.

Just six members of CJAP are women. When I asked Kashif why there weren't more, he told me that going out and about to report on breaking news, especially as a Christian, can be dangerous work, and women weren't always willing to take those risks. Additionally, CJAP doesn't advertise for members, and journalists come to hear about it only through word of mouth. As more women join, he hopes that will help spread the word among female journalists, and more of them will sign up.

The White Post website, which led me to Kashif, is a more recent development and is a place for CJAP members to post articles about minority issues that might not be welcome elsewhere. It strives to amplify the voices of underserved communities and, as it aspirationally claims, simultaneously uphold peace, pluralism and democracy. Its website states that it covers 'news without engaging in political theatrics or narrative wars, choosing to report real stories from real places and people'. As well as these goals, it is not commercially bound to any external interests and welcomes the participation of its readers who are invited to 'rate our stories, advocate on our behalf, provide constructive suggestions for enhancing our work, and respond to calls for assistance in developing stories'. I was impressed and a little daunted by its full-on professionalism.

Having spoken to Kashif myself, the man behind these words, I sense that he is a born collaborator and networker. He is one of those people who, if you mention any topic to him, will know someone involved in the issue. I love how he encourages joint working, and when I asked if he knew a female Christian journalist, he had no hesitation in putting me in touch with Saima, one of a handful of female contributors to the White Post.

Kashif had come across Saima's blog towards the end of the pandemic lockdowns. He thought her work had potential. The two of them spoke by phone, and she later told me that she immediately felt comfortable working with him. For her, being part of a professional body was a welcome opportunity. To become a registered journalist in Pakistan requires an in-person visit to the Press Association Office, which is staffed entirely by men. For a female to even enter their office invites harassment, so barely any women feel courageous enough to register with the organization that is supposed to represent their interests. No wonder there are so few female reporters.

Since their first conversation, Saima has taken up CJAP's offer of free coaching and met Kashif several times, becoming a key contributor to the White Post. She was especially thankful for the multiple opportunities to receive training in a safe environment. The week prior to my conversation with her, she had gone with her daughter, who is also interested in becoming a reporter, to a training session organized by an international news firm. When they arrived, she and her daughter were the only women in a room full of over thirty men; they found it very intimidating.

Saima and I were talking on Zoom one Tuesday in late March. For once, the sun was blazing through the window of my house in Belgium, and probably all Saima saw of me was my face in silhouette, even though I closed the curtains next to me. It was early afternoon in Lahore, and Saima had recently arrived home from the school where she teaches geography and history. I hope she had already eaten lunch because our conversation lasted almost two hours.

As always, I wanted to understand Saima's personal history and heritage. Her parents are both from Martinpur, an isolated village in the district of Sheikhupura in Punjab. It's easy enough to find on Google Maps, and a quick glance reveals that it is far from any major thoroughfare. It's evidently a Christian area, though, as all the landmarks are named after saints. Saima's family still owns land in the village, but it has always been a poor area. Since Saima's father wanted a better life for his family, he upped sticks and moved to Karachi, Pakistan's cultural capital on the coast in Sindh province.

Saima was born in Karachi and told me, 'I opened my eyes and was a Christian.' Like many Pakistani families I have spoken to, she does not know which of her ancestors was the first to convert to Christianity. Neither does she know how they first heard the gospel; her family has always believed in a Christian God.

Saima's education took place at a Muslim school, and I noticed a tinge of bitterness as she spoke about her father's decision not to place her in a Christian school. At Muslim schools, Islamic studies were mandatory, but her father argued that she and her two younger siblings should be exempt from those classes as they were Christian. His arguments were successful, and the three children played outside in the schoolyard while the Islamic lessons carried on. However, her father's decision came with a significant cost for Saima and her school marks. End-of-year grades and assessments were scored out of the total marks possible, including Islamic studies. Since a large proportion of the year's grade was earned from a student's marks in Islamic studies, the most Saima could ever hope to score was around 75 per cent, which meant a B or C grade at best. Even if she aced every other exam, she would always score near the bottom of her class.

During her primary school years, Saima felt discouraged that she consistently scored low grades but, by the time she was a teenager, she had hopes and ambitions and knew that, if she was to achieve her dreams, she needed higher test scores. She spoke with her father and the school, eventually persuading them to allow her to learn Islamic studies. This meant embarking on a course designed to venerate Muslim martyrs and glorify the Islamic faith. However, she memorized what she had to for her exams and, in the first year alone, she caught up with her peers. They had been learning about Islam from their families and at school for many years, so they had a considerable advantage, but she was bright and passed the assessments with distinction.

According to her school results, Saima was now all set to follow her dreams, which at the time were to become a weather reporter. With a cheeky glint in her eye, she told me she used to practise presenting weather forecasts at home and hoped to one day appear on one of Pakistan's national television channels. However, her dreams were shattered when she was not admitted to work and study at the state-run Meteorological Office. As a Christian, the government was biased against her to begin with and didn't recruit female Christians. The only way to beat the system was to obtain a letter of recommendation from someone already working there, but she didn't know anyone and could not get in.

Saima spent her entire childhood and adolescence in Karachi before accompanying her parents when they relocated back to Punjab, where she lives today. Saima's father had always intended his stay in economically vibrant Karachi to be temporary, but returning to their home province was expedited when there was, unfortunately, a robbery at their house. Saima tells me these types of incidents happened all the time in Karachi, so her family weren't particularly targeted, yet it left her parents feeling unsettled. Her father had accumulated a fair amount of savings working as a realtor in Karachi, so they returned to Punjab and purchased a spacious house in Lahore.

The family's move back to their ancestral region coincided with the decision to find Saima a husband, and they sought out a Punjabi Christian for her. A second cousin on her mother's side was chosen, and the couple was given two years to get to know each other and to go on dates. Although the marriage was arranged, Saima had every opportunity to pull out of it if she had wanted to, and she confirmed, with a shy grin, that after two years she had fallen in love, and she and her match agreed to become engaged. Again, there was no rush or pressure on the couple; their families took another two years to plan the wedding, which gave her and her fiancé further time to discover more about one another.

Throughout this period, Saima was a student at the University of Lahore, where she studied geography and environmental science. By the time she graduated, she was both married and pregnant, yet despite being constantly tired she graduated with a gold medal in geography. Since her hopes of becoming a weather presenter had been dashed, she now focused her efforts on becoming a teacher. In her view, there are only two possible careers for educated Christian women in Pakistan: teaching and nursing. Although it isn't straightforward for Muslim women, they have many more opportunities to work in the media.

Saima gave birth to a daughter and began teaching at a Christian school. Unfortunately, her salary was low to start with and fell even further as annual increases did not keep pace with inflation. Eventually, she concluded that working as a Christian educator wasn't sustainable, so she switched to a semi-government-run Muslim school where the pay was better. She teaches classes in geography and the history of Pakistan.

At the large school where she is employed, Saima is one of only three Christian teachers on the girls' campus. Among the pupils, only one or two in each year group are Christian. Given that some year groups have as many as eight hundred students in them, Christians are vastly in the minority. She says she faces constant badgering and pressure to convert to Islam from her fellow teachers, who show off about their Muslim faith. In their eyes, Islam provides women with many opportunities, such as working as a well-regarded teacher. They tell her Muslim women are respected, and Islam requires great discipline, of which they are proud. Initially, Saima felt anxious that to get through her day, she had to constantly ignore their remarks; she feared she would irritate her colleagues. Now, however, she is confident, though tired of the comments. She knows her colleagues will continue to deride her Christian faith, but they are unable to do anything to her; she patiently has to disregard their comments and not react when they say the same things day after day.

A couple of years after her first daughter was born, Saima fell pregnant again. Sadly, her second pregnancy resulted in a miscarriage. A small operation was performed to remove the tissue; however, attempts to conceive after the operation were unsuccessful, and she required medical assistance to do so. Thankfully, she conceived successfully with this help and gave birth to her second daughter. Several years later, she became pregnant again, and despite constant pressure from others to find out the baby's gender, she put it off until the eighth month when she discovered she was due to give birth to a boy. Even among Christians in Pakistan, there is tremendous pressure on women to produce a son and heir. There was huge relief because now society would view her favourably, but she knew she would have loved her child the same whether they had been a boy or girl.

Saima's three children get on well with each other and make videos, which they post online. She proudly tells me that she has a great relationship with her son; similarly, her husband is close to their daughters. She and her son will go on excursions, and her husband makes a point of going on outings with his daughters. This is one of the key ways the two of them teach their children that they have value and is part of their Christian discipling.

I cautiously asked Saima if she was worried about her daughters being taken by Muslim men. She explained that girls can be ensnared in one of two ways. Either they can be abducted, in the ways I have detailed in earlier chapters, or they can be enticed into relationships by men who prey on them. Many young Christian women in Pakistan become tired of their underdog status and believe life would be easier with a wealthier Muslim. When a Muslim man shows interest, they can be easily persuaded to abandon their Christian families and elope with them. Yet, all too often, once the man has these young girls alone, he will quickly begin abusing them. It is this second scenario that Saima fears more for her daughters. To protect them, she is raising her daughters to provide for themselves and wants to dispel the fantasy that marrying a rich boy solves all of life's problems. Christian faith is also integral to this, so she trains her children in the Bible. Her elder daughter is now a youth leader and discipling others, and all three of Saima's children have been baptized.

Saima's Christian faith is precious to her and influences every aspect of her life. Although wider society judges her for her religious label, she knows it is much more than a category, and she nurtures her personal relationship with God. As a member of the Presbyterian Church of Pakistan, she counts herself as part of the third largest Christian denomination in the country after the Catholic and Anglican Churches. During her childhood in Karachi, there were few Presbyterian churches, and so she went to a Catholic Sunday school. In Lahore, however, the Presbyterian denomination is sizeable, and she feels strengthened by being part of a larger group of Christians.

To those who don't share her Christian faith, larger numbers might inspire more fear and be perceived as a more significant threat. To keep the church under control, the Government of Pakistan requires that consent be sought for any new church buildings. Saima explained to me that regional governments permit churches to be built. Yet, once they are erected, the local community may not welcome a new church congregation in its midst, and threats might be made. If the threats are viewed as genuine, the government advises churches not to meet; purportedly, for the safety of their own congregants. Churches have indeed been targeted for attacks across many cities in Pakistan. As I sat down to write this chapter, I received an article from Kashif observing the ninth anniversary of the twin bombing of two churches in Youhanabad, Lahore, when 27 people died and another 100 were injured.[2] In response, Pakistani police officers are regularly assigned to stand guard on church compounds, but they can do little to stop determined terrorists. Despite these dangers, Christians still want the freedom to meet together and continue to boldly attend services.

There is plenty of outrage among church leaders at the treatment of minority Christians. To help ease tensions, they meet regularly with Muslim and other faith leaders, but these interfaith dialogues seem to lead nowhere. In Saima's view, the church leaders are voiceless, and although initiatives to protect Christians are promised, rarely is action taken. After the bombings mentioned above, some Christian youth took matters into their own hands and went on to the streets, where they burned tyres to cause congestion and create a disturbance. The police promptly arrested these young Christians, and they have been held without trial ever since. Although Saima doesn't condone the actions of these young people, she wants them to receive impartial treatment and be put on trial fairly.

Recently, Saima has studied for a bachelor degree in ministry training and missions. It's possible she may travel as a missionary educator in the future. Her pastor has asked her to consider taking on a full-time role doing this work but, so far, it hasn't felt to her as if it's the right time. She regularly has dreams and visions, and although she doesn't call these prophecies, she occasionally foresees violent events. Sometimes, these dreams have occurred so regularly that she is scared of sleeping, and when she tells her friends about them, they think she is boasting. I'm not sure if it's wise to judge her experiences, but they certainly testify that she faces many battles, including those that are spiritual.

Thankfully, Saima's daydreams are much more pleasant, and she has fantasized about becoming a journalist since she was a teenager. Since then, she has devoured books by notable western authors whenever she can get her hands on them. She mentioned Sidney Sheldon, Jane Austen and Danielle Steele as her favourite authors and said she enjoyed reading *The Notebook*.[3] For many years, she had no outlet for her writing but, five years ago, she began her blog, which is how Kashif discovered her. Through her own contacts, she arranged for specialist training in three areas that were of specific interest to her, namely animal rights, environmental degradation and juvenile justice, hence her interest in child marriage and abductions. She covers many other topics and regularly speaks with Kashif; together, they decide what she should write about and how to frame articles. Attending Islamic studies classes as a schoolchild has benefited her, as she can now write knowledgeably about Islam when it is appropriate and safe to do so. As always for minority Christians, the threat of a life-changing blasphemy allegation needs to be considered, and she writes with caution. When we spoke, she was drafting a piece about World Water Day,[4] which would be observed three days afterwards and was a safe topic.

Not only can CJAP help with training, but it also provides equipment such as microphones when Saima goes out on location to report. This can be threatening work, though, and she matter-of-factly told me that she is regularly harassed, laughed at, mocked, groped and spat at by male correspondents when she is reporting. As a female journalist, she has so much to overcome; I was shocked. She agreed that in severe instances, she could report this behaviour to the authorities, but she did not believe anything would be done, and it might make her the target for more crass deeds. In this, she is similar to the countless women in Pakistan who suffer abuse at the hands of men. The fear of making their situation worse all too often prevents them from reporting violence to the police. Typically, Saima is paid 20,000 PKR (£60) per 1,000 words for all her efforts and the risks she takes.

CJAP is also a source of much-needed encouragement to Saima and its members, and through the group, she hears many stories she might otherwise not know about. Recently, a fellow journalist was beaten up by a plain clothes police officer; she rallied to his help. She's also aware, through another CJAP colleague, of a 12-year-old Christian girl who was abducted and, though the girl's family feared talking to the mainstream press, word was spread among Christian reporters, and prayers and offers of assistance were readily made to help free this girl. I sense there is a strong camaraderie among the CJAP group.

In Saima, I recognize the same longing I have: to enthusiastically explain events to my readers and help them know the incredible people I meet. I love sharing my thoughts and experiences with others. She also finds the world fascinating but is aware of great injustices; her desire is for people to understand what is happening so they can work to make life better. She hopes that influential people in critical offices and roles in Pakistan will read her articles and take action to make the country more equitable for everyone. Incredibly, you can play a part in this by following the White Post on Facebook and X (Twitter) and amplifying their posts by re-sharing and adding your comments and re-sharing. The upside to social media is that disparate parts of the body of Christ can now easily connect with each other.

When I asked Saima to describe what persecution is like for her, she expressed it as 'inequality entrenched', which seems to me to sum it up well. She is constantly battling to have the same opportunities as Muslim women, let alone the advantages of being a Muslim man. In every situation, from girlhood to adult life, she swims against the tide, either being the only woman, the only Christian or frequently the only Christian woman. I sense that she longs for her life in Pakistan to be different, and she would prefer the tide to move in a different direction so she wouldn't have to go against it.

Despite this, I see glimmers of hope for her and Pakistan; in Lollywood movies (Urdu language films made in Lahore), the hero frequently stands up against tradition and the excesses of patriarchy. All too often, these heroes are male, but women are gradually being portrayed as the ones initiating change.[5] Indeed, on social media, many voices are crying out for greater rights and for women to be better treated in general. However, as Awais Khan writes in his brilliant novel, *Someone Like Her*, sadly, an uproar on social media may not mean much in the real world.[6] It can be a case of two steps forward and one step back.

Regrettably, Saima feels as if the treatment of minorities in Pakistan is getting worse and not better at the moment. She looked gloomy as she told me, 'Pakistan is a majority country'; she believes many do not want a place for minorities. She and her husband take their role as parents and role models very seriously and try to equip their children to cope with whatever comes their way, but holding out hope is hard.

As we ended our discussion, the sun was still shining, and I offered to pray for Saima. I felt unable to do much to help her, but simultaneously admired her resilience and willingness to keep speaking out. She knew trials would be ahead but wasn't about to shirk them and would keep swimming against the tide. I was reminded of Jesus in the garden of Gethsemane.

He also felt the looming oppression of events and knew persecution was inevitable. His request at that juncture was for his disciples to stay awake with him and pray (Matt. 26:36–46). We can do likewise for Saima; we may not face the same pressures nor share her calling, but we can keep watch with her as she bravely speaks out and documents the truth.

10

One of Us – Behien

It's wintry outside and, as usual in Belgium, it's gloomy. It seems as if there are always grey skies outside my window. Michelle Chaudhry and I are online and waiting for a lawyer to arrive at Behien's home and connect to our call. In the meantime, we are having a quick chat over Zoom about what it's like to be part of a military family. I wish that continents and circumstances didn't separate us, as I'd love to know Michelle better. She looks somewhat wrapped up, too; the nights in Lahore are cold, but temperatures still rise to around 20 °C in the day. Shady indoor rooms don't heat up much, though.

We had been waiting almost two hours, sporadically checking in with each other, before the lawyer appeared on our screens. He was a middle-class, middle-aged man dressed in a dark suit and tie but with a warm smile. He apologized profusely for the delay; it seemed he had come directly from court in Faisalabad. As he joined our online meeting, he walked into a busy room; a young-looking woman with a curious smile was sitting waiting for him, and on her lap perched a girl with short hair whom I knew was her child. Settled beside them was an older woman who was Behien's mother. I began to sense that this would be a group interview and wondered how to organize my questioning. When there are many people on a call, they tend to interrupt and talk over each other. Even so, it was wonderful to see that Behien had the support of her family.

The interviewees were gathered in a room that appeared to have no windows or natural light. Although it was mid-afternoon for them, the lights were on, making it impossible to tell what time it was. So many of the women I interview are in hiding and spend their days indoors and away from daylight. I feel immensely sad for them but also chastened for complaining about the grey skies in Belgium; at least I can go out and about as I please.

The lawyer bossed them around for a minute or two to arrange their seating positions but did so in a friendly way as if he knew them well. Then, he handed the phone to Behien, who looked attentively into the phone at me; I liked her immediately. I told her that I would begin with some straightforward questions. Michelle translated, and I was grateful that she had kindly sent me a synopsis of Behien's story, which included pregnancy and a shooting; I knew I needed to ease into the conversation slowly before I could ask her about more troubling topics. We began with her family.

Behien was born in Faisalabad and is the eldest of four daughters. She attended a mixed school where Christians and Muslims mingled freely, and there she continued her studies until the seventh grade when the 'incident' occurred. The kidnapping and ensuing events have ended her education but, before then, she loved school and, even during breaktime, she would continue reading and studying rather than joining her friends to play. Her favourite subject was Urdu, but she also learnt some English and confidently told the child on her lap to say hello to me. We waved at each other momentarily.

Though the family was nominally Christian, their attendance at the local Catholic church wasn't frequent. Her parents were often too busy to take their daughters to the services or Sunday school. Both Behien's parents were sanitary workers at the Civil Hospital in Faisalabad, and the family was desperately poor. Shifts were long, and her parents were gone all day, which meant that Behien and her sisters had to take themselves to and from school. There often wasn't enough money to buy food, so her parents would bring home some of the canteen meals provided for hospital workers. They shared what they had, but splitting two meals among six people meant they were often hungry. However, they were fortunate to have inherited and own the rudimental home they lived in, and it is where they continue to live. Behien and her sisters grew up surrounded by their extended family, and cousins were always nearby to play with. Cricket was a favourite among them all.

Needing to move on to the disturbing part of her story, I suggested that Behien might want to let her child go elsewhere. The sympathetic lawyer picked up on my suggestion and excused himself, too. He knew Behien would find talking to Michelle and me easier if he wasn't there. Behien continued her story, and her mother listened in.

An uncle who lived nearby had a Muslim friend who would often visit them. They called this man 'Chachu', and he was well known to Behien's family, who always welcomed him. His home wasn't far away, so they saw him quite often. Although Chachu was married with three children, his wife had abandoned him to run away with another man; he lived with his three children, a sister and his mother.

In late 2019, when Behien was just twelve-and-a-half-years-old, this man dropped by as usual. He had brought two boxes of juice with him, which he shared among Behien's family, although she didn't drink any herself. Within minutes, her mother and father began to feel sleepy and, pretty soon, they passed out. Chachu then pulled out a gun and forced Behien out of the house and into a waiting rickshaw. Behien was frightened and confused. By now, she had figured out that her parents had been poisoned; however, when she was ordered to drink some of the contaminated juice, she complied. After all, he was pointing a gun at her, and she had no choice. I can't help wondering what the rickshaw driver thought and if he could have intervened, but I suppose that when a passenger wields a weapon, you do what you're told.

When Behien came around, she found herself in a rural area with only a few houses. She was hauled into one of them and, as she became more alert, she began to scream for her mother and father. Chachu told her that she had been kidnapped and that she must be quiet. When she wouldn't pipe down, he administered some more sedatives to knock her out.

At this point, I realized I hadn't asked how old Chachu was when he abducted Behien, so I interrupted the story to find out. I was repulsed to discover that he was around 50 years old when he snatched her, and one of his children was, in fact, older than Behien. I was further disgusted when she told me that while she was drugged and unconscious, he raped her.

Behien's mother was anxious to talk to me, so Behien passed the phone to her. Back in Faisalabad, Behien's mother and father slowly regained consciousness and quickly realized their eldest daughter was missing. It took a while for their memories to return fully, but as soon as they could walk and talk, they headed directly to their brother-in-law's house, who was their and Chachu's mutual acquaintance. As Behien's mother tells me this, she becomes breathless and agitated. I imagine it must have been a living nightmare in those early moments as they were frantic for Behien but struggling to overcome the effects of the toxin in their bodies.

Their brother-in-law showed them where Chachu lived, but he was not there, and nothing could be done. Even when the police showed up, they received no answers to their questions.

Meanwhile, back in the village, Behien spent her days tied to a chair. Chachu repeatedly raped her and gave her more poison to drink; most of the time, she was oblivious to what was being done to her. It is perhaps a blessing that she cannot remember all the violent details.

At some point, Chachu dragged Behien out of the house and into another rickshaw before taking her to a nondescript building where an imam awaited them. Once there, the imam forced her to sign both a false certificate stating she had converted to Islam, and a phoney marriage certificate. Due to the drugs she had been plied with, she doesn't know if this happened soon after she was kidnapped or later.

At another time, she vaguely recalls being moved to another house. Apparently, this was Chachu's family home, so she was not far from her family. Behien's mother continued to come to the house, demanding to know where her daughter was. It was then that Chachu's mother and sister abetted Chachu. Now in possession of the falsified marriage certificate, they waved it in Behien's mother's face and told her to go away; Behien was theirs now. Despite their arrogant assertions, Chachu and his family underestimated the police in Faisalabad and were unaware of the power of community in Behien's neighbourhood.

I think Behien's lawyer had been listening to our conversation all along, and he now appeared on screen. He was keen to share his part of the story, too, and explained how his legal clerk, who lived near Behien's family, had heard about her abduction and asked his boss to assist them. As a Christian lawyer and father, he wanted to help and did not shy away from becoming involved.

Behien's mother strongly suspected that Behien was inside Chachu's house. She gave this information to the police and lawyer and, for once, the legal process worked as it should. Chachu was arrested, and Behien was taken into custody as well; the next morning, they appeared in court together, at which point Behien cried out to her mother. The sensible judge made the right decision and restored Behien to her family. Praise God!

There were several shocks in store, though, and it became apparent that Behien had no idea what had happened to her. Chachu had been sedating her repeatedly for four months by this time. Prior to her appearance in court, a medical examination was mandated. It was during this that Behien discovered she was pregnant. Given that she didn't know she had been raped, this must have come as a terrifying shock. Second, in conversations with the kindly lawyer, Behien showed concern for Chachu and wondered when he would be released. She had no idea that he had been abusing her and was the father of her unborn baby.

Behien and Chachu's court appearance took place in February 2020. Having read the medical report and seen how Behien, who was still only 12 years old, responded to her mother, the judge courageously convicted Chachu of abduction. This wasn't his first crime, and he was sent to jail. Yet, awfully, his imprisonment wasn't to last.

In March 2020, the world began to reel from the consequences of the Covid pandemic, and Pakistan did not escape the turmoil. Faisalabad's prison was unsanitary and overcrowded, and the virus spread rapidly between inmates. To ease pressure on the ailing and overworked prison guards and medical staff, many prisoners were released.[1] In theory, only prisoners who did not threaten public safety were supposed to be let out but, regrettably, Chachu was among those given freedom.

Back at home with her family, Behien was coming to terms with her pregnancy. Although a nominal Christian, her mother was horrified by the idea of caring for this monstrous man's child and wanted Behien to have an abortion. In Pakistan, abortions are permitted if the life of the mother is at risk but, since Behien was healthy, they would have to arrange an illegal termination. This was out of the question, though, because the court knew that Behien was pregnant. If they broke the law to obtain an abortion, they might have been prosecuted. The pregnancy continued, and Behien remained hidden and at home.

Throughout the pandemic, Behien's mother and father continued to work; Faisalabad Civil Hospital was extremely busy, so they were needed night and day. Behien's mother was returning from a night shift one morning, and it was still dark. She did not notice a man in the shadows until it was too late. Several shots rang out; it was Chachu with a gun. He had hit Behien's mother five times in the leg, but she was still breathing. He ran off, and an ambulance was called, which rushed Behien's mother back to the hospital she had just left. Mercifully, the bullets had missed all her vital organs, and the injuries to her leg were only flesh wounds. She stayed in the hospital for around a week but was discharged in time to accompany her daughter back there for the birth of her grandchild just a month later. Although her treatment at the hospital was free, the follow-up medicine to ward off infection was costly and put further strain on the family.

Behien carried her baby to full term and gave birth in September 2020. She was the young girl I had seen sitting on Behien's lap at the start of our conversation. Behien was extremely relieved that her mother was able to accompany her.

The doctor in charge of delivery saw Behien's mother's negative reaction to the baby when she was born. She asked a few questions and discovered that the pregnancy had come about through rape. When Behien's mother continued to speak disparagingly about the baby, the doctor admonished her. Firmly yet kindly, the doctor told her that it was neither Behien nor the baby girl's fault that she had been conceived in this way; Behien's mother should love them regardless. These words were precisely what Behien's mother needed to hear, and her heart softened towards them both. Since then, she has considered the baby girl one of her own children and counts herself as having five daughters. However, the child's birth certificate accurately shows that Behien is the mother; they chose not to name a father, so that space remains blank.

This period was incredibly traumatic for Behien and her family; in the space of a year, they had gone from living ordinary lives to coping with a new baby and the aftermath of a shooting. All the while, the Covid pandemic raged around them. However, they were not alone in their struggles and had made new friends. The lawyer and his assistant were still in contact with them, and they encouraged the family to go to the police and register an FIR against Chachu for the shooting and attempted murder. Perhaps knowing that Behien's case against Chachu had been upheld before, this time, the police were quick to act. Though he was in hiding, they traced

Chachu by putting pressure on his family and, once found, he was arrested and placed in police custody until a second trial.

A month or two later at the court in Faisalabad, Behien's mother bravely testified against Chachu; he and his threats had not cowed her. As their lawyer describes what happened, he is quick to praise Behien's mother's courage. Once again, the judge was sympathetic to their situation and locked Chachu up. He spent almost three years in jail but was released just a week before my interview with Behien and her family. None of the family appeared worried about him, though; I could tell that they drew strength from one another, and there was solidarity and calm.

This attitude might be due to their increased involvement in church. When Behien was first abducted, the family did not have time for Christian activities. No one from the congregation they occasionally attended was brave enough to reach out to them. However, thanks to the interest and help given by the Christian lawyer, who has worked on their cases *pro bono*, they have found a new welcome and are more involved in prayer and services. They have been practising Christmas songs recently since it is Advent.

It is extraordinary that the lawyer has successfully won their cases and got Chachu locked away, even if his incarcerations have been too short. There are, however, a couple of situations where justice is yet to be served. The first concerns Behien and her marriage; since Chachu has not been convicted of rape (at the first trial, he was found guilty of abduction), his marriage to Behien has not been annulled. She is now over the age of 18, so it is far harder to invalidate it by arguing that she was a minor when it took place.

The other unresolved issue has to do with her daughter's birth certificate. Currently, the space for the father's name is blank since they do not want any formal link between Chachu and the child. However, this undermines their accusation of rape, which is needed to annul the marriage. Their helpful lawyer has proposed taking the case to court and calling on 'the Government of Pakistan' to be named as the father. This would protect the girl from any claim that Chachu may make on her. However, there is no precedent for this, and the process is highly complex.

I wrapped up our time together by asking Behien about her hopes for the future. Above all, she longs for justice and would like to see Chachu locked away. Her dreams for herself are much more modest. She spends most of her time out of sight from prying eyes but, when required, she accompanies her eldest sister to carry out beauty treatments in people's homes. Apart from household work and caring for her daughter, this is all she does at the moment, but she would love to study and is keen on taking some online courses. These would be perfect for her as she could stay safe indoors while obtaining the qualifications for a new kind of life. Behien's feisty mum interrupts to tell me that she is proud her daughter did not resort to suicide or prostitution after everything that happened. I'm pleased, too. Behien has her whole life ahead of her, and I'm glad shame isn't holding her back. Instead, I fear poverty might be the most significant hurdle to overcome; I'm sure she doesn't own a computer. Behien also has her daughter to think about; she doesn't attend school yet, but they hope to enrol her soon.

I'm also encouraged that Behien is surrounded by people who support her. They have endured so much together but are sticking by one another. As we ended the call, the lawyer spoke directly to Michelle; apparently, one of his Muslim co-workers had been waiting to speak to her all through our Zoom interview. As Michelle is the daughter of the famous fighter pilot and war hero, Group Captain Cecil Chaudhry, this colleague wanted to pay his respects to her father. She graciously listened to his compliments and thanked him. For me, it was encouraging to see admiration given by a Muslim to a Christian. If Behien is part of a community like this, with respect for all, then she is in a good place. I hope that Chachu was just a very nasty exception.

I'm finishing this chapter on 17 December 2024, known in the church calendar as Antiphon Day, which I first discovered ten years ago and have come to love. No other day in the church calendar seems to sum up so well how I often feel: stuck in the here and now of tragic stories such as Behien's, yet longing for and knowing that our Saviour will be arriving soon, at Christmas, bringing light to the world. The traditional O Antiphon prayers, which are read out on this day, are addressed to various names of God, such as O Emmanuel or O King of the Nations. Each prayer is a cry for wisdom, power and rescue, articulated beautifully in the time-honoured carol, 'O Come, O Come, Emmanuel'. Two especially moving lines call on God to 'free those who sit in darkness' and 'close the path to misery'. These are my prayers for Behien, both figuratively and literally; I'd love her to escape the confines of her house more and enjoy the bright Pakistani sunshine. I'm also reminded of some words from Psalm 35:6 (CEV) that state,

> Make them run in the dark
> on a slippery road,
>   as your angel chases them.

For now, this is my prayer for Chachu, though I hope that one day he, too, will walk in the light.

11

Unexpected – Allam

Have you ever wished for something only to discover that it's nothing like you expected once you receive it? Rather than feeling disappointed, you may feel confused or pleasantly surprised, or most likely a mixture of all these emotions. This describes my meeting with Pastor Allam. He was nothing like I imagined and has had me scratching my head ever since. I think I have more questions now than I had before I met him.

Right from the beginning of my research into the abductions and forced marriages of women and girls in Pakistan, I have wanted to get my theology right. Suffering is one of those massive stumbling-blocks that keeps many people from faith in God and, for those of us who are Christians, unwarranted disaster and tragedy can cause us to fall away from faith. Reconciling a loving and all-powerful God with the desperate hurting we see in the world is not easy. Sometimes, we shy away from these big questions, presuming that asking them is a sign of faithlessness. However, in my view, wrestling with these questions is not a sign of spiritual weakness; rather, the more someone knows God and truly understands his goodness and might, the harder it is for them to comprehend why he appears to permit tragedy. It's only those who think God is feeble or absent who are tempted to believe suffering is unavoidable.

In my own life, I have experienced the regular ups and downs of suffering that everyone goes through. I, along with my friends and family, have had miscarriages, cancer diagnoses, mental health problems and lost loved ones. Additionally, the women helped by the charities I run in Nepal have borne the brunt of terrible violence and pain caused by others. Whenever I encounter suffering, I try to take my questions to God, and I discover he is pleased when I seek him for answers. He wants to be in dialogue with us, and I have regularly been aware of his deep empathy and sympathy for pain. Jesus suffered terribly, and he knows how much we hurt. On other occasions, he tells me that I must trust him, and he won't explain why tragedies have occurred. This is hard, and having faith in him isn't always easy, but it eventually leads to peace and forgiveness.

These thoughts and wonderings led me to seek out a Christian leader in Pakistan with whom I could discuss the question of suffering. I wanted to know what it is like to shepherd a spiritual flock through dark times and whether that led to great insight and wise theology beyond what I, in the spiritually stagnant West, could come up with. I hoped for a softly spoken theologian and imagined a kind of Father Christmas figure who would remain unflustered while gently caring for the families of girls who had been abused. Maybe spiritual pastors like this exist in Pakistan, but Pastor Allam was not one of them; in fact, he was quite the opposite.

Once again, it was Joseph who arranged for us to meet online and surprised me. I should know better by now. Although we had arranged to talk at some point during the last week of April 2024, Joseph needed to bring the meeting forward by three days; he wasn't sure if Pastor Allam could speak fluent

English, so he needed to be present as well. Thankfully, Joseph gave me twenty-four hours' notice this time to at least prepare some questions. It turned out he was flying to Pakistan when we had been due to talk. It was a last-minute trip as he was hoping to help a woman called Rashida,[1] who had been enslaved in a forced marriage for ten years. She had been abducted at the age of 13 and had given birth to five children during her subjugation. More recently, her abductor had violently attacked her and, among other injuries, had cut off the tip of her nose and all her hair, which are plain to see in the article cited in Note 1.

I created the Zoom link for our three-way meeting and, just as I was about to click on it to start the interview, my phone rang. It was Joseph. Of course, I assumed there was a problem – maybe Pastor Allam wasn't available, or we had to shift the time. But no, Joseph was calling to tell me that his trip to Pakistan was a secret and that I must not mention it to Pastor Allam. Essentially, he was going to Punjab on a rescue mission to free Rashida, and the element of surprise was crucial – brave, brave Joseph. Once again, I felt proud to know this fearless man who keeps me on my toes.

After finishing my call with Joseph, I began the Zoom meeting. Pastor Allam appeared in a bright yellow shirt and looked very young; I believe he was in his twenties. He was nothing like I imagined, and he spoke in a fast, business-like patois. He was more wheeler-dealer than passive pastor. Yet I knew he had much experience with persecution since he lived in and led a church in Jaranwala. In this city, widespread and orchestrated violence against Christians occurred in August 2023 (see Chapters 2 and 4 about Abhita and Mashaka respectively). Throughout our conversation, Pastor Allam referred to the savagery that arose as 'the incident'.

I began by asking him what Jaranwala was like before the incident. He described an old city predominantly inhabited by Christians since the 1800s. Most of these Christians were from the lowly sweeper caste, considered to be untouchable and, consequently, the area was impoverished; their working conditions were practically slave-like. Yet the area had begun to change in the last couple of decades. Christians were breaking free from their traditional caste roles and becoming entrepreneurs, setting up small businesses that served the local Christian community. The church was also growing, and there were regular conferences and crusades. At these, nominal Christians became more robust in their faith, and there was an occasional Muslim convert. Although there had been incidents of violence and persecution meted out by jealous Muslims and landowners, these had not been enough to stop the Christian community from becoming more empowered. They had even elected one or two Christians to political roles.

Pastor Allam had a small family and was a business owner. He ran a successful restaurant and pastored Elohim Church, which had around seventy members. He told me his restaurant was the largest one in Jaranwala, and many people worked for him. His brothers were also becoming wealthy, and his family had caught the attention of envious landowners.

On the day of the incident, he was out of town helping a friend move home and business to Islamabad. He was on a road near Peshawar when his assistant and usual driver rang him. As soon as Pastor Allam answered, he could hear panic in the man's voice as he said, 'Something have happened, very bad.' This man went on to state that his photo, and that of his brother, had been put on a poster along with some anti-Islamic scripts that opposed the prophet. A crowd of Muslims were gathering in Jaranwala and were trying to find the two men to punish them for blasphemy. If found, this man knew the angry crowd would be likely to kill him and his brother, so he was hiding in fear for his life.

Pastor Allam explained that he wasn't in Jaranwala and couldn't come to this man's immediate aid, but he did his best to reassure him and advised him to continue hiding or flee if he could. As soon as Pastor Allam hung up, he began receiving countless other calls from Christians in Jaranwala asking if he knew where the wanted men were.

Meanwhile, back in Jaranwala, the mob was growing and threatening to burn down the old city. Telephone calls and messages between the Christian inhabitants were frenetic, as they hid in their homes and tried to determine what would happen next. Very quickly, Christians began to flee the city. If they had a car or motorbike, they took those. Otherwise, they took buses or rickshaws. As the violence had probably been pre-planned, the mob was well-organized and knew which houses, businesses and churches they wanted to attack. They had brought along petrol and set about lighting multiple blazes. The fires burned for several days and, by the end of it, twenty-eight churches had been damaged or destroyed, and hundreds of homes had been gutted.

By the grace of God, Pastor Allam's assistant and brother had managed to escape the city. However, they knew they could not hide forever and were terrified that the mob would catch up with them. Just one day after the attack, they courageously handed themselves in at a courthouse and were taken into custody. Similarly, Pastor Allam knew he could not return to Jaranwala, so he made his way to his childhood home in Wazirabad, where he stayed with an uncle. His wife and children met him there, having fled Jaranwala. However, a day or two after arriving here, the police turned up and arrested Pastor Allam. At the same time, the police also rounded up the restaurant manager and a female server, both of whom were Christians. A Muslim security guard who also worked for Pastor Allam was apprehended. Unlike the Christians, he received favourable treatment and, although he was intimidated and questioned in the back of a police van, he was not taken into custody.

The police had five people in custody: Pastor Allam, the two men who had been accused of blasphemy and the restaurant manager and server. They were each taken to different police stations and detention centres. Thus began repeated interrogations and various tortures. Yet, after one month, Pastor Allam, the manager and the server were each released. It wasn't until 1 March 2024, seven months after the unrest and when their case finally went to court, that the other two men were freed, yet remarkably, everyone is now at liberty.

In the first few days and weeks after the incident, various videos and photos of the violence that had taken place in Jaranwala circulated on social media. This evidence eventually ended up in the hands of the police and courts. Consequently, around one hundred men who had been involved in instigating the fires were identified and arrested. Although these men were primarily Muslim, they had been manipulated by a nominal Christian convert to Islam who was a drug-dealer; he was a known criminal and had been held in prison countless times. His wife alleged that he had been visiting madrassas and imams for six months prior to the Jaranwala attack, and the blasphemy allegation was just a ploy to stir up hatred and mob violence against someone with whom he had a personal grudge.[2] His trial continues as I write, but all the Muslim vigilantes whom he incited have been released without charge.

Regrettably, Pastor Allam tells me that life in Jaranwala is utterly different now. Tensions between Muslims and Christians in the district are exacerbated, and he no longer feels safe out and about. In general, Christians keep inside their homes and away from Muslim neighbours. Community relations, which were fragile to begin with, are now broken. Although most Christian families have returned to their houses and, having cleaned them up, can live there, he and his staff must live elsewhere. He returns to Jaranwala to lead church services but leaves quickly afterwards. His restaurant has closed, so he can no longer provide jobs for his former employees who were arrested and now need an income; they all had to pay hefty legal fees, and some are in debt. The furnishings and fittings from the restaurant were destroyed in the fires, and he currently has no income.

Unfortunately, the mob violence in August 2023 isn't the only persecution Pastor Allam has been witness to. He, like every other Pakistani Christian, is all too aware of the threat of forced marriage and abduction faced by young Christian girls. He described three instances to me, and I believe he knew of more. They varied from seduction and abuse to outright kidnap and rape.

The first case he described to me concerned a girl who was around 13 years old when she was taken just a few months before 'the incident'. She attended a Catholic church in Jaranwala, but Pastor Allam knew her because she had sometimes visited his restaurant with her family. Her father was a gardener in a government-maintained public park. They had a housing quarter within the park and, sickeningly, she was snatched when she was playing outside their home. Pastor Allam's description of her playing outside disturbed me; she was only a child if she was young enough to play.

Her elder brother immediately began searching for her. When he discovered her whereabouts, the Muslim family who had taken her told him she had converted to Islam and was now married to their son. Thankfully, since she was taken before the Jaranwala incident when the Christian community was growing in size, wealth and political clout, there were influential Christians whom her community could call upon for assistance. Pastor Allam spoke with the family, which he found extremely hard because the girl's father broke down and cried uncontrollably. Pastor Allam reassured them that their situation was not hopeless and that, by God's grace, their daughter would be rescued. He connected them with a local politician known as Bhai Khan (Brother Khan), who was able to exert his authority and, fantastically, the girl was returned. It's hard to say whether her situation would be so quickly resolved nowadays after the incident.

Another instance involved Pastor Allam's own family. In 2017, a Christian cousin had been seduced by a Muslim man. She had begun talking with him, and they agreed to marry with the proviso that he would convert to Christianity afterwards. His promise turned out to be a lie and, as soon as they married, he forced her to convert to Islam. They had two children together, but then he tired of her. He, as well as his entire family, with whom she lived, began to abuse her. They mocked and insulted her, referring to her as a chura, which is the name of her sweeper caste but has the more literal meaning of 'garbage eater'. They continued to treat her as if she was dirty and untouchable so, eventually, she ran away from them and divorced her husband. Tragically, she had to leave her children behind, and they remained with this cruel family.

In another case, a Christian girl just ten-and-a-half-years-old was promised a day of fun but was instead abducted. Her Muslim neighbours asked if they could take her out as a treat, but instead, their 30-year-old son forcibly married her. Pastor Allam explained that even if Christian families suspect that their Muslim neighbours may have ulterior motives, they cannot say no to them for fear of causing offence and potentially triggering an allegation of blasphemy. In this case, the girl's family certainly would have been wary of letting their daughter go out for the day with a Muslim family, but they wouldn't have been able to say no to their neighbours. Given the enormous outrage and violence sparked by the false blasphemy charge against Pastor Allam's staff member, the fear of offending is genuine. Christian parents teach their children to be silent and, when required, to always say 'yes' to Muslims.

Thankfully, this young girl has also been rescued. Yet, although the family have repeatedly asked the police and government to prosecute the abductor, they are ignored, and there has been no justice. There is enormous frustration among the Christian community because of this. In each of the three situations Pastor Allam described, the girls were repeatedly raped and expected to fulfil their 'wifely' duties. Once home, their emotional scars remain, and their family is left feeling powerless and vulnerable.

Given all this opposition, it's admirable that Christians remain true to their faith and carry on attending church. The temptation to convert to Islam and make life easier for themselves must be strong. Yet, the church in Jaranwala has experienced many miracles, which encourage Pastor Allam's faith. He grew up in Wazirabad (where he still has family and to which he fled immediately after the incident) but moved to Jaranwala in 2012 as a teenager. At that time, Wazirabad was a tribal village, and family feuds were commonplace. His uncle murdered someone in a revenge killing. Since Pastor Allam's father was working in Saudi Arabia and was not around to protect his family, his mother made the move to Jaranwala to shield her children from further violence.

Once living in Jaranwala, the family joined a lively Pentecostal congregation called Jehovah Jireh (The Lord Will Provide) Church, and Pastor Allam assisted the lead pastor with events. A significant crusade in 2014 occurred when between twenty and twenty-five thousand people attended huge meetings. Missionaries came to preach, people were healed and demons were cast out. Even Muslim converts shared testimonies of how God was changing their lives. As a result of seeing these miracles first-hand, Pastor Allam decided he wanted to become a church leader, and his pastor advised him to attend seminary in Faisalabad, the nearest major city.

It's fair to say that Pastor Allam doesn't lack self-assurance. When he arrived at the seminary, he thought he already knew a lot about church and theology. However, he soon discovered he had a lot to learn. His year group had fifty students in it, and the pastoral course took three years to complete, so there were one hundred and fifty students all told, including women. Everyone knew everyone else and, when he graduated in 2017, the entire class carried on in Christian ministry; no one dropped away. He believes all the students he took courses with are still going strong with God today, a sign of remarkable faithfulness among his contemporaries.

Despite this, when the Jaranwala incident occurred and Pastor Allam's name was being bandied about on social media, none of his fellow graduates contacted him to offer their support. He tried to reach out to a few friends from that time, but only a female pastor in Sindh province offered him a place of escape. She knew of a safe house in Karachi, over 1,000 kilometres from Punjab, to which he could flee. Regrettably, the police caught up with him and arrested him in Wazirabad before he could take her up on the offer.

When I asked Pastor Allam what he liked best about being a pastor, he said he enjoyed the prestige and respect it gave him. His wife, who had joined us on the call, also found the prominence it gave her within the community gratifying. I admired their honesty. Given that they hail from a caste and religious group that has languished at the bottom of social strata for centuries and been treated terribly, this is understandable.

Despite government promises to rebuild the churches in Jaranwala that were destroyed or gutted by fire, nine months after the event, little work had been done. Only three out of twenty-eight churches had received assistance from the local municipality. However, church members have contributed to the rebuilding and helped with the clean-up and renovations. Pastor Allam's church can meet again, and he visits the city three times a week to lead and attend services.

As we spoke, there were occasions when Pastor Allam's Wi-Fi signal cut out. As the Zoom link reconnected, his profile photo would appear, showing him dressed in a gold tunic and sunglasses like a Bollywood star. He was nothing like I expected a pastor to be, but we hadn't discussed theology yet.

I began by asking him if his faith had become weaker or stronger since the incident. Remarkably, he told me it was far more robust. Although he lost his business and had no income from the church since its members also lost their businesses,

God still provided for him and his family. He also highlighted his imprisonment and torture. He was held by the police for just a month, which was so much shorter than the time other Christians had spent in jail in Pakistan for similar charges. He mentioned Asia Bibi, who was on death row for nine years, and Joseph's sister, who was held for seven years. In comparison, his one-month detention was nothing, and he gave God all the credit, saying, 'By his right hand he saves us, it's all by the grace of God.'

Pastor Allam's wife vehemently interrupted at this point. She wanted to give God all the credit for protecting every single Christian life in Jaranwala when the mob descended. No one died, which is astonishing, given the number of churches and homes that were burnt. She had been resting in bed when she first heard reports that a crowd of angry Muslims were gathering. Initially, she dismissed the information as fake news; however, when she began receiving multiple videos and messages showing churches burning, she took the reports seriously, grabbed her phone and some cash and fled.

She told me that God provided a means of escape for everyone. Those who had cars and scooters discovered they had enough petrol to flee, even though the petrol stations in the city had been told not to serve Christians that day (further evidence that the violence was pre-planned). Like the miraculous jar of oil in the Bible (1 Kgs 17), which did not run out during drought and famine, every family had enough fuel to reach garages on the city's outskirts. Here, they could buy as much as they needed. Similarly, buses and rickshaws, which often break down or aren't kept topped up with petrol, kept moving, and there was space for everyone. It was miraculous, and God deserved all the glory.

I'm sure I was wrong to expect a cuddly, soft pastor; what do I know about the type of Christian leader persecuted Christians need? God had clearly been working in Pastor Allam's life, and his faith was refined and pure and, just like gold, a little showy, too. If I were faced with opposition and difficulties, wouldn't I appreciate a pastor who knew what it had been like to be held in prison and tortured? His testimony of a quick release would encourage me, and his life is much more like Jesus' than most pastors I know. As Christ's followers, we worship a man who was accused, beaten and killed and who understands what it is like to go through pain and suffering (John 15:18–20). Pastor Allam presents a similar example to his congregation.

Reflecting on my church experiences, I realize that much of my faith journey has been about learning the right things. Determining if someone is a Christian has seemed to be more a test of knowledge than whether it is revealed through their behaviour and the fruit of their lives. I came to Pastor Allam with questions about his beliefs, but they don't seem relevant compared to the miracles he has seen and the glory he gives God as he relates his testimony. I've been asking the wrong questions and looking in the wrong places.

When looking to the future, Pastor Allam admits that he fears that similar events, including abductions and mob violence, may occur again. He knows that many Muslims are jealous of the Christian community in Jaranwala, although he says his church prays for and loves Muslims. He's not naïve about existing hatred and will respond to events with faith and not walk by sight. Having gone through circumstances that left him feeling powerless, it is now easier to give control to God, knowing he will take care of every tomorrow.

He urged us, as western Christians, to join him and his church in prayer for ongoing safety.

Fiery Joseph chimed in with his thoughts at this point and chastised the Western Church for paying no heed to violence in Pakistan. He felt it could do so much more but was too inward-looking. I know he is right.

I caught up with Joseph at the end of May, during the week of Pentecost. During that same week, I reached the end of my daily Bible reading scheme and asked God what I should read next. He prompted me to return to an Old Testament plan for Ignatian prayer produced by Grove Books.[3] I had previously read through this scheme over several years, beginning around 2016. It was a prayer plan I adored, but I wasn't sure if I should go through it again. However, I discovered that at the beginning of the plan, there were some suggestions for Pentecost week, which seemed ideal timing, so I began there.

Pentecost is a celebration of the birth of the church in the New Testament. It marks the occasion when the Holy Spirit first descended on the disciples in tongues of fire, and they were enabled to speak in multiple languages about what Jesus had done. Since my Bible plan was an Old Testament resource, readings for Pentecost might be expected to cover the Tower of Babel or occasions when the Holy Spirit brought dreams and visions to Old Testament characters. Yet the first passage it suggested I use for Ignatian prayer was nothing like any of these 'easier' stories. Instead, it began with 1 Samuel 11. It's one of those Old Testament stories full of gratuitous violence that can be tough for modern Christians to reconcile with the God of love and mercy we know more about.

In 1 Samuel 11, Saul had just been anointed King of Israel by the prophet Samuel. Yet because Israel hadn't had a king before, there was no palace or capital city for him to live in. Saul returned home and waited for God to reveal what to do next. Meanwhile, the Ammonites, Israel's enemies, laid siege to an Israelite town called Jabesh-Gilead and warned the inhabitants that, after one week, they would gouge out the right eye of each of them and make them their slaves.

The besieged town sent messengers across Israel asking for back-up, and when the message reached Saul, verse 6 says the Spirit of God came mightily upon him. To begin with, Saul cut up two oxen and dispatched the pieces across Israel with the intimidating message that whoever did not join him and Samuel in battle to defend the town would have their oxen cut up, too. The Israelites responded to Saul's call to arms and gathered to fight. Then, Saul mobilized this newly formed army and led them as they marched on the Ammonites. The Israelites attacked before dawn, and the slaughter was so great that no two of the Ammonites were left together.

As I read this gnarly Bible story, I felt as if I might be the only person in the world thinking about this passage during Pentecost week. Yes, the Spirit of God is mentioned, but the outcome is gruesome and bloody. A day later, I sensed I needed to return to the passage and grapple with it again; I was missing something God had for me. Ignatian prayer encourages those who use the method to linger with difficult ideas, which it calls desolations. I also recalled advice from the New Testament about testing what claims to be of God by examining the fruit of those actions (Matt. 7:15–20). The fruits of the Spirit are love, joy, peace, patience, kindness, goodness, faithfulness, gentleness and self-control (Gal. 5:22–3, NLT) so I went through 1 Samuel 11 and looked for these. They weren't hard to find; in the middle of the story, verse 9 states, 'So

Saul sent the messengers back to Jabesh-Gilead to say, "We will rescue you by noontime tomorrow!" There was great joy throughout the town when that message arrived!' In several other versions, the town's inhabitants are 'elated'. I concluded that Saul's actions were right; the Spirit of God had been upon him, and I could see it clearly now.

I immediately went from reading my Bible to opening up a series of media files from Joseph showing Rashida's rescue (as mentioned above).[4] First up was a video of Rashida and her family describing events that took place at the beginning of 2024. By this time, Rashida had been held captive for ten years, subjected to daily abuse. When she was first abducted, her parents had tried to secure her release through the police and courts, but this had only invoked the anger of her captor, who had become incredibly violent and threatened to kill them all. Consequently, her family fled their home and, since they had no savings, they ended up as bonded labourers in a brick-kiln. Here, they worked punishing hours to pay off their debt, which they now owed to the brick-kiln's owner, who had provided a room for them to live in. Bonded labourers rarely pay off these ever-increasing debts; spurious interest rates mean their work is never enough to reduce the amount owed. In the short film, Rashida's mother describes how the family often went without food, and Rashida's younger brother explains how, after coming to the brick-kiln at age 10, he never returned to school.

Rashida herself also made an appearance in the video and described her 'husband's' violence at the start of the year. He had become totally enraged and slashed her hair, the end of her nose and cut her private parts. His actions almost killed her and, to cover up what he had done, since the injuries were so blatant, he imprisoned her at his house. In late February, after two months in captivity, Rashida managed to escape to her family in the brick-kiln. It was then that the family tried to obtain help, and their story first reached Joseph.

Rashida's abductor pursued her and arrived in the brick-kiln compound with a gun, demanding that her family release her back to him. Enraged again, he ended up shooting Rashida's younger brother in the leg before fleeing. Although Rashida remained with her parents, her abductor kept on turning up, breaking into their home and making endless threats. No one knew what would happen next; the family had no money with which to escape and, if they did, they knew the brick-kiln owner would track them down, as well as Rashida's violent 'husband'. They were trapped.

Meanwhile, in Europe, Joseph was considering what to do. He receives many requests for help from persecuted Christians in Pakistan and can't respond to all of them, but he knew Rashida's situation was particularly horrific. He decided to intervene and began making plans to rescue the family. Simultaneously, a Catholic priest contacted Joseph out of the blue and told him that military personnel were interested in training and planning rescue missions. Joseph took them up on the offer and, miraculously, was able to comprehensively plan Rashida's escape using military-grade maps and even drone footage. This mysterious planning team identified alternative routes in and out of the brick-kiln and suggested places for vehicle swaps and locations for safe houses. Wonderfully, the plan worked.

As I continued to open the photos and videos of Rashida's rescue that Joseph had sent me, I was increasingly sensing God at work. The Holy Spirit was somehow pouring out of the images, which was overwhelming. I see many photos of terrible situations in my roles running charities in Nepal and writing books about women in Asia. Yet there was something enormously powerful about this collection of images. One photo showed Rashida slumped and asleep in a car being driven out of the brick-kiln; I felt overjoyed to see her finally able to rest after so many years of abuse. Another snapshot was of her family crouched in the back of a car, hiding below the windows as they, too, were driven away. Joseph told me he paid €2,000 to the brick-kiln owner to pay off their debt and secure their release. He had been doubtful about doing this but wanted reassurance that the brick-kiln owner would not pursue them.

Similarly striking is a photo of Joseph and his team of lawyers and security guards eating a meal with Rashida and her family when they are finally safe. At one end of the room, Joseph's team fill up several sofas, and they look like giants compared to Rashida's family, who sit together on one couch and are visibly malnourished and emaciated.

Most potent is a video of Joseph and his suited-and-booted team striding purposefully into the brick-kiln. They are accompanied by black-clad security guards who have 'Vision of God' written on their backs and are carrying guns. Joseph later told me these Christian guards were volunteers who put their lives at risk to rescue persecuted Christians. I am not a fan of guns and, despite being married to an Army officer, I am rather a pacifist at heart. Ordinarily, I would not be a fan of anything like this but, as I watched the video, I became intensely aware that God had prepared me to see these images by prompting me to grapple with 1 Samuel 11. As I watched the video again, it became apparent that the same mighty Spirit that had led Saul against the Ammonites was also working in Joseph and this team to rescue Rashida. She, like the residents of Jabesh-Gilead, also faced mutilation. It was astounding. Not only were all the images Joseph sent me hard-hitting on their own, but God had caused me to reflect on this difficult passage for two days before viewing them.

Moments like this are rare, and I felt the Holy Spirit seeping into me with new understanding. I had been praying for deeper theology and better insight, and God responded by pushing me out of my comfort zone. Thankfully, the Christian guards didn't have to use their guns, and Rashida's family got out of the brick-kiln without further violence.

They now live together in another city, around 400 kilometres from where they were rescued. Joseph and his wife have arranged a furnished home for them just 100 metres from a church that will support and comfort them. Joseph's organization, Teach the Children,[5] finances these efforts. All told, the rescue mission cost €5,500, which includes the ransom paid to the brick-kiln owner and Joseph and his wife's flights in and out of Pakistan. It's not much to secure the rescue of an entire family, and I hope people will be prompted to give when they read this. Joseph's wife – who was changing the smoke detector, causing Joseph to regularly look up at the ceiling as we spoke (she always seems to be doing something a little random but practical) – said that with more money, they could buy out more Christian families from the brick-kilns; they don't all need complex rescue plans.

Regrettably, Rashida has had to leave her five children in the clutches of her abusive 'husband'. Sadly, even if they could join her, they probably wouldn't want to. Rashida's captor and his parents subjected her to endless name-calling and abuse.

Their treatment of her has influenced how her children feel about her and so they, too, now call her names. It is utterly heartbreaking that they have been poisoned against their mother. We need God to perform another miracle to restore this fractured family and undo years of brutality.

Joseph, like Pastor Allam, faces difficult decisions about the future. He would like to carry out more rescues and is excited by the prospect of further military assistance, which made the escape plan for Rashida so easy to execute. In the end, their strategy ran like clockwork. However, the more advocacy work he does in the West, the greater his profile becomes in Pakistan, which makes him a target. He has a young family to consider and ponders where God is leading him. Please pray for him and all those who must practise their theology in life-threatening situations. My prayer is that the Spirit of God would be poured out on them mightily, it's astonishing what can happen when God takes the lead.

12

Apple of His Eye – Emaan

If you were a Pakistani Christian, how bad would things have to get before you fled the country? Knowing you would become a stateless asylum seeker at the mercy of global whims towards migrants, would you be willing to escape your mother country to keep your family safe? And once you fled, how would you support your family? Would you be able to protect them in a new destination where you might know no one? These questions, and many more like them, plague the minds of Pakistan's Christians. Some, though, have had no choice; when loved ones are killed, they know beyond a shadow of a doubt that it is time to run.

Emaan and I know each other from Kathmandu. We attended the same international church, where we served together in a ministry to help displaced persons. She is a refugee herself, who somewhat unwittingly found herself living in the city after a traumatic and hasty escape from Pakistan. When I was thinking about writing this book back in 2021, she was the first person I spoke to, and she encouraged me to share the stories of families like her own. Always bubbly and forthcoming, Emaan was also patient with me. She took the time to explain matters I didn't know much about then, but have familiarized myself with during the two years I have been authoring this book. She and I used to meet at a coffee shop in Jhamsikhel, and although we talked about serious matters, we laughed a lot, too.

There are many rules that determine what refugees are and aren't allowed to do, and the laws vary from country to country. Since Nepal isn't a signatory to various global conventions, refugees there are prohibited from taking on registered employment. Instead, they are permitted to earn 'pocket money' by making and selling items on the side. Emaan had a jewellery-making business when she lived in Pakistan and continued this work in Kathmandu. In 2022, when I lived there, the United Nations organized a craft market in the grounds of its main building and invited refugees to sell their creations. Emaan had set up a stall with her husband and, since the building was within walking distance of my house, I went along and bought several items from her, including a necklace made with wooden beads. I decided to wear this necklace for our Zoom interview, and she recognized it as soon as we connected.

Two years had passed since I last spoke with Emaan, and it was lovely to see her again. It was a treat to begin an interview with someone who was already at ease with me. She looked beautiful, and her black glossy hair was loosely tied behind her, attractively framing her face. Although I already knew parts of her story, we began by reminding each other of the similarities between our families. She is just a year younger than me and also gave birth to a son in 2004. Her daughter is just six months older than mine, and it is these parallels that remind me how, had I been born in Pakistan, I too might have found myself living perilously as a refugee. The blessings I have had from birth by being born in a western country are hard to comprehend and appreciate without direct comparisons like this.

Emaan was born in Lahore, Punjab, to a large Catholic family that lived in a Christian colony (housing section within the city). Prior to Partition, some of her family had lived in Amritsar (present-day India) and practised Hinduism, but she only remembers being surrounded by Christians; she is one of five siblings. Though they grew up going to Catholic Sunday school, when a new Pentecostal church established itself in the area, her sister-in-law persuaded the younger members of the family to try it. Although the church had some connections to Pentecostal churches in the West, it was set up by native missionaries, and everyone who attended was Pakistani.

At first, Emaan and her siblings just went to the new Sunday school. However, when their classes put on performances and singing shows, her parents came along to watch and gradually decided to switch denominations and join the new, livelier church. A few years later, when Emaan was 13, she asked if she could be baptized, and her parents consented immediately. There was no opposition to the family's conversion from Catholicism to Pentecostalism since Emaan's father was a respected community member. Although he had received training to become a nurse, he had years of experience and was called 'Doctor'. Throughout Emaan's childhood, he ran his own clinic within their neighbourhood, and her mother, who was also medically trained, worked at a nearby hospital.

During Emaan's teenage years in the 1990s, she did well at school and went on to college, where she studied for a master's degree in computer science. During this period, her church also received regular visits from western missionaries who led crusades and held revival-type meetings. I wondered if she found the idea of white missionaries turning up as celebrity pastors rather imperialistic, but she thought not. Many of their church members could not read or write, and they were greatly encouraged by the thought of these missionaries travelling such a long way to speak to them. I was glad to hear her perspective on this.

A native Bible teacher at her church helped to interpret for an older Australian woman missionary. I asked Emaan what she meant by older, and she described the lady as probably in her fifties. When I reminded Emaan that we are almost in our fifties, and I certainly don't want to be described as 'older', we both laughed. So, I'll describe this Australian lady as being in her prime. When she thoughtfully asked her interpreter how she could pray for him, he confessed that he wanted to find a wife since he was in his late twenties. The strangest events then occurred; I can only presume that the Australian missionary had absolute faith in her convictions and was confident she was hearing from God. Upon her return to Australia, she continued to pray for the Bible teacher. She then received a message from God that the woman he would marry had a name beginning with E. Despite seeing the woman in a vision, she couldn't pronounce her Pakistani name. So the Australian lady asked the Bible teacher for photos of the single women at his church whose names began with E. After seeing them, she promptly declared that Emaan was the woman he should marry. Perhaps most astonishing was that Emaan and the Bible teacher agreed to the match.

Emaan confessed to me that although she felt privileged to have been chosen like this, she also felt enormous pressure. The Bible teacher was quiet and seemed aloof; he was eight years older than her. Apparently, she wasn't his type either and he thought she was too skinny. They hadn't spoken much before the Australian missionary's prophecy, yet they have been married for over twenty years now. I met her husband at church in Kathmandu, and I think his demeanour was just shyness; he is a natural introvert, whereas she is radiant and lively. They are opposites of each other, but that is often a successful combination in a marriage. Despite their mutual trepidation, the two of them started a new life together, and she moved to his home, just a few hundred metres from where she had been born and raised.

I was somewhat surprised to hear that the common belief among Christians in Pakistan is that those involved in Christian ministry should not ask for a salary from their church. If gifts from church members are offered, then those can be accepted, but Christian workers are encouraged to have regular jobs and provide for themselves. This tallies with Pastor Allam's experiences in Chapter 11, too, as he ran a successful restaurant as well as leading a church, and I presume it follows the example of the Apostle Paul in the New Testament.[1]

Emaan could not find work that directly utilized her degree in computer science since, in that sector, hours were long, and it wasn't safe for women to travel on their own early or late in the day. Consequently, both Emaan and her husband worked as teachers. She taught several subjects at a primary school before moving on to a secondary school where she could teach computing and eventually use her specialized skills. Her husband began teaching at one of Lahore's most prestigious Christian schools and worked his way up to become vice-principal.

Throughout Emaan's childhood, Muslims and Christians in her part of Lahore had lived side by side in relative harmony.

Though she had heard of persecution taking place elsewhere, the Muslims near her were good to the Christians among them, and each had a respectful attitude towards the other. A drastic change was to come, though, in the mid-2000s. Just as she was getting used to her new role as mother to a baby and toddler, a younger generation of Muslims began to hate Christians. There are probably many contributing factors, but a crucial part of this was 9/11 and the subsequent war on terror in neighbouring Afghanistan. Pakistanis watched the battle unfold and felt forced to take a position. Pakistani Muslims sided with their Afghan neighbours and began to view Pakistani Christians as western allies, leading them to scapegoat Christians for the violence tearing their region apart.

Emaan and her husband were relatively wealthy; they owned their home outright and had vehicles. Since they had enough money to meet their basic needs, they were also able to invest in stocks and some small businesses, including the jewellery-making enterprise. Simultaneously, they rose in the leadership ranks at their church and became co-leaders. When western missionaries came to visit, they hosted them and continued to arrange public crusades to which Muslims were invited. Miracles occurred and, wonderfully, some Muslims chose to convert to Christianity. All of this activity meant they became well-known to Muslim community leaders who were jealous of their success and wanted the church to close.

In 2009, Emaan's husband began to receive regular calls warning him to stop their church activities. The phone numbers were unknown to them, but the area code for each was Karachi. This made them nervous because rather than just neighbours being a little grumpy with them, it appeared that a more expansive network might be displeased with their

Christian activities. However, they tried not to be deterred by the calls and carried on with church meetings.

Then, in 2010, Emaan was riding on a motorbike with her uncle and cousin (she hastily added that riding three to a bike was legal in Pakistan at the time), but since it was in the cool season, her uncle was wrapped up, and was mistaken for being her husband. A motorbike cut across in front of them, and the rider yelled at them to stop preaching to Muslims. This dangerous and intimidating action caused the bike Emaan was riding on to crash, and she ended up in bed for the next two months as she recovered from her injuries.

Meanwhile, Emaan's husband repeatedly tried to register an FIR at the local police station regarding the motorbike incident. Despite his family's apparent injuries and damage to the motorbike, the police kept trying to dissuade him and told him the verbal threat was a figment of his wife's imagination. The police firmly believed that Christians and Muslims lived in peace. After several visits, the police eventually relented and registered the confrontation. However, they told Emaan's husband that if he wanted them to investigate the case, he would have to pay all the police's expenses. Given that the initial telephone threats were made from Karachi, any investigation would mean travelling there. Proceeding would cost a fortune, so Emaan's husband abandoned pursuing the matter through the police.

Having come so close to critical injury, Emaan and her husband took seriously the warning that had been bawled at them, and rescheduled all the church's meetings. They began gathering in members' homes rather than in the church building, where they were vulnerable. This still allowed large meetings since many houses had open courtyards, and it was warm enough for most of the year to sit outside. Emaan and her husband also arranged for services to take place at irregular times so, unless you were in the know, it would be hard to predict when the next service would take place. Crusades continued, but these were 'closed', meaning only those trusted and invited could attend; sadly, their open invitation to Muslims to hear the gospel had to be withdrawn.

Despite these adjustments, the threats continued for the next five years. A crude crucifix was daubed on their compound wall, marking the household as Christian, and this resulted in fire-bombs being thrown into their property. It sounded incredibly frightening, but most intimidating was when the wall opposite their entrance gate, which ensured they would see it every time they went in and out of their home, was painted with a threat in Urdu. It read, 'In reverence of Muhammed we are willing to cut heads.'

Emaan's husband felt powerless, but he had a close Muslim friend whom he had known for many years. This man was part of a well-established family in Lahore and had influence. Emaan's husband went to see him and described both what had happened on the motorbike and at the police station. He asked for the man's protection and help but was completely let down. This man told him that he should not have come to his home and that he had cousins who worked in eleven police stations across Lahore. If Emaan's husband came to him again, he would have him arrested. I can see in Emaan's eyes that they both felt utterly betrayed by these words and the man's lack of compassion and action. These sentiments, perhaps more than any physical violence, hurt them most deeply.

I began this chapter by asking how bad things would have to get before you left your home. Would this be the point at which you would have fled? It's hard to put ourselves in the situation; although Emaan and her family felt immense danger, all of their extended family was around them; how could they abandon them? They felt loyal to their church and country; surely God wanted them to remain in Pakistan as his witnesses. Besides, where could they possibly go? Escaping anywhere is expensive and, globally, migrants aren't welcome in many places. As I'm writing this chapter, riots and mob violence are taking place in cities across the UK. Social media was awash with misinformation after young girls were stabbed at a summer dance class in Southport. Asylum seekers housed in hotels are being targeted night after night by far-right mobs. It's easy to feel a sense of despair; who will welcome and care for the persecuted?

Tragically, in 2015, Emaan and her family suffered a significant attack by Muslim vigilantes, and they were left with no choice but to leave Pakistan. They, their parents and siblings were gathered at her parents' home to celebrate her sister's birthday. All told, there were around eighteen adults downstairs and a boisterous gaggle of children playing upstairs on a terrace. The house was situated near a central intersection within their colony, and they later learned that two gangs of men on motorbikes approached the house from opposite directions, allowing them no escape. However, they were completely surprised by the attack, and there was no time to run away.

Just after dark, the gangs converged on the house and knocked on the gate. When it was opened, they rushed into the compound. Emaan's initial feelings were overwhelming confusion, and the gang were similarly bewildered. They thought they were attacking a church meeting rather than a birthday party and expected to find everyone gathered in the same room; instead, the family was dispersed throughout the house. Emaan had no idea what they wanted but, pretty soon, the men started beating and hitting the male members of her family and toppling furniture and appliances. Emaan rushed upstairs to the children and locked them in an upstairs room to prevent the mob from reaching them as the carnage unfolded downstairs.

Emaan's mother had a similar instinct and rushed in front of her adult sons to protect them; the gang was beating them with sticks and using the butts of their rifles to batter them. Her selfless act was not enough to stop the violence, and she, an elderly lady, was shoved against a wall and she collapsed to the floor.

Though it seemed like an age, the gang left quickly before any police could arrive, and Emaan's family was left bloodied and terrified. All the men in the family had been attacked, although the women, except for Emaan's mother, had mostly been spared. The family immediately called for ambulances, and everyone rushed to the hospital.

The family's injuries were various. As well as cuts and bruises on their heads, Emaan's brothers had been kicked in the stomach; their internal organs were damaged, and some of them continue to have kidney problems to this day.

Emaan's husband had been brutally beaten about the head and, in other circumstances, would have been admitted to hospital for brain scans. Given that their lives were in danger, however, after a couple of hours, when he was conscious, he discharged himself and went with Emaan and their two children to his aunt's house on the periphery of Lahore. Emaan's father-in-law wisely advised them not to return home, and they have never been back.

Most upsetting were the injuries to Emaan's mother, who was named Gloria. She had bravely tried to save her adult sons but did not wake up after the incident. Three days later, while still in hospital, she died. Heartbreakingly, Emaan was not able to be with her mother when she passed away. I asked Emaan for permission to use Gloria's real name in this chapter because I want to pay tribute to such a courageous woman.

Emaan and her family lay low at their aunt's house. They had barely begun to recover from their physical and psychological wounds when a young man from the neighbourhood told them that several strangers had turned up nearby and were asking about them. On the night of the incident, they had noticed that one of the men who attacked them had a prominent scar across his cheek. They asked their friendly informant if any of these strangers had such a scar, and he confirmed that one of them did. Hence, Emaan and her family knew the gang was after them; they were still in danger.

While Emaan's family had been sheltering with her aunt, their entire family across Pakistan had found out what had happened, and those who could, offered to help. An uncle, an accountant for an engineering company in Khyber Pakhtunkhwa province, 400 kilometres away, had room to accommodate them. He worked away from home, and his position entitled him to a house in the company's compound. On discovering that the gang was still after them, Emaan acted quickly and immediately booked bus tickets to Tarbela to travel that night.

They made their escape less than a week after the attack, and Emaan's husband was still covered in injuries. Although it was July and very hot, he had to make the long, bumpy journey covered in a shawl to conceal his wounds from the other passengers. He felt hot and sick the entire way as there was no air conditioning on board. Emaan, reeling from the death of her mother, tried to take care of their children and reassure them. It must have seemed like a very long bus journey that night, but they were there by mid-morning the following day.

Their stay in Tarbela was temporary. Khyber Pakhtunkhwa has even fewer Christians than Punjab, and it has been a hotbed for terrorism as it borders Afghanistan. The province saw a great deal of violence during the war on terror and was where Osama Bin Laden was later found and killed. Going there, for Emaan and her family, was like jumping out of the frying pan into the fire, but it was perhaps the last place the Muslim gang expected them to go, and it bought them another week to plan what to do next. It was becoming increasingly evident that only leaving Pakistan would save them.

Back in Lahore, Emaan's father hastily visited a travel agent, the passport office and a couple of foreign embassies. According to Emaan, a Pakistani family can't take their children out of the country unless they can prove they are going on a holiday. For those reasons, her father obtained month-long visas for Thailand and the Philippines to give the impression that they were going on an Asian tour. Secretly, though, they thought they might escape to the Philippines since it is the only Christian country in Asia. Emaan's sister bravely returned to their home and collected some of their belongings, and Emaan and her immediate family took another bus from Khyber Pakhtunkhwa directly to Lahore's international airport. The family met in the departure hall, where they handed over the travel documents and belongings just before the flight.

Emaan had not left Pakistan before this, and she had never been on an aeroplane. Travelling in these circumstances was extremely daunting, and she was desperately praying for their nightmare to end. There was a brief stopover in Thailand, and then they flew on to Manila, the capital of the Philippines. They had no family in this country, but a friend of a friend who was Filipino now lived in the United States. She had left behind an empty house when she had emigrated fifteen years beforehand, and she still had family in the country. This kind Christian woman, who had never met them, asked a family member to meet Emaan and her family when they touched down and to take them to the empty house inconveniently located over four hours from the capital.

The Philippines is located in the tropics, with almost constant humidity and heat. In these conditions, any building quickly becomes dilapidated, so the place needed a thorough cleaning when they arrived. Their priority, though, was to get some sleep and then register with the United Nations High Commission for Refugees (UNHCR) to begin the asylum process and obtain some help. Their travel and food costs alone were quickly eating into their savings.

Although they hoped to make the Philippines their home, they remained there for only a month. They traipsed to the main UNHCR office in Manila every other day. It was gruelling; the journey into the city took several hours each way, and their visits were fruitless. On each trip, they were met by the same secretary who spoke no English and couldn't register their case. They were repeatedly told they must speak with the human rights department, where English speakers were available. However, despite leaving their contact details several times, no one contacted them, and they couldn't get an appointment.

By the end of the month, with their visas about to expire, it seemed their only option was to seek refuge in another country. As they left the Filipino Department of Justice, where a lawyer had promised to meet them but hadn't shown up, they were distressed and entered a travel agency to find out their options. The agent who spoke to them happened to be a Christian, which was a great comfort, and she counselled them wisely. By now, they were thinking about trying to get to Sri Lanka, where the UNHCR has a good reputation, but the travel agent advised them to try Nepal as it is the only country where South Asian Association for Regional Cooperation (SAARC)[2] citizens can obtain a free one-month visa on arrival at Kathmandu's airport. They booked four tickets for Nepal.

Once again, the body of Christ jumped into action and, when Emaan and her family arrived in Kathmandu, Christian friends of friends from Pakistan met them at the airport. This family had escaped from Pakistan a year before them and already attended the international church where I was to meet Emaan in 2020.

I wondered how Emaan felt about coming to Nepal. After all, it is an impoverished country, though the capital, Kathmandu, is progressing quickly. As much as I love the place, I found living in the city challenging, as pollution levels are high and there is very little green space. Yet she was positive about ending up there; it is a relatively cheap place to live, many people speak English, and the climate is good. For a capital city, it is exceptionally safe, particularly for women, who can dress with a fair amount of freedom and move about without intimidation.

The two Christian families spent a week living together, which was a huge relief as Emaan and her husband had been doing everything for themselves since the incident. These kind Christians also helped Emaan and her family find a place to rent. Registering with UNHCR wasn't easy, but they managed it thanks to the helpful advice they received. They also attended the international church that Sunday and were introduced to the pastor who ran the displaced persons' ministry. Their situation was improving, but it was still only six weeks since they had been stripped of their home and family. It was a dark time, and the mental repercussions were just beginning.

Thus began a bureaucratic battle that continues to this day. First, they had to register as asylum seekers. Following an interview at UNHCR's offices, they were issued with a letter confirming their asylum status. Then they had to familiarize themselves with what that entitled them to. It turned out that it didn't give them much: only medical treatment from Kathmandu's busy teaching hospital and 3,000 Nepali rupees (NPR, approx. £20) per month for six months each year while their children were under the age of 16 to cover education costs. Not only were the rules tight, but they were also constantly changing. After a year, the education cost was paid out only to children under 14 years of age, and now it has completely stopped (for all children). Additionally, only medicine up to the value of 500 NPR (approx. £3.50) is now covered.

Emaan's husband was still suffering from his injuries, so they had to make frequent visits to the teaching hospital. I also wondered if there was any provision for trauma and PTSD counselling; apparently, UNHCR has a department to deal with this, but none of Emaan's family have utilized their services.

UNHCR helped them open a bank account, but there was little to put in it as they were prohibited from taking jobs in the formal sector. Without contracts, there is a real risk of exploitation. When I was in Kathmandu and part of the displaced persons' ministry, we heard how one refugee had found work with a Nepali road gang for several weeks, carrying out back-breaking manual labour. When it came time for him to be paid, the gang leader refused and threatened violence if he complained. There was nothing this refugee could do; he had no proof that he had done the work.

Emaan has heroically voiced her concerns about the employment situation to the UN representative in Kathmandu. However, the representative believed there were plenty of opportunities in Kathmandu for refugees to find informal work and to be paid in cash. Emaan has not found this to be the case. She and her family continue to struggle and rely on their family back in Pakistan to meet many of their needs.

After six months in Nepal, they received official recognition of their refugee status and were no longer asylum seekers. This meant they could apply to resettle elsewhere, and they promptly submitted paperwork to go to Canada, which currently operates the most promising refugee resettlement programme with a small but significant quota for applicants from all over the world. This was eight years ago, and they are still waiting to leave. Emaan's husband sent over three thousand emails to churches in the West, asking for protection and sponsorship, and only one replied positively. They are now working with this church in Alberta, to finally move to safety. I asked Emaan if she was looking forward to trying skiing, and she looked a little nervous but laughed at the idea. I think she'd appreciate some instruction when she finally gets there.

Canada is not the only country offering a sanctuary for refugees; most western nations have programmes that welcome and settle migrants fleeing persecution and conflict. In the UK, churches and community groups can sponsor and welcome a refugee family, and the Sponsor Refugees website[3] has full details about what is required. The steps involved are as follows: build a group of volunteers; get consent from your local authority, complete your sponsor application, fund-raise £9,000, find a property, welcome the family, support them with language and employment; and prepare the family for independence. In my view, none of these steps would be prohibitive for the average UK church if it were to instil a vision for helping refugees among its members. The only caveat is that the church cannot name a specific family it wishes to help; it is obliged to assist the refugee family that UNHCR selects to send their way. However, the more churches that can provide homes and help for refugees, the better. I'd love to inspire churches to take up the challenge of welcoming a persecuted family and, if you can't get your church on board, you can join an existing welcome group through the Sponsor Refugees website.

The biggest barrier, and the one that I find most infuriating, to Emaan and her family's future life in Canada comes from Nepal's government. At the start of their stay in the country, they were given visas to remain in Nepal for one month. When they were officially recognized as refugees, these visas ended, and Nepal does not have a procedure for extending or providing refugee visas. This has two disastrous consequences. First, they cannot leave Nepal, as they have no means of re-entering the country and are therefore stuck. Visiting their family in Pakistan or meeting midway in a safe country is impossible. The second is that they now owe Nepal's government overstay fees. At the rate of $8 per person per day, over the last eight years, these fees have amounted to $87,000 worth of debt. It's an absurd amount. Most countries either provide refugees with visas or don't charge overstay fees, but Nepal's government is so chaotic that it hasn't decided what to do with the refugees in its country. I feel heartbroken as I observe Emaan living in limbo, unable to plan for the future, as she has no idea when it will begin.

Emaan would love us to pray for Nepal's government to remain stable long enough to enact a law allowing refugees to move forward with their lives. I'm part of a WhatsApp prayer group with the specific aim of praying for this issue; it would be encouraging for the group if I could let them know that others are praying for them; do let me know if you feel burdened for this issue. Additionally, Emaan is eager for more churches and communities in the West to welcome refugees, and she encourages us to learn more about how to do this as the processes in each place vary hugely.

In the meantime, her children spend their days at home and cannot finish formal schooling. The standard Nepali qualification (like GCSE) requires a module in the Nepali language, and since they don't know Nepali, they can't complete this section of the course.

At times, they feel that no one cares about their situation. Living long-term out of their home country means they no longer feel fully Pakistani but are neither Nepali nor Canadian. Their identity hangs in limbo, and the usual progression people make in their career or church leadership is impossible. On one occasion, Emaan's husband prayed about this and received a promise from God based on Isaiah 61:4–7. It's a passage that I think those of us with secure citizenship will never fully appreciate. In it, God promises to restore Israel and that foreigners will someday come to serve us. Their status will be recognized, and their leadership qualities will be acknowledged. Within an hour of receiving this promise, some foreigners from the international church turned up unexpectedly at Emaan's home with furniture, including a much-needed cupboard and mattress. It was a reminder that God remembered them and would honour them.

Being members of the international church has been an enriching experience for Emaan. Her husband has come out of his shell as he interacts with the constant stream of passing church visitors who come from overseas to take up short-term positions in the city (as my family did). They have each enjoyed getting to know Christians who stick around for more than a few years too. In Pakistan, they can 'read' someone quite quickly to understand their background, but learning to do this in an international context is a new skill that Emaan enjoys.

Unfortunately, being part of the Pakistani refugee community in Kathmandu has not been all that positive. Yes, they received a warm welcome, and some families have supported them through thick and thin, but the overall context is not good. The UNHCR barely provides enough to get by, and this feeds into a narrative that it could do more if there were fewer refugees. Similarly, and unavoidably, the situation at the international church is the same. They have limited resources, and the more refugees it chooses to assist, the less it can provide for each. This breeds a sense of competition between the refugees, which is detrimental.

One newly arrived Pakistani family asked Emaan and her husband to help them prepare for the in-depth assessment interview that UNHCR carries out. A lot hangs on this interview as it determines whether a family is officially given refugee status and, therefore, their allowances and future options for relocation. Emaan and her husband did their best to coach this couple but, in the end, UNHCR rejected them because there was insufficient evidence of persecution. Unfairly, the couple accused Emaan and her husband of giving them bad advice and spread malicious gossip about them.

The uncertainty and pressure that refugee families live under can also cause conflict and may even trigger forms of domestic abuse. Emaan tried to help another family that had fallen out and no longer wanted to live together. Again, she was accused of interfering and blamed for the mess. It's sad that divisions like this occur, but also understandable given that these families are unable to plan for the future; it's a form of mental torture keeping them in limbo; they exist in no man's land. I think it's also important to recognize that they are adhering to all the rules laid down by UNHCR. I'm sure they must be tempted to try to reach another country illegally, by boat or by foot, as many others do. Media and governments in the West must do more to recognize and help those who place themselves at the mercy of our legal systems.

While they wait in Kathmandu to move on with their lives, Emaan and her husband are, naturally, ageing. He, in particular, still struggles with some lasting health effects from the attack that slow him down. They know it will take a lot of energy in Canada to begin again, which worries them, so they would prefer to get there sooner rather than later to give themselves the best chance of thriving.

When Emaan lived in Pakistan, she taught and preached to her congregation. Then she had head knowledge only of the Israelites wandering in the wilderness. Though she knew the Bible stories of miraculous manna and springs of water, she now has first-hand experience of God's provision and awareness of her needs; she has been amazed at his timely goodness towards her family. Although she often feels as though she is going round in circles, waiting for her future to begin, God is there with her. In Deuteronomy 32:10, God promises to find his chosen people in the desert and to guard them as 'the apple of his eye'. I am confident this is how the Lord feels about Emaan.

After conducting interviews, I always feel sweet exhaustion. It takes enormous concentration to follow a story and ask the right questions, but I feel humbled and privileged to hear from people who have overcome tremendous hardships. I am left cherishing precious memories and eager to honour the person's experiences. With Emaan, these feelings are even more intense since she and I are friends; I hope I have managed to convey how brave and wonderful I think she is, and I pray that even before this book is published, she will have begun her new life in safety in Canada. She may have even taken up skiing!

13

Seeker – Anna

How do you go about finding someone you last saw in 1993 and whose name you can't even remember? That challenge faced me as I thought about trying to track down my classmate, whom I mentioned in the introduction to this book. She had been sent to Pakistan immediately after our GCSEs to marry a distant relative, and now that I knew so much more about the treatment of women in Pakistan, I wanted to understand how her situation fitted into the broader picture of what life is like for women there.

Apart from our English oral exam, we hadn't spent any time together during school as we weren't in the same classes, and she lived nowhere near me. The only information I had to identify her with was what she had told us during her oral presentation.

I remembered that she was British-Pakistani and, like all the girls at our school with that heritage, she wore shiny white tapered trousers over her legs. The school uniform concealed the rest of her body, but she didn't cover her hair.

During our English oral, she spoke last in our group and, when she did so, she immediately launched into the facts; over the coming summer, she would be sent to Pakistan to be wed to an uncle or cousin, and she did not know when she would return. I remember asking why she didn't simply refuse, and that was when she told us she would be injured or possibly killed by her own family if she didn't comply. This part of her story just didn't compute for me. I had never heard of a parent killing their own child, and it seemed preposterous.

I don't remember her using the word 'honour' during her presentation, but she did talk about 'shame'. She stated that, if she didn't go along with the proposed marriage, it would bring shame on her family and, in their eyes, that would warrant murdering her. According to her, Pakistani parents in Britain were more conservative and protective of their daughters than their counterparts who had remained in Pakistan. She felt they were more vigilant about holding on to traditional ways for fear of being corrupted by British morals. As a result, they wished to avoid shame at all costs, even if it meant losing a daughter. Although she was evidently talking about an 'honour killing', I later discovered that, in 1993, the term had not yet been coined.

I had spent months planning how to contact my classmate, but I also knew that anything I did to find her could be totally ignored. To say I was nervous was an understatement. (I had already signed the contract to write this book, so the pressure was on me to write something!) Although I needed to go public and use social media to find her, I also knew that making too much of a fuss would be likely to frighten off the very community and person I needed to reach. Tracking down someone affected by honour-based violence would not be easy.

I planned to use Facebook for my search since a Facebook group already existed for my year group and had over one hundred members. Hopefully, one of them would know how to find her. I began by tidying up my profile; it felt rather like going for an interview. I knew the first thing any of my school-friends would do, especially if they didn't remember me, would be to check my profile. What did I want them to see first? I decided an old photo of me in school uniform would do the trick.

It was the coronation weekend in May 2023, and my daughter was in the middle of her own GCSE exams. Since the UK had been granted an extra bank holiday to enjoy the coronation celebrations, she had decided to spend the long weekend with her grandparents by the seaside. It was a good plan since they could spoil her while she revised. While she was there, I tasked her and my mum with digging out an old school photo of me in uniform. I cringed when it arrived via WhatsApp; though it wasn't awful, the thought of splashing it all over social media made me clammy!

The following day was the Monday bank holiday itself, and I thought people would be likely to be at home, with perhaps some time available to help me search for my classmate. I posted the photo of me from 1991 and added some words about my excitement at being given a contract to write a new book. I also made a subtle reference to 1993; I hoped to distract people from actually looking at my photo! Thankfully I received a fair few likes and some kind comments. I felt a little better.

Morbidly, it also occurred to me that I ought to check the online archives for the local paper in Reading, where Bulmershe School is located. I needed to ensure there wasn't an honour-based killing near the time that my classmate felt threatened. I pulled up the *Reading Chronicle* website and, to my relief, there have never been any officially recorded honour killings in Reading. Phew!

I then spent the rest of the afternoon pacing. Why is contacting former school-friends so tricky? I felt sick whenever I looked at their photos in the Facebook group. Messaging them all to ask for help about such a sensitive topic gave me heart palpitations! In hindsight, I was scared of their responses, of which I expected three. First, I thought I might be ignored entirely, which would be hugely frustrating. Second, I might receive some pleasant responses and possibly some help; this would be the best outcome, but I also feared the final possibility, which would be to stir up some animosity between Muslims and Christians. I know there are far more Muslims in the UK trying to end forced marriage than those who practise it, but I didn't want things to get nasty. I am a Christian author, after all.

Just like removing a plaster, I knew I had to send out my plea for help, and I would feel better once it was done. I had a stern word with myself; I had spent the last few years writing about women with genuine problems, and here I was, pathetically worrying about social media. It was 3 p.m., and the day was passing quickly. I decided to send private messages to each of the Facebook group members, knowing that, due to the nature of my search, anyone wanting to respond would be likely to want to communicate in private as well.

Here is what I sent out:

Hi, I'm not sure if you remember me, I was at Bulmershe School many years ago in class 'M' and took my GCSEs in 1993. My maiden name was Jaques.

I'm now an author and write about women in Asia. I want to track down someone we went to school with.

You might remember that, when we took our English GCSE, we were put in randomly assigned groups to present and discuss a topic. I ended up in a group with a British-Pakistani girl who said that, following our GCSEs, she would be sent back to Pakistan for an arranged marriage. She told the group she would be killed if she didn't comply with her family's wishes . . . I would love to find her, but sadly I don't even remember her name.

Maybe you know who she is, in which case, please reply to this message or send an email to annamtarbonne@gmail.com. If you don't know who she is, please could you help me by forwarding this message to everyone we went to school with. Hopefully, we can find her; she could be in Pakistan or the UK or perhaps elsewhere.

Rest assured, I will treat anything you share with me in the strictest of confidence, and I will not publish any details you share with me without your express permission. Thank you for your help.

I also posted this in the Facebook group itself, hoping to spark the interest of those people that Facebook prevented me from contacting.

Hi, I wonder if you remember me, I was at Bulmershe School many years ago in class 'M', my maiden name was Jaques.

I'm trying to track down someone we went to school with. The details are somewhat sensitive, so I've sent out private messages to everyone who is part of this group. If you'd like to help me and haven't received a message, please just let me know. You may need to check your Facebook security settings to allow the message to get through.

Thanks, everyone.

I began by sending the message to my Facebook friends from school. I suppose I was hoping for an immediate positive reaction, some encouragement that what I was doing was worthwhile and not weird, but there was nothing. I nervously continued to the list of non-friend group members, people whom I vaguely recognized but had never been close to.

As I sent my message to them, I began to feel discouraged; almost everyone I contacted was white and male, not exactly my target audience. I knew I needed to reach the British-Pakistani community and the girls who had attended Bulmershe School with us. It dawned on me how little we had truly integrated and, thirty years later, this was reflected in the make-up of our year-group Facebook page. Where were they?

Eventually, my laptop began buzzing away, my message was being seen, and friends were starting to respond. As I continued to copy and paste my message to more people, there were recurrent 'bings' as interest grew. Should I stop to react or continue reaching out to more people?

My curiosity got the better of me, and I took a peek at the reactions so far to discover my enquiries had triggered an outpouring of compassion and emotion. One man confessed that he had tried hard to forget his time at Bulmershe but hoped I would find her. Another man suggested a charity for me to contact; he had watched a documentary about them and thought they did incredible work. There is more information about them below.

Then I hit a problem. It seemed Facebook algorithms were fine-tuned to pick up when someone sends the same message over and over to group members, so I was flagged for spam. I continued to be able to contact those I had already reached out to but could not send any new messages. It was hugely disappointing, but I felt relieved that I had set the ball rolling. In all, I had contacted thirty schoolmates and, given that I had asked them to forward my request, I hoped my impact went beyond what I could see.

Of course, responses continued to roll in from those I had been able to communicate with, and then I started to receive snippets of valuable information. One friend suggested the girl I was trying to contact was someone she had tried to befriend who once arrived at school with scald marks from an iron. Her parents were known for being strict. This jogged a memory; I recalled that this girl was relatively small and may have had some learning difficulties. She was bullied sometimes, and I remember her as troubled. However, she was not the girl who had participated in my English oral. The girl I remembered was outspoken and fearless; she was not the type to allow anyone to push her around.

Other messages of support started to arrive from the 'white males' I had contacted; they were so kind. Although no one knew the name of the girl I was trying to reach, they hoped I would find her and that she was safe. Given how little I had grasped in the nineties about the experiences of some girls I attended school with, I expect these boys were utterly clueless back then.

I asked a close Christian friend, who had also switched schools with me to attend a different sixth form, to pray for the search process; I had expected it to be challenging but didn't think Facebook would close down on me. Facebook even began to stop me from sending messages to 'friends'; I was definitely on their block list. I wondered how long it would last. I was curious to know if my close friend recalled if I ever shared with her what had been revealed in my English oral. She didn't think so, but she did recollect a conversation in a changing room about girls who were not expecting to return to Bulmershe after the summer holidays. They were due to visit Pakistan and were uncertain that they would be back at school the following year.

When another message arrived from someone who recalled a sense of sadness that permeated everything at school, it resonated with me. There were many unseen and unspoken challenges at home for many pupils, and the cultural gulfs between us were huge. Thirty years later, they were still proving formidable to cross since no British-Pakistani person had responded to me.

I suppose my initial message showed that I was compassionate, and my allusion to being an author prompted some to look up my books on Amazon. Presumably, it was clear from them that I was a Christian, so it was lovely to hear from some friends about their own faith. Another woman shared with me how she had lost her partner, leaving her alone to raise their two children. I was heartbroken for her, but I was glad we could connect. I shared about the two miscarriages I had experienced and how they had prepared me to take on the challenge of caring for women in Nepal who also suffered through no fault of their own. We both understood that suffering is almost always wholly undeserved.

The practical-minded among my school group suggested I take a look at our year-group photo, which I believe was taken during our GCSE year in either 1992 or 1993. Sadly the image was grainy and, although I stared at every face, trying to determine if they were the girl I was looking for, it was hard to identify anyone. I could barely recognize myself! Several people suggested I also speak to Bulmershe School directly, which was already my intention. However, I did not have an up-to-date contact there so, thankfully, a friend was able to put me in touch with a current teacher. I would email them after this search to learn more.

Yet another contact responded that there was no way that a British-Pakistani girl would be sent away for marriage like this now, or at least if she was, her friends would know to do something. I wasn't sure about this, although I agree they would be more likely to act. I resolved to find out more and to discover if there is more awareness and prevention now.

Just before bed, I received a message from another friend saying that a British-Pakistani girl who had been in our form knew precisely who I was searching for. However, I wasn't in contact with this mutual classmate myself. I hurriedly sent her a friend request and a message and hoped she would reply. Until that moment, I had been unable to penetrate the British-Pakistani community and desperately needed a breakthrough.

Sadly, it never came.

Despite persistently trying to get hold of my school-friends and reaching out to the one girl who said she knew what had happened in 1993, I heard no more about forced marriages and threats of violence from them. I felt devastated that my search had gone cold, but I was convinced that stopping honour-based violence today was critically important. A spark within me had been lit; it seemed to be a God-thing.

It also became apparent to me that, just like the persecution of Christian women within Pakistan, British-Pakistani women in the UK were being exploited by some men in Pakistan to further their own ends. Marriages were arranged for the benefit of men in Pakistan who desired an easier life in the West. Like their Christian counterparts, single British-Pakistani women often felt unsafe within Pakistan's borders whenever they travelled there.

The more I strove to understand forced marriage and honour crime in the UK, the more often I saw the organization Karma Nirvana mentioned. I began researching their work on the recommendation of a Bulmershe friend, and I also put out some feelers to Pakistani Christians in the UK. Amelia Jacobs, Britain's first Pakistani-born priest, responded to me with her insights. She also recommended Karma Nirvana to me as they would know the latest situation regarding forced marriages in Britain. It seemed obvious that I should find out more about their work.

Based in the Midlands, Jasvinder Sanghera set up Karma Nirvana in 1993 to help women from a South Asian heritage in the UK. Since I was keen to learn as much as possible about them, I was in luck. As it turned out, Jasvinder Sanghera had written three books: *Shame (S)*, *Daughters of Shame (DS)*, and *Shame Travels*.[1] This was both a blessing and a curse. It was fantastic that so much information was available to me, but also overwhelming – how would I ever sift through it? My husband, Simon, was due to be away for two weeks, so I committed myself to reading her books.

Reading Jasvinder's books wasn't easy; for me, delving deeply into stories about trauma, family murders and suicide while living on my own was tough going. By the time I had finished them, though, I knew I had to share what I'd discovered. It is vital that more people become aware of what is going on behind closed doors across the UK. Honour crimes are nearly impossible to expose because they are essentially crimes of secrecy and façade; knowledge is the best weapon against them.

By the time I finished Jasvinder Sanghera's first two books, *Shame* and *Daughters of Shame*, I had taken thirty-eight pages of Kindle pdf notes. If I was still harbouring any doubts about whether honour killings occurred in the UK, they had been obliterated. Her books are comprehensive and cover instances of violence in the name of honour from up and down the UK. She doesn't hold back; a torrent of upset and trauma floods from her pages.

I find it strange that the name for this type of abuse is 'honour-based', when there doesn't seem to be anything honourable about it. Instead, everything seems to be about shame. Fear of shame dictated every decision made by Jasvinder's family, and I suppose that is why she named her first book, *Shame*, to highlight this negative feature of her upbringing.

I felt a pang of recognition as I continued to read about Jasvinder's childhood. She attended Littleover School, and this area of Derby is a name I recognize. My dad was sponsored through university by Derby-based Rolls-Royce. His good friend from that time became my sister's godparent and, when I was young, he and his wife sent us Christmas presents. In return, my mum made us write thank you letters; their address was in Littleover, and I remember writing it on the envelope. Yet again, this personal connection reminded me that honour-based violence and forced marriages occur in neighbourhoods I know.

Unsurprisingly, Jasvinder detested the thought of an arranged marriage for herself. However, once a trunk appeared and began filling up with wedding clothes, she knew she would be whisked away soon; she was only a teenager at the time. I wonder if my friend from school experienced the same with her mother. Did she also have a sense of foreboding as the end of her GCSEs got closer? I presume she must have also seen some warning signs of an imminent wedding.

Jasvinder told her mum she didn't want to marry and was locked away in her room, only being allowed out of her bedroom to go to school. She 'used to wonder if other Asian girls in my class were going through the same thing as me. But I never dared ask them because I'd been so indoctrinated not to talk outside the family' (S, p. 55).

Thankfully, I don't believe she thought her family would murder her if she didn't comply with their wishes to marry. Still, she did fear household imprisonment so she ran away. Just like my friend at Bulmershe, she saw her school as a possible means of escape. School was Jasvinder's 'link with the wider world' (S, p. 52), and where her mother never ventured. Knowing that the law in England mandated school attendance, she had noticed that 'Every year, a couple of Asian girls would disappear from Littleover during the holidays. It was easier if they went then, when the teachers weren't expecting them, weren't making accusatory "absent" marks in the big black register each day' (S, p. 74). It pains me to read that she 'used to fantasize about telling a teacher and asking them to help' (S, p. 55). I wonder if my friend from Bulmershe had similar dreams about what her revelation might lead to. Jasvinder was realistic and commented, 'Even if I had been brave enough to tell a teacher, I didn't think they'd understand' (S, p. 55). Regrettably, I think she was right; in the 1980s and 1990s, there was very little knowledge of honour-based violence. I am hopeful that teachers are more clued-up now and, by reading this book, my aim is that many others will be too.

Although Jasvinder managed to avoid a forced marriage, her sister Robina wasn't so fortunate and, tragically, took her own life. Disturbingly, 'the suicide rate among young Asian women is three times the average for women of other ethnicities' (*S*, p. 312), and suicide rates among young females have been steadily increasing over several years.[2] In Berkshire, where I grew up and Bulmershe School is located, an alarming number of women jump in front of high-speed trains along the route to London Paddington. These trains pass through predominantly Asian areas such as Slough and Southall.

In memory of her sister Robina, Jasvinder set up Karma Nirvana. She wanted to help other girls who felt trapped and under threat because of honour-based abuse. Having escaped herself, she knew the support girls in similar circumstances would need. Over the years, Jasvinder heard many stories of honour-based violence and abuse from girls raised in homes and families akin to hers. She comments that she 'had no idea of the scale of the problem I was tapping into' (*DS*, p. 14).

Sometimes, girls were brave enough to talk about the difficulties they faced at home and the pressure they were under with their school teachers. However, social workers would go to the girls' homes rather than following up with them at school: 'I thought they would come and see me at school, but they didn't, they went to my house while I was at school, and what did they see? A nice house and my mum all smiling and full of lies, and that was that. They never came back. But when I got home, I got the beating of my life' (*DS*, p. 50).

In another case, a girl wrote accurately about her life and described her brutal family and the pressure she was under to maintain honour. Rather than seeing her words as a cry for help, her teacher thought she was joking and couldn't believe anyone would describe their supposed carefree teenage years in such horrifying terms (*DS*, p. 160). This teacher's attitude is similar to how I had felt all those years ago at Bulmershe School when I first heard about shame and its impact on girls of my age.

In the UK's first successful prosecution for an honour killing, the victim, Heshu Yones, apparently asked her teachers for help on three separate occasions. Yet her pleas for intervention were not taken seriously. Her father murdered her just weeks later and, shockingly, when he arrived at the prison to begin his sentence, he received a hero's welcome (*DS*, p. 26). In the eyes of many, he had acted honourably by murdering his daughter.

Sometimes, a girl may be unable to explain what is going on to her teachers, but her actions will highlight that something is amiss. Once girls have reached puberty, they might be considered eligible for marriage by their families and, from then on, the risk of being sent abroad to marry is increased. If a girl is consistently playing truant, schools can investigate her absences but, rather than going to the girl's home, those responsible for safeguarding should speak to her alone at school. Away from listening ears, hopefully she will feel safe enough to divulge the truth about any honour-based abuse she is encountering or if there is emotional pressure to marry.

Despite all the evidence that forced marriages are taking place, school leaders are unfortunately not doing enough to prevent forced marriage. Head teachers might attempt to avoid the issue for fear of causing offence and stirring tensions among different communities. Theirs is a difficult path to tread; on the one hand, needing to demonstrate that their schools offer equal opportunities and do not discriminate and, on the other hand, being sensitive to the particular needs of various demographics.

I spoke to a staff member at Bulmershe School who has particular responsibility for safeguarding; she said they could do little besides refer the issue to children's services at the local authority. She had been trained to spot honour-based violence and received missives from the Thames Valley Police Commissioner encouraging staff to keep their eyes peeled. Heightened awareness was especially needed in the run-up to the long summer holidays. It is then that many families take the opportunity to return to India or Pakistan for what they claim will be a holiday but, in reality, includes a marriage ceremony for their unsuspecting daughters.

The local authority for Bulmershe School is Wokingham Borough Council. Once WBC takes up a girl's case, it follows guidelines issued by the Safelives charity that operates nationwide. It begins by assessing the situation using the DASH (Domestic Abuse, Stalking and Harassment and 'Honour'-based violence) risk checklist.[3] A lengthy blurb at the beginning of the questionnaire reminds the assessor that, in the case of honour-based violence, there may be more than one abuser and that, often, these may be female family members. Staggeringly, victims of honour-based violence are seven times more likely than other victims of domestic violence to endure abuse from more than one person. Further questions seek to understand the level of threat and control the victim is enduring and how this began, such as by being told what to wear. Once again, in the case of honour-based violence, this prompts the appraiser to consider the influence of the extended family upon the victim.

Since the lines between love, control and abuse are often blurred in honour-based situations, on average, victims of honour-based violence typically wait two years longer than other abuse victims before seeking external assistance. It is hard to recognize yourself as a victim when your own family carries out the offences.

Thankfully, Safelives also provides awareness training through videos, podcasts, blogs and reports that educate front-line workers about the dangers girls face if they are raised within honour and shame cultures. In addition, the charity also organizes frequent live events on X (Twitter) and webinar platforms. These enable safeguarding practitioners to hear the latest research and ask questions. Jasvinder is a regular contributor and, thanks to input from many others with similar experiences, the Safelives website is a fantastic resource.

Among all the stories that Jasvinder tells in her books, only one describes a savvy girl who takes pre-emptive action just in case her family forces her to marry someone during a planned family holiday to Pakistan. In Chandi's case, she told a friend, 'Here's where I'm going. If I'm not back in a month, tell the police' (*S*, p. 312). How I wish my classmate at Bulmershe had done this. In Chandi's case, her words were a necessary precaution since she did not return, as planned, at the end of the summer holidays. Her loyal friend bravely took action and contacted the police. They, in turn, contacted the British Embassy in Islamabad, which swiftly rescued Chandi from the clutches of her extended family. This remarkable story shows that, with awareness and action, forced marriages can be avoided, and girls can outsmart their oppressive families.

Of course, not every girl raised in a British-Punjabi family will experience pressure to partake in an arranged marriage. One notable exception is Anita Rani, the BBC Television presenter. In her book, *The Right Sort of Girl*, she describes a progressive childhood during which she was encouraged to make the most of her family's new life in the UK. She attended a private school and was allowed to dress as she wanted. However, Anita experienced a certain dislocation within this freedom and resorted to self-harm for a short period in her teens. Now, as a grown woman, she still depicts herself as falling in the gap between her traditional British-Punjabi community and her successful British life, for which she has fought so hard. She finishes her book with a letter to her younger self, encouraging her to 'dismantle some of [her] cultural conditioning to live the life [she] want[s]'.[4]

As I was completing this chapter, a relative reached out to me. He was working in Pakistan and had a female colleague who wanted to talk to me about marriage in her culture. I made preparations to speak with her but, as I did so, I realized that I too had gone through the motions of travelling to Asia to meet and stay with a man I didn't know, just as my school-mate from Bulmershe may have done.

When I was 20, I went to Delhi to meet up with a pen-pal who was the same age as me. She was originally from Calcutta, and we had been corresponding since we were 11 years old; our birthdays were just days apart. As it happened, I had a distant cousin who lived in Delhi, near her college, since he worked in the country for an international NGO. My relative was already married with a young child, but he offered me a chance to stay with them. I had never met his wife and child, but I had seen him at some previous family weddings, and he was around ten years older than me. Had we been born into different cultures, I could so easily have been travelling to marry him. He was the oldest son of my gran's favourite cousin and, as her eldest granddaughter, the two of us might have made a match that the wider family would view favourably.

Like many couples whose marriages are arranged, meeting beforehand at a few family weddings would have been deemed sufficient acquaintance.

When I think back to flying into Delhi on my own that summer, I can easily imagine the fear and helplessness girls born and brought up in the UK would face. The heat and humidity were oppressive and disorientating. As I looked out of the plane window before landing, there were only a few lights to break up the night-time darkness (thousands of street lights illuminate the city today). Consequently, I was completely vulnerable on my arrival. With no sense of where I was going, I jumped into a car with my cousin and set off for his home. I had no idea where I was, and I could have been taken anywhere. Of course, I was entirely safe; my cousin, his wife and their cheeky son were wonderful and hospitable. I thank God for my culture and family; the trip was simply a summer adventure, not the beginning of a lifetime of submission to a man I barely knew.

When I spoke with my cousin's colleague, Juni, I discovered that she, too, had been born into a family where she could make her own decisions. Chatting with a Pakistani woman with a mind of her own was a great relief. As if to make her point, she was three hours late for our Zoom chat as she had been going to and fro across Islamabad rescuing a stray cat. She told me this was unusual behaviour in the same way that her decision to turn down every marriage offer was. In her mid-thirties now, as a single woman, she was a rarity in Pakistan.

To begin with, Juni wanted to know what I meant by 'forced marriage'. We talked at length; she felt that not many girls were made to marry by violence or force, but the expectations of family and society were the driving factors. Unseen emotional pressure to comply with a match was ever-present and firmly applied. It was difficult to parse the difference between a forced and an arranged marriage, but it came down to choice. If a girl can truly and honestly say no to an arrangement, then it is not a forced marriage but, in reality, this type of free-will yet arranged marriage is very rare.

As a single woman, Juni felt extremely vulnerable. She felt that men ogled her, and they believed they were entitled to do so because she was unmarried. She received bad service from workmen and shopkeepers because she was alone. At every point in her day, her culture pressured her to conform and marry like everyone else, yet she resisted. She did not want to settle down with just any man and believed there might be love for her.

Countless friends of Juni's had gone through with arranged marriages, some with more force applied than others. In some instances, there were major benefits for the girl; she may have married and moved abroad or gained access to a higher quality of life.

I asked Juni what she would do if a friend were being forced into a marriage she did not want. First, there was no way Juni would involve herself in an issue like that unless her friend actually asked her. Juni admitted that almost nothing could be done to prevent a wedding and, if she intervened, she might invoke violent retribution on herself, her friend or both of them. There might be some possibility to help if she could do so in secret, perhaps give her friend some money to escape and hide, but this might require a lifetime of resources, and Juni couldn't afford that.

Juni mentioned two promising signs that women are no longer prepared to tolerate forced marriages and the ensuing abuse, whether it is emotional or physical. The first is the increasing divorce rate in Pakistan. Although, as a Christian, I don't believe a high divorce rate should be encouraged, neither do I think marriage should be against the couple's will. I am glad women are freeing themselves from men they didn't choose and it is striking that more women in Pakistan feel emboldened enough to initiate divorce proceedings. Although women may be ostracized by their families if they divorce, they are increasingly economically independent and can support themselves if they choose to. The second factor Juni mentioned is the increasing number of women like her who choose to remain single. Nowadays, more and more Asian women are deciding to move abroad to countries where being single is not such an anomaly. I'm encouraged that Pakistani women can now defy stereotypes and make their own decisions.

I'm hopeful that times are changing for women brought up in honour and shame cultures. In the UK, there is much more awareness about the pressure on girls to conform to their families' wishes, and I encourage everyone to read Jasvinder's books to know more. After all, knowledge is power. In Pakistan, pioneering women are taking on age-old traditions and freely expressing their will. They need our support, so please pray for them.

14

Magnifier – Becky

It was spring again, and almost a year after I began my search for my friend from school. I had continued writing the first half of this book. Activists and women in Pakistan, for the most part, were keen and willing to share their stories, and I could recognize God leading me to people and arranging things ahead of me. Though many of the people I interviewed didn't know each other, I sensed their stories formed a patchwork picture of what life was like for Christian women in Pakistan and those boldly standing up for them.

Consequently, it came as a massive encouragement when, in early 2024, I received an email from the Evangelical Alliance (EA) with news of its South Asian Forum. Included with it was an invitation to an online event entitled 'Loving your South Asian Neighbour'. The EA has been a bastion of the British church since it was established in 1846; it seeks to unite Christians and churches so they can make Jesus known and, therefore, impact society. I was overjoyed to find that they were seeking to build bridges between different cultural expressions of the church in the UK. This was the first time I had come across a genuine desire from the established UK church to train and equip Christians to reach South-Asian communities. I hoped they would share my passion to show the love of Christ to victims of honour-based abuse too. Of course, I signed up for the online event.

There was a real mix among the attendees who joined the virtual event. Most, but not all of us, were white, and most but not all of us were women. Some knew a lot about South-Asian culture, having served as missionaries in the region and had now returned to live in the UK. Others were ethnically South-Asian but, having been raised as Christians, knew little about their ancestral religion. It was fascinating. We all shared a passion for reaching the South-Asian community with the gospel in the best way possible. Our two event hosts, Rani Joshi and Amita Sudra, encouraged us to be gentle, pray, and love well. Rather than seeing other faiths as wholly opposed to Christianity, we were encouraged to find grains of truth in the beliefs of others and then use these gems as stepping-stones. I loved the mixed metaphors, which made complete sense as they were presented. The online event was a taster for a longer course that the EA runs. The extended course takes place over twelve hour-long sessions and is called 'Love Your Neighbour'.

Towards the end of the forum, attendees could share why they had joined the training and what help they needed going forward. Becky chimed in with her distinctive northern accent to explain how she had set up a women's refuge, that most of the women she supported were from Pakistan, and they had experienced honour-based abuse. I almost fell off my chair. She had already been able to chat with many of these women about their faith but needed help with how best to share her Christian beliefs. My heart leapt; I simply had to speak with Becky and learn more about her story. She was an answer to my prayers, not only for this book but for all the women she helps out of violent situations.

When we met online a few weeks later, Becky told me how she had spent many years working in safe houses that helped victims of modern slavery. This had involved working far from home and, when her children were young, the hours no longer suited her. Though she was reluctant to step away from her work with trafficking survivors, she found a similar job at a women's domestic abuse refuge that allowed her to work from 4.30 p.m. to 11 p.m. and then sleep at the refuge overnight rather than remain awake. It doesn't sound all that easy to me; I think she must have had buckets of energy; however, the role was an answer to her prayers and allowed her to be around for her children during the day.

One of Becky's jobs at the refuge was answering the organization's helpline. Calls might come in from anywhere in England, and she would triage the cases. Depending on whether the shelter had space at the time, she would determine whether to offer the woman and any children a room. She could direct the callers to other services if the hostel was full.

Besides the telephone where Becky received calls, there was a large sign with the words 'No NRPF' written on it. NRPF refers to an immigration status, meaning 'No recourse to public funds'. This status can be applied to anyone who has arrived from outside the UK and means that person cannot claim state-provided benefits. Many of the callers to the helpline were affected by this condition; if they had arrived from overseas to marry a British citizen and only had a spousal visa, they would also be likely to have an NRPF condition attached to their residency. Refuges are not centrally funded by the government but rely on women being able to claim housing benefits. Consequently, Becky could not offer these callers a space at the refuge because they had no funding.

Over and over, as Becky spoke with women (or those who rang on their behalf if they spoke little English) who had NRPF status and had to turn them away, she became more distressed about their plight. These women either had to remain with their cruel husbands or partners and continue to endure abuse, or they ended up living on the streets. In almost every situation, these women refused to contact the police for fear of being deported back to Pakistan (or elsewhere), where they might face more honour-based violence for having abandoned their husbands and purportedly bringing shame to their families. It was excruciating for Becky that she couldn't help them, and it seemed utterly immoral to her that she couldn't assist women in desperate situations simply because of their immigration status.

As a faith-filled Christian, Becky took her anger and frustration to God and cried out to him. As she tells it, she prayed a dangerous prayer and asked him, 'What are you going to do about these women?'

God's response to her was, 'What are you going to do?'

As she quickly realized, God asks Christians to be his hands and feet on earth, and he was calling her to start serving him by assisting women with no one else to turn to. Around the same time, a man she didn't know all that well came up to her at church and told her he was going to buy a house to rent out. He inquired if she would be interested in renting it from him for a refuge. The offer was somewhat vague, and it was a little early for Becky to take him up on his idea, but she tucked the suggestion away for the future.

Becky believed she was already obeying God's calling to help women with NRPF status since in October 2019, she began running a satellite shelter. She had spoken to her management about her idea to admit women without recourse to public funds, and they discovered a legal way of working within the current limitations. If a child was at risk, under Clause 17 of the Children's Act, the local authority had a statutory obligation to ensure the child's well-being. This applied to all children, regardless of their immigration status. It was a small start, but they began to assist women with NRPF status.

Yet God kept speaking to Becky; it seemed as if news stories about honour-based violence were being reported every day, and anti-immigrant prejudices were always in the headlines. These stories distressed her so much that she had trouble sleeping. Although she wanted God to act while leaving her to continue the work she was already doing, it became increasingly clear that he wanted to use her to answer her own prayers. Simultaneously, he reminded her that his church had a responsibility to the sojourner: 'You shall not oppress a sojourner. You know the heart of a sojourner, for you were sojourners in the land of Egypt' (Exod. 23:9, ESV), and he would raise up other people to help.

As it turned out, her work at the satellite refuge was perfect training. Not only had she become familiar with the particular needs of victims of honour-based abuse, but also the independence she had running it by herself meant she had been in charge of everything from health and safety to paying rent.

Though Becky was holding out against God and trying to stay put in her current job, she signed up to attend a Christian conference in November 2019. The programme had been organized by Press Red, a faith-based umbrella organization committed to developing new ways of highlighting gender violence and helping people make a difference. Press Red was established by Michele Hawthorn, wife of Andy Hawthorn OBE, who set up the Message Trust. Focused on reaching young people with the gospel and equipping the church for evangelism, the Message Trust began in Manchester but now has global reach. By God-coincidence, immediately prior to my chat with Becky, I had been listening to the 'Inspired . . . with Simon Guillebaud' podcast[1] and hearing some of Andy's story. Amazingly, I was now familiar with some of the names Becky mentioned, although I had been oblivious until just an hour earlier. It was fantastic to know that Becky was a part of God's larger work in the north-west.

At the conference, Becky heard from incredible and passionate speakers and was encouraged to read Elaine Storkey's fiery book, *Scars Across Humanity*,[2] which challenges Christians to overcome violence against women. It was as if every speaker at the conference talked directly to her; she could no longer hide from God and knew she was being called to set up a refuge which would expand the limited provision for women who could not benefit from public funding. These women truly were the least, the lost and most vulnerable. Before the meetings ended, she presented her idea to several speakers and explained what she thought God was calling her to do. Everyone she spoke to was enthusiastic and encouraging. Just as I can sense God's call on her life as I listen to her share her story, they could also recognize God at work. Despite this, Becky quickly points out that if she hadn't obeyed God, he would have called someone else; she is confident that the women she now helps are loved by and precious to him. There was no way he would have abandoned them.

As a result, in early 2020, Becky began making plans to start a charity called Beauty for Ashes Refuges. The phrase 'beauty for ashes' is taken from Isaiah 61:3, in which God proclaims his favour towards his people after they have been almost destroyed. He assures them that restoration and healing will come, and the poetic language is evocative and beautiful. Since God also promised Becky the church would help her, she would be able to say yes to supporting all the women she'd had to deny help to until now. Having received such positive responses to her idea at the conference, she approached many of the women she had met there to join her board. All these women represented the Black and Minority Ethnic (BAME) community, whom she was so passionate about reaching.

Of course, with hindsight, we know the Covid pandemic was just around the corner. Becky's plans were put on hold for a while. She became a designated key worker and continued to run the satellite refuge, where three women remained for the duration of the lockdowns. Those women, and her family, were her Covid bubble. The wait gave her time to apply for charity status, raise money and, since it was lockdown, attend countless Zoom meetings with her new board and panel of experts. The vision for Beauty for Ashes began to take shape,

The newly formed board decided to approach Green Pastures, a unique Christian social enterprise, to help fund the purchase of a home. This organization uses invested funds loaned by (mostly) Christians to buy properties that charities can use to provide secure homes for people in need. I had seen Green Pastures displays at various Christian conferences over the years but had never entirely understood how any deposit I made with them would be invested. Hearing Becky explain the process, it became clearer. Not only does Green Pastures help Christian charities off the ground and enable them to do God's work, but they also offer ethical and profitable investments to Christians looking to do good with their money. The board of Beauty for Ashes met with the Green Pastures team and received approval in principle to go ahead and buy a property. Green Pastures would provide the finance; Becky praised God.

As Becky began to look for properties, she encountered a problem. During the year after the pandemic, the housing market was racing; prices were high, and homes would sell in a day. Given that she required board approval and clearance from Green Pastures for any purchasing decision, even if she did find a suitable property, they couldn't act fast enough to secure it.

Right from the start, Becky knew that Beauty for Ashes would be a group effort and that she wasn't being called to work alone. During the pandemic, she attended a lively online prayer meeting organized by Press Red, the same Christian ministry that had organized the conference. Once the plans for Beauty for Ashes became more concrete, she was invited to address the prayer meeting and present her ideas. The lockdowns had ended by then, but the prayer meeting was still online. But, since life was back to normal, attendance had dropped to a skeleton few. Before delivering her message, she had an awful day; her children were being difficult, and when she logged in to give her talk and saw that only a handful of people were online to hear her, she admits that this dampened her mood. She told God he had to speak through her.

After Becky presented the vision God had given her for Beauty for Ashes, a woman asked how the group could specifically pray for the new charity. Becky shared that their immediate need was for a property and that they were having trouble keeping pace with the housing market. Without saying the exact location where they hoped to find a house (the addresses of shelters need to be kept secret to prevent the women who live in them from being found by their abusers), Becky asked them to pray that God would provide a home and they would be able to sign for it before anyone else. She likened this to putting a fleece out like Gideon did in the Bible (Judg. 6:36–40). She knew that, without God, Beauty for Ashes would never find a property but, if God provided one, she would know for sure that this was his idea.

The day after the prayer meeting, one of the ladies who had been there called Becky. She was friends with a Christian father-and-son team who were property developers. They were working on a house nearby, and she had asked them if Becky could look at it. The property was tentatively promised to someone else, but progress wasn't being made for some reason. It was rather a cheeky favour to ask, but Steve, the dad, said OK and agreed to show Becky around. They made arrangements to meet, and Becky was shocked and delighted that the house was in the precise location she was praying for. The woman at the prayer meeting hadn't known this but, of course, God was able to provide exactly what Beauty for Ashes needed.

When Becky entered the house, she knew this was it. The building was perfect; it had high ceilings, period features and large communal areas. Becky poured out her heart and vision to Steve, who was there to meet her and was probably rather taken aback by her story and passion. She remembers him looking at her rather oddly. Since his son wasn't with him, he couldn't immediately say yes or no to her offer but promised to get back to her soon.

In the meantime, Becky needed to resolve some other issues. Although the overall size and location of the property were ideal, it needed to be converted to make it suitable for a refuge. She hadn't got the money for that. Additionally, the house was in an Article 4 area, where it is almost impossible to obtain planning permission for a house in multiple occupation (HMO). Yet she knew deep down that this was the property God had promised Beauty for Ashes; she had a sense of calm and conviction that could only be from the Holy Spirit.

Becky prayed and felt led by God to obtain a quote from Steve and his son for the renovation work. It wasn't cheap, but she approached Green Pastures to see if they would lend her the additional amount and, fantastically, they agreed. She tells me it was a miracle; Green Pastures were already having to devise new ways of working with Beauty for Ashes because the ultimate beneficiaries had no recourse to public funds. They had to adapt their processes to use the Children's Act for surety, but she gives them enormous credit for being willing to do this.

The process of applying for planning permission took a lot longer than anticipated, and in her mind, she expected Beauty for Ashes' first home to be this newly renovated property. Yet God had other plans. As the planning process rumbled on, in August 2022, the man at her church approached her again and asked if she still wanted the property he had mentioned three years before. It was vacant and ready to be used as a refuge since it would be used by only one family with up to five children; it could be rented out as a standard property with no HMO licence necessary. Within a month, Becky quit her job at the satellite refuge and began working for Beauty for Ashes. She readied the home this man offered for its first occupants, and when planning permission in the Article 4 zone was miraculously granted for the period place, she kept in touch with Steve and his son as they carried out the renovations. In January 2023, Beauty for Ashes opened its first refuge in the house offered by the man from her church. Then, in June 2023, the keys to the renovated home were handed over to them. Hallelujah!

Becky is so thankful for all the people God used to launch Beauty for Ashes. She marvels at what the church can achieve when it follows God's leading and works in unity. Just before opening, she appealed for women's toiletries and was overwhelmed with donations. She tells me a cupboard at the refuge now smells like the Body Shop. Of course, there are days when she feels down and wonders if she is 'enough', but God's response is always the same. He tells her that he is enough, and all she can say in response is, 'Yes, you are'. She has learnt that her relationship with God is more important than all the work she does for him. The refuges come second.

The first refuge has three bedrooms and houses one family with up to five children; the second has six bedrooms and could accept women with up to two children. Sadly, demand was high, and both quickly filled up as word spread that there was a place for women with NRPF status. Whenever she has available spaces, Becky adds these to the Women's Aid Platform, which is a live database that can be accessed by police forces, hospitals, domestic abuse helplines and many other agencies up and down the country that assist women fleeing violence. Referrals are also made by word of mouth, and she works closely with other specialist organizations in the north-west. On occasion, women who are experiencing domestic abuse themselves reach out to her directly.

Tragically, 98 per cent of the women Becky and her team help have experienced honour-based abuse, which she points out can also occur in Christian homes. During the week prior to our chat, Becky had attended an event at Manchester Law School where they had highlighted the desperate need for an agreed-upon definition of honour-based abuse so that the needs of victims can be better understood and, in turn, they themselves can be protected. As Becky sees it, honour-based abuse is different from other abuse in two key ways. First of all, there is usually more than one abuser and, sometimes, an entire family can band together to oppress a victim. On occasion, women have told Becky that a 'meeting of the elders' influenced how they were treated. On hearing these words, alarm bells ring, and Becky knows that she is dealing with a case of honour-based violence. Second, the victim's blood relatives (i.e. a woman's birth family rather than her in-laws) might not come to her aid for fear of the supposed shame she will bring on them, whereas, in other domestic abuse cases, a woman can often escape to her parents or siblings. Together, these two factors leave women ostracized and extremely vulnerable.

When a woman arrives at the Beauty for Ashes shelter, the first step is to complete a DASH risk assessment. This is the same national questionnaire used in Wokingham that I mentioned in Chapter 13. It is designed to measure the risk of further domestic abuse and stands for 'Domestic Abuse, Stalking, Harassment and 'Honour'-based Violence Assessment Tool'. It can be completed more than once for each woman as her situation changes and measures to protect her are put in place. Despite mentioning 'honour' twenty-two times, the form has no singular definition, which Becky regards as a glaring omission. Instead, determining whether the abuse is honour-based relies upon a professional's judgement and on whether they can pick up clues about cultural barriers, involvement of the wider family and community, family history towards siblings and if the victim is being 'policed' at home and/or having their public behaviour monitored. It's no wonder then that when Becky reported a safeguarding concern to a local authority, the operator had not heard of honour-based violence. Without a clear definition, it remains challenging to identify and even harder to prosecute.

Once a woman is offered a place and welcomed to the Beauty for Ashes shelter, everything possible is done to make her feel at home. As a faith-based Christian organization, they realize the importance the women place on being able to practise their faith and that it is integral to their identity. As Becky says, religion isn't just a tick box on a form. The refuge provides prayer mats, halal meat, and pots and pans designated for preparing halal food. The team, which Becky counts for me on her hand, currently comprises five Christian women. They each know when Muslims will want to stop and pray and can signpost women to nearby mosques.

All these efforts to accommodate faith practices help encourage the women to stay longer at the shelter rather than return to dangerous situations. Everyone calls each other 'sister' and, frequently, the women open up about their beliefs. Becky often tells them she prays for them and is building up to a time when residents and staff pray together. She is keen to speak more about her Christian faith and tells me there are opportunities, which is why she joined the Love Your South Asian Neighbour forum when I first came across her. She knows that respect for other religions has to go both ways and wants her conversations with the women to be natural and not pushy. Since women typically stay with Beauty for Ashes for six to nine months, there is plenty of time for God-inspired conversations.

Throughout their stay at Beauty for Ashes, Becky and her team repeatedly tell the ladies they believe them. Many of them will have been told they are liars by their abusers and wider families, and these accusations and psychological labels need to be erased. When the women can trust that their story and words will be believed, they can open up about what has happened to them and begin the process of healing. The women need to hear that the team believes them many times, and Becky finds herself saying, 'I believe you' over and over.

Sadly, despite all of Becky's efforts to welcome women in different circumstances, she says more groups and scenarios always fall between the gaps. One of those gaps was refuge space for women with more than two children. She sought God about this, and he provided the house through her fellow church member.

Another huge gap in provision was lodging for single women since the law to provide children with protection can't be extended to them. Although women with children might need to be prioritized so that youngsters are protected from abuse, single women, who might have only recently arrived in the UK on a spousal visa, have particular vulnerabilities that need to be cared for. For instance, they may not speak English or own a mobile phone. Becky prayed about how to meet this need; she was sure God had not forgotten them, and that's when the new building immediately next door to the home that Steve and his son renovated became available. She couldn't believe they were again granted planning permission for an HMO in the same Article 4 zone. It is currently being fixed up and will have nine rooms.

Regrettably, some of the women Beauty for Ashes has helped have been children themselves. One girl was 18 years old, and her parents had booked her on a flight to Pakistan the day immediately after her last A-level. She discovered she would be married while overseas and sought help from a teacher. I'm so relieved that, in this case, her plea for help was heeded, and the local safeguarding plan was initiated, which resulted in Becky and her team offering her protection.

Beauty for Ashes will continue to support a woman if she decides to take her abuser to court. Child custody cases are tried in the family courts, which Becky tells me are far from perfect. They can be especially traumatic for a woman who has to stand up in front of a judge and answer questions. Additionally, most cases are heard behind closed doors, and the media is not usually admitted. This is helpful for privacy but, as I have mentioned in earlier chapters, the press plays a vital role in holding public bodies to account. There is a lack of consistency between verdicts and, in Becky's opinion, some of the judges are misogynistic. I checked that she wanted to say this on record, and she confirmed that she did.

To back up her opinion, Becky described a recent case to me. Beauty for Ashes had supported an honour-based violence survivor through a child custody case. The woman co-operated with everything the judge asked of her, including prolonged fact-finding. Once in front of the judge, her abusive husband presented himself as humble and contrite, yet the woman expressed herself vehemently and came across as angry. In Becky's view, this woman exhibited these emotions because she was desperate to hold on to her children and, in her culture, it is appropriate to express oneself loudly. When her husband called her a liar, the male judge believed him and, tragically, the judge appeared to dismiss the woman as hysterical. All other evidence was overlooked, and partial custody of their children was awarded to their violent father. Understandably, the woman was heartbroken, and Becky vividly remembers her sobbing when she returned to the refuge. What this woman feared most is that with access to his children temporarily assured, her husband might decide to abduct them and take them overseas. Becky knew this was a real possibility, so she felt furious and frustrated that day.

There is mounting pressure to allow journalists and bloggers to report anonymously on decisions made in the family courts. In turn, this should increase consistency and hold alleged chauvinistic judges to account. In early 2024, a pilot scheme that permitted access to 3 family court centres was extended to 19 out of 43 jurisdictions across the UK. Sir Andrew McFarlane, President of the High Court's Family Division, has described the move as a 'huge step to increase transparency and improve public confidence and understanding of the family justice system'.[3] Praise God!

Becky's passion for justice is driven by her resolute faith. It turns out that I'm interviewing her on her birthday; it's the only time she has free to speak to me. She talks animatedly, and it's a struggle for me to keep up. Her red hair suits her fiery determination to do whatever she can to help women. Having grown up attending a house church, she has always considered church to be family. She has fond memories of church services in living-rooms. When Becky was at the age of 8, the church her family attended split and they began attending a Pentecostal church; she found it all very formal.

At 14, she began to drift away from church; Becky never lost her faith but didn't make any effort with it either, always telling herself that, after the next party, she'd start attending church again. Throughout these years, she was aware of God constantly and gently calling her back to himself. While at university studying journalism, she began seeing a local lad, Chris, who was neither a Christian nor knew she had been one. However, when she realized things were becoming serious with him and God was still on her case, Becky decided to tell Chris that she was going to be a Christian again. Her lukewarm attitude towards God couldn't continue; she had to be all in or all out with him. I can tell she still has that attitude today. She and Chris had just returned from the local pub when she blurted out her decision to recommit, which surprised her as much as Chris. He told her he needed a few days to think about her faith declaration but was intrigued and began coming along to church with her.

Not long after, Becky and Chris were at an evening church service when 'Bill the bus driver' shared his testimony. It was a simple gospel presentation, which didn't impact Becky much, given that she had known the good news from a young age. However, sitting beside her, Chris was in floods of tears and gave his life to Christ there and then. A year later, they were married.

After graduating, Becky took a job at a press agency in the north-west. None of the UK's leading newspapers have offices in the north of England, so they use press agencies to cover stories. She told me that she wrote features, and I immediately felt nervous about my interview skills; what was she thinking of me as I jotted down her story? While working for the agency, she discovered that she loved listening to women and giving them a voice. Some of the issues she covered included rape and childhood sexual abuse. I wondered aloud if those had been hard to cover when she was only in her twenties, and she confessed she had felt overwhelmed sometimes.

When Becky's second child was born, there were some complications, and she ended up being rushed into surgery for an emergency C-section. She found herself struggling to breast-feed her son after all the trauma but received some wonderful help from breast-feeding coaches. Consequently, rather than returning to work at the press agency, she told Chris she wanted to give something back and become a breast-feeding coach herself. Chris was surprised but gave her his full support, and this was her first step into working full-time supporting women. Her breast-feeding coaching skills are still helpful today at the refuges.

Having worked as a coach for three years, Becky realized there was no chance of further promotion. To proceed further, she needed midwifery qualifications, which she didn't have. This prompted a change of employment, and she found a job in a safe house for victims of modern slavery. Though she didn't know it then, God was steadily nudging her toward establishing Beauty for Ashes, and she was picking up valuable skills along the way. She moved from the safe house to the shelter where she was obligated to say no to women with NRPF status, and the rest is His-story.

Nowadays, she jokes that Chris is often at the refuges more than she is. He's the handyman and on call to fix whatever is broken. Becky's children, who are 11 and 15, have witnessed the remarkable way God has worked through Becky and have seen the origins of Beauty for Ashes first-hand. Her favourite sound is hearing her two children sing in church. Becky tells them to ignore anyone who says Christianity is boring. As she puts it, God is more than willing to roll up his sleeves and get involved in the messiness of our lives; very often, we just get in the way. And, she adds, don't be surprised if he does something left-field.

I inquired about the future. What's next for someone who keeps saying yes to God? For now, she tells me three refuges are enough for her. She's looking forward to a more settled season once the third home is fully operational. However, there are multiple changes she'd like to see regarding legislation; the most urgent need is to alter the No Recourse to Public Funds regulations. She highlighted the work being done by Nicole Jacobs, the Domestic Abuse Commissioner,[4] and Karma Nirvana. Lately, Karma Nirvana has been running a campaign that tells vulnerable girls to put a metal spoon down their underwear if they are being taken against their will through a British airport and suspect they are on their way to a forced marriage. The spoon will set off alarms during the security process, and the girls will be taken to a private area where immigration officials can speak to them confidentially. It's a novel idea.

Throughout my interview with her, Becky has been radiant. God has done so much in her life, and she has witnessed so much provision and favour as she has set up Beauty for Ashes that she could barely contain her excitement to tell me. The stories kept pouring out, and if she hadn't had plans to celebrate her birthday, I'm sure she would have told me more and more instances of God's goodness. She reminds me of Mary, who said yes to becoming the mother of Jesus. Immediately after Mary obeyed God, she poured out a song of praise to him that is labelled the Magnificat (Luke 1:46–55). Like Mary,

Becky's praise stories are linked to her obedience. She praises God because she has submitted to him and can see what he can do when she says yes. That's why I've described her as a 'Magnifier' in the chapter title. I think she will continue to sing her beautiful song of praise to God. There is so much more for her to tell, and I'm glad I have been able to hear her sing about God's goodness and replay some of it here.

Conclusion

In presenting these chapters and stories, I feel as if I have sewn together a patchwork of personal narratives and motifs. Each experience in the book has graciously been entrusted to me by the men and women I've spoken with. In coming to the end of the book, I realize there are quite a few loose ends, and initially, I had hoped to tidy them up with one last chapter. However, after some prayer and reflection, I realized it wouldn't have been accurate to tie up the loose ends so neatly and present a tidy conclusion.

The reality is that women in Pakistan are still on the run from their abusers, activists are still campaigning for justice, and refugees continue to wait for somewhere to call home. Their lives continue to unfold, and there is still much work to be done before we declare a happy-ever-after ending to their stories. I long for the day when Christians and women especially can live without fear of violence. So, although it feels difficult, leaving some loose ends is a much more accurate reflection of their lives.

All the accounts in this book are linked by the way in which some men use women for their own ends. In the beginning, I focused on the experiences of Christian women in Pakistan, and the later chapters examined the impact on women in the West who face honour-based abuse in the wake of forced marriages to men from Pakistan. The outcome of the varied abuses each of these groups of women face is that none of them feels secure within or travelling to Pakistan. Although everyone I've spoken to is fiercely patriotic and longs to see Pakistan become a stable, just and prosperous nation, they each believe that it isn't a safe country for them to remain in or visit. All of them expressed immense sadness because of this.

The outcome is that many people within Pakistan, not only the country's Christians, frequently consider leaving the country, even if they don't do anything concrete to migrate. The thought is always at the back of their minds and, as a persecuted minority, Christians find it especially hard to see a future for themselves in their home country. The corrupt judicial system means that anyone lacking resources can become a victim, and there is a permanent state of insecurity. The poorest in the country, from any religion, fear they may be turned on next and will be unable to defend themselves. This, in turn, fuels the desire for arranged and forced marriages with those already living overseas and has led to numerous Pakistani refugees seeking asylum in safer countries, where they face long waits (the average is over fifteen years[1]) to be resettled.

Getting to know Pakistan and all its idiosyncrasies has been like becoming acquainted with a distant cousin. In 2025, I was able to visit Pakistan, meet many of my contacts and gather more stories; it was wonderful to finally see for myself this incredible country. So much is similar to Nepal, where I lived for four years; the sights and sounds of everyday life are much the same but, historically and religiously, the two countries are like chalk and cheese, or perhaps kebabs and momos are a better analogy. I have loved my introduction to the country; all the Pakistanis I've spoken with and the books I've read have been fascinating and absorbing. The country has a rich literary history, much of which has been written or translated into English, in which I have happily immersed myself. What an incredible and beautiful place with a fascinating culture.

Pakistan is a relatively new country, and it is ambitious, anxious to be taken seriously on the world stage and seeking international treaties. Yet the nation had a brutal and bloody birth at Partition and now engages in mutual loathing with its closest neighbour, India. Like a divorced couple, the two countries claim to have moved on but constantly compare themselves to each other and hark back to their former alliance.

The two countries' race to outperform each other is not only about nuclear arms, military might and who has the best academic institutions but is a competition between religions. Will the Hindu ideology in India or the dominant Muslim world-view in Pakistan lead to better outcomes for their citizens?

Islam tells its adherents that it is through their own efforts they will achieve salvation and enter paradise. There is no gift of grace and so, when a Muslim cannot purify themselves, which is inevitable given the human propensity to sin, it is no surprise that they look to blame someone else. When applied on a national level, this has led to the scapegoating of Christians and other minorities. As Pakistan tries to achieve wealth and develop, when its efforts fail, those on the margins are blamed.

Hence the wildly popular blasphemy laws. Until I began my research, I had no idea how popular they were among the general population of Pakistan. Though I had been hearing about them for years, I imagined that the average citizen did not approve of physically punishing someone for simply saying the wrong thing. I had presumed that free speech was a more prevalent value, but I was wrong.

As a Christian, I'm not entirely without sympathy for the blasphemy laws, though. Perhaps you also recognize the prick of irritation felt when someone nearby says, 'Oh, Christ', in anger or frustration. Listening to a podcast interview with comedian Frank Skinner recently, I'm encouraged to know that I'm not alone in this.[2] But I'm certain neither of us would ever want to chastise the person who blasphemed and offended us, let alone beat them up for it. As Christians, forgiveness is our superpower.

In my speech at the UN Parallel Event, I likened the blasphemy laws to a network of laser beams that criss-cross a room. The slightest wrong move will trigger alarms and an overwhelming response. This is the terror that Christians and other minorities live under in Pakistan; they constantly fear saying or doing the wrong thing and that the Muslims they live among will administer swift vengeance. Although I made my speech before my conversation with Pastor Allam, I had the opportunity to ask him if he agreed with my laser-beam metaphor, and he gave it his seal of approval.

Sadly, in the few weeks after I finished the majority of this book, there were two utterly horrific and contemptible murders of Pakistani Christians. I read about a 72-year-old man who was stoned to death in Sargodha for allegedly burning pages of the Koran. I, unwittingly, clicked on a link and saw images of his shrouded body covered in dust on the ground, with a mob around him. The image seared my soul; if you have ever wondered what hate looks like, this was it. The gathered mob had utter disdain for the humanity of a small elderly man.

Just three weeks later, another Christian man was killed by a mob in Swat. On this occasion, he was burnt alive for purportedly desecrating the Koran. At the time of writing he has not been named, but it is known that he was a Punjabi tourist to the area.

In both tragic instances, the police were utterly powerless to help the Christians they were supposed to protect. In Sargodha, they may even have been complicit in handing over the man to the furious crowd and, in Swat, the police station was burned down. Though some arrests were made after each tragedy, to date, no one has been prosecuted nor punished for the role they played in the violence. It is this profound lack of justice that propels Christians to seek out safer lives elsewhere.

Deplorably, there are sexual predators in every country; however, the extent to which they can act on their deviances is determined largely by the law of their nation and its culture. In my view, there is nothing about Islam that makes men abuse women or encourages them to prey on Christians. However, the blasphemy laws provide a cover for them to get away with abuse since the Christian minority is so vulnerable within Pakistan. Police officers readily ignore the testimony of Christians and, if a Muslim feels at all threatened by a Christian, they can 'cry blasphemy', and popular opinion will come to their rescue. It appears to be quite easy to rally a mob to enact summary 'justice' on your Christian rivals. Consequently, a Christian family cannot safely bring men (of any religion) to account for violence against them because they fear being accused of blasphemy and the possible ensuing mob violence.

In her groundbreaking book, *Why Men Rape*, Tara Kaushal[3] examines the situation of abuse against women in India (rather than Pakistan). She comes to the same conclusion: Islam does not promote rape; however, some of the cultural practices around separating men and women, especially concealing women from their sons under layers of clothing, may interrupt maternal bonding. When these are taken to the extreme, some young boys may not learn to read emotional cues and body language from their mothers and sisters, leading them to objectify all women and potentially leading to sexual violence.

Once a man no longer has empathy for women, the blasphemy laws enable sexual predators to prey on the weak, which in Pakistan's case includes Hindus, Christians and certain Muslim minorities such as the Ahmadis. If we want to stop forced marriages and conversion, then we must act to end the blasphemy laws. But how?

Whenever a violent attack takes place against Christians in Pakistan, in the days that follow, a flurry of politicians and various institutions within the country decry the attacks. They make statements and put out press briefings asserting their abhorrence of the hatred and bloodshed. These groups are generally made up of elite older men, with perhaps a token woman sitting alongside them. They do not reflect the youthful make-up of Pakistan, where the average age is just 20.[4] If we are going to see a wholesale change in attitude towards Christians and eventually a repeal of the blasphemy laws, then change must come from below. The man or woman on the street, or in the market, needs to believe that the blasphemy rules are unfair and are being twisted to further the cause of those who already have power. Endless missives from above and appeals from concerned observers, such as the UN, will do nothing if the hearts and minds of average Pakistanis aren't changed.

My favourite Pakistani author is Mohsin Hamid. He is a novelist and a columnist for publications such as the *New York Times* and the *Observer*. Furthermore, having lived in the USA and UK and then choosing to return to settle in Lahore, he offers an insightful and optimistic view of Pakistan. Yet even he agrees that 'Our problems are not insurmountable. Pakistan is, simply put, a land that mistreats its minorities and its majority. It is ripe for a revolution, except that it already has many trappings of democracy: elected assemblies, free media, independent judges. A revolution in our thinking and behaviour, brought about by sustained pressure from below, is what is really called for.' He hopes that 'We might, for example, shift from disputes over blasphemy laws to actually delivering due process of law'.[5] I concur with his prognosis, and both Cecil (featured in Chapter 1) and I are encouraged that a secular writer also sees the urgent need to better protect minorities.

Lasting positive outcomes for Christians in Pakistan are possible, but achieving them will require changing the mindset of the majority of Pakistanis who are currently in favour of the blasphemy laws and, if anything, wish to see them toughened. The first step in social change on this scale is inspiring a 'silent majority'[6] who agree on the need for reform but don't yet feel bold enough to call for it. I also sought Cecil's opinion on this to understand whether he thought a silent majority currently existed within Pakistan. His response saddened me, as he doesn't think such a group exists yet, but I can't help feeling a clear sense from God that, as Christians in the West, this is what we should be praying for. Pakistan needs a silent majority who will, in time, become a vocal majority who will call for the blasphemy laws to be applied without bias before eventually being repealed.

Another term for achieving sweeping change in the hearts and minds of a nation's people is 'revival'. It feels like a crazy and ambitious desire, but I pray for a Christian revival to transform Pakistan, too. Prayer can move mountains but, often, organizations working in Pakistan who stand up for Christians ask for prayer only after significant acts of violence and persecution. I believe our prayers need to be continual. We can persistently ask God to soften hearts, for the bright light of the gospel to come, and for justice to be done.

Cecil is also a staunch advocate for using the school curriculum and textbooks to promote the positive and patriotic role that Christians have played in Pakistan's history. By accurately reflecting the actions and sacrifices of Christians and Hindus, he believes that, from a young age, all Pakistanis could learn to view minorities favourably. This is in keeping with the opinion of the founding father of Pakistan, Muhammad Ali Jinnah, whose vision for the country was reflected in the white stripe of the flag, which represents the inclusion of minorities. It would improve the status of Christians in Pakistan if more of the country's citizens also shared Jinnah's vision.

Thankfully, there has been good news from Pakistan in the past few months, too. Nationally, the marriage age for Christians has been upped to 18 years[7] which, provided it is implemented in every court of law, is promising news for Christian girls who are abducted and forced to marry. So long as they can appear in court, and their birth certificates are believed, there is now greater opportunity to have their sham marriages annulled. Sadly, since the law does not apply to Muslim girls, if a falsified conversion certificate is produced, the girl would not be protected, but at least some progress has been made. Let us pray that the law can be extended to girls from all religions; I congratulate all the Christians and other people of faith who presented the bill before Pakistan's Senate.

If you want to do something concrete in addition to praying, I urge you to contact the organizations listed in the back of this book to see how you can donate and volunteer your time. To understand more about forced marriage, it is possible to register for a free training course developed in conjunction with the Foreign Office. Perhaps the easiest way to make a tangible impact and become relationally involved is to work with refugees, either by sponsoring a family to safety or aiding those who have already arrived in your country.

If you are a campaigner, please consider contacting your government representative and calling on them to open up more safe routes for refugees. Our media makes a lot of noise about illegal asylum seekers, but little is written about refugees who adhere to UNHCR's processes and wait many years before being brought to safety. Why not explain Emaan's story to someone with influence who may be able to help other families like hers?

While writing this book, I have experienced many God-orchestrated 'coincidences' that have led me to the right people at the right time. However, I was most overcome with God's presence when I read the Bible story in 1 Samuel 11 immediately before receiving photos of Joseph carrying out his daring rescue at a brick-kiln. I still have goosebumps when I think about it. The message was clear; the Spirit of God was with him and enabling him to bravely free a young Christian woman who had been mutilated and forcibly married for years.

What does this mean for us, though? Should more Christians hire bodyguards and take up arms so we can attempt similar rescues? I don't have a clear answer; however, I recently listened to an interview with Dave Eubank, who founded the Free Burma Rangers.[8] He is an American Christian and former marine who provides military training to ethnic Burmese freedom fighters so they can document atrocities and help free their fellow citizens from the violent oppression meted out by the Burmese Government. It's inspiring and ridiculously dangerous work, captured powerfully in a documentary film.[9] Dave and his family even go behind the frontlines in Iraq to use their skills to rescue the forgotten.

Do Joseph and Dave have exceptional callings, or should we imitate them? I honestly don't know; my theology on this is still developing. However, I don't think God will sit idly by forever, watching his people in Pakistan suffer. There are many occasions in the Bible when he hears his people crying out to him before he takes decisive action. In these instances, his followers are called to be attentive to his voice and to obey. That is not easy in hostile situations with a genuine risk to life. If you believe you may be called to go to Pakistan and become involved like this, I'd love to pray for you; please get in touch.

Thank you for choosing this book and for reading it to the end. I believe God has put it in your hands for a purpose, and I pray that you will readily and easily discern what that is. There is so much need and oppression against Christians in Pakistan. I hope you can find a way to be a light to those who live there and are crying out to God to remember them; they are Our Sisters

Bibliography

Ahmari, S. *From Fire by Water* (London: Hodder & Stoughton, 2019).
Aid to the Church in Need, *Religious Freedom in the World Report 2023* (Königstein: ACN International, 2023).
Anonymous. *A Woman in Berlin* (London: Virago Press, 2005).
Aslam, L. *Building Bridges: The Role of the Church and the Bible in Supporting Immigrants and Refugees* (Seattle, WA: Amazon, 2024).
Brooke-Smith, R. *Storm Warning: Riding the Crosswinds in the Pakistan-Afghan Borderlands* (London: I.B. Tauris, 2013).
Center for Social Justice. *Human Rights Observer: A Factsheet on the Rights of Religious Minorities in Pakistan* (Lahore: Center for Social Justice, 2022).
Gourevitch, P. *We Wish to Inform You that Tomorrow We Will Be Killed with Our Families: Stories from Rwanda* (New York: Picador, 1998).
Gul, I. *The Most Dangerous Place: Pakistan's Lawless Frontier* (London: Penguin, 2010).
Gupta, R. (ed.) *From Homebreakers to Jailbreakers: Southall Black Sisters* (London: Zed, 2003).
Hamid, M. *Exit West* (London: Penguin, 2018).
— *The Reluctant Fundamentalist* (London: Penguin, 2007).
Hanif, M. *Our Lady of Alice Bhatti* (London: Jonathan Cape, 2011).
His Majesty's Chief Inspectorate of Constabulary. *How the Police Respond to Victims of Sexual Abuse when the Victim is from an Ethnic Minority Background and may be at Risk of Honour-based Abuse* (Birmingham: HMICFRS, 2022).

Husain, M. *Broken Threads: My Family from Empire to Independence* (London: HarperCollins, 2024).

Jacob, A. *The Priest from Pakistan* (Rickmansworth: Instant Apostle, 2023).

Kazmi, W.A. *Asia Bibi: A Christian Woman's Plight through the Eyes of a Muslim* (Seattle, WA: Kindle, 2018).

Khan, T. *Determination* (London: Footnote Press, 2024).

Mai, M. *In the Name of Honour* (London: Virago Press, 2006).

McCord, K. *In the Land of Blue Burqas* (Chicago: Moody, 2012).

Meroff, D. *SOS: Save Our Sisters: An Action Guide for Helping Girls and Women at Risk Worldwide* (Secunderabad, TG: Authentic Media, 2014).

Mission Frontiers, *The Power of Honor* 37. No. 1 (Pasadena, CA: US Center for World Mission, 2015).

Nordberg, J. *The Underground Girls of Kabul: The Hidden Lives of Afghan Girls Disguised as Boys* (London: Virago Press, 2015).

Open Doors International. *The 2024 Gender Report* (Witney, Oxon: World Watch Research, 2024).

Pinault, D. *Notes from the Fortune-telling Parrot: Islam and the Struggle for Religious Pluralism in Pakistan* (London: Equinox, 2008).

Robinson, S. *In Our Own Language: The Story of Bible Translation* (UK: Peldon Press, 2019).

Safe Lives, *SafeLives Dash Risk Checklist for the Identification of High Risk Cases of Domestic Abuse, Stalking and 'Honour'-based Violence* (Bristol: Safe Lives, 2015).

Shamsie, K. *Kartography* (London: Bloomsbury, 2011).

— *Best of Friends* (London: Bloomsbury, 2022).

Sheikh, B. and R.H. Schneider. *I Dared to Call Him Father: The Miraculous Story of a Muslim Woman's Encounter with God* (Old Tappan, NJ: Chosen, 1978).

Sidhwa, B. *Ice-Candy Man* (London: Daunt, 2016).

Singh, J. *Helium* (London: Bloomsbury, 2013).

Taylor, C. *New Yorkers: A City and Its People in Our Time* (London: John Murray, 2021)

Thanasingh, P. *Rev. Robert Clark: Missionary to Punjab and Pakistan* (Nashik, MH: Eternal Light, 2021).

Voice for Justice, *Conversion Without Consent: A Report on the Abductions, Forced Conversions, and Forced Marriages of Christian Girls and Women in Pakistan* (Fairfax, VA: Jubilee Campaign, 2022).

Wilson, K. *Where No One Has Heard: The Life of J. Christy Wilson Jr.* (Pasadena, CA: William Carey Library, 2016).

Woodberry, J.D. (ed.) *Muslims and Christians on the Emmaus Road* (Monrovia, CA: MARC, 1989).

Yousafzai, M., and C. Lamb. *I am Malala: The Girl Who Stood Up for Education and Was Shot by the Taliban* (London: Orion, 2013).

Zakaria, R. *Against White Feminism: Notes of Disruption* (London: Hamish Hamilton, 2021).

— *The Upstairs Wife: An Intimate History of Pakistan* (Boston, MA: Beacon Press, 2015).

— *Veil (Object Lessons)* (London: Bloomsbury, 2017).

Websites

Aid to the Church in Need International, 'Women Often Targeted in Discrimination of Christian Minorities' (2022) https://acninternational.org/violence-against-christian-women/ (accessed 14 Mar. 2024).

Alford, F. 'The Trauma of Rape can be Told' (2015) https://www.academia.edu/19830543/The_trauma_of_rape_can_be_told?source=swp_share (accessed 10 Nov. 2022).

BBC, 'Pakistan Blocks Wikipedia for "Blasphemous Content"' (2023) https://www.bbc.com/news/world-asia-64523501 (accessed 5 Feb. 2023).

— 'Pakistan: More than 100 Arrested after Churches Burned' (2023) https://www.bbc.com/news/world-asia-66517901 (accessed 27 Sept. 2023).
— 'Pakistan Overturns Christian Couple's Blasphemy Death Sentences' (2023) https://www.bbc.co.uk/news/world-asia-57347604 (accessed 16 Feb. 2023).
— 'What are Pakistan's Blasphemy Laws?' (2015) https://www.bbc.com/news/world-asia-48204815 (accessed 23 Jan. 2023).
Berkshire Live, 'Honour Based Violence Remembrance Day: Thames Valley Police Pledges Its Support' (2015) https://www.getreading.co.uk/news/reading-berkshire-news/honour-based-violence-remembrance-day-9647798 (accessed 8 May 2023).
British Asian Christian Association, 'Pakistan's Notoriously Draconian Blasphemy Laws Now Even Stricter' (2023) https://www.britishasianchristians.org/baca-news/pakistans-notoriously-draconian-blasphemy-laws-now-even-stricter/ (accessed 7 Feb. 2023).
Christian Solidarity Worldwide, 'Blasphemy Allegation Triggers Mob Attack on Christian Colony in Punjab' (2023) https://www.csw.org.uk/2023/08/16/press/6059/article.htm (accessed 9 Oct. 2023).
Deutche Welle, 'Why are More Pakistani Women Choosing to Divorce?' (2022) https://www.dw.com/en/why-are-more-pakistani-women-choosing-to-divorce/a-63116481 (accessed 5 Jul. 2023).
Development and Cooperation, 'Autocratic Governance: Decades of Military Rule' (2018) https://www.dandc.eu/en/article/brief-history-military-rule-pakistan (accessed 24 Jan. 2023).
European Parliament, 'European Parliament resolution of 29 April 2021 on the blasphemy laws in Pakistan, in particular the case of Shagufta Kausar and Shafqat Emmanuel (2021/2647(RSP))' (2021) https://www.europarl.europa.eu/doceo/document/TA-9-2021-0157_EN.html (accessed 16 Feb. 2023).

Glessener Höhe (2023) https://de.wikipedia.org/wiki/Glessener_Höhe (accessed 28 Apr. 2023).

Ground Report, 'UK Muslims to Root Out Forced Marriages' (2008) https://www.groundreport.com/uk-muslims-to-root-out-forced-marriages/ (accessed 13 May 2022).

The Guardian, 'A Short Walk to Tragedy' (2005) https://www.theguardian.com/theguardian/2005/sep/08/features11.g23 (accessed 15 Jun. 2023).

—— '"I Fear They Will Kill Me for Talking": The Pakistani Poet Abducted for His Activism' (2024) https://www.theguardian.com/world/article/2024/jul/22/i-fear-they-will-kill-me-for-talking-the-pakistani-poet-abducted-for-his-activism (accessed 22 Jul. 2024).

Inayat, S., and N. Sadiq, 'Empowerment or Subjugation? Women Through the Lens of Lollywood Films' (2019) https://doi.org/10.1007/s12119-019-09664-w (accessed 8 Apr. 2024).

India Today, 'No, Pakistan's Non-Muslim Population Didn't Decline from 23% to 3.7% as BJP Claims' (2019) https://www.indiatoday.in/india/story/pakistan-bangladesh-non-muslim-population-citizenship-amendment-bill-bjp-1627678-2019-12-12 (accessed 27 Jan. 2023).

Kross Konnection, 'Blasphemy Law, Capital Punishment and Psychological Loopholes' (2022) https://krosskonnection.pk/2022/11/blasphemy-law-capital-punishment-and-psychological-loopholes/ (accessed 1 Jul. 2024).

La Stampa, 'Pakistani Couple Sentenced to Death for Blasphemy' (2015) https://www.lastampa.it/vatican-insider/en/2015/02/16/news/pakistani-couple-sentenced-to-death-for-blasphemy-1.35295238/ (accessed 26 Mar. 2023).

Pontificio Istituto per le Missioni Estere, *Asia News*, 'Blasphemy a Pretext to Attack Christian Churches and Homes in Jaranwala' (2023) https://www.asianews.it/news-en/In-Jaranwala-blasphemey-used-as-pretext-to-attack-Christian-churches-and-homes-58980.html (accessed 27 Sept. 2023).

— *Asia News*, 'Islamabad Tightens Blasphemy Laws' (2023) https://www.asianews.it/news-en/Islamabad-tightens-blasphemy-laws-57582.html (accessed 24 Jan. 2023).

— *Asia News*, 'Not Only Naval'nyj: Torture in Russian Lagers' (2024) https://www.asianews.it/news-en/Not-Only-Naval'nyj.-Torture-in-Russian-Lagers-60267.html (accessed 4 Mar. 2024). Naval'nyj (all one word) is the way this website is showing the name Alexei Navalny, who died in Russia.

— *Asia News*, 'Okara: Fleeing Abduction and Forced Marriage, the Clavary [bravery] of a Christian Teenager' (2023) https://www.asianews.it/news-en/Okara:-Fleeing-abduction-and-forced-marriage,-the-clavary-of-a-Christian-teenager-59221.html (accessed 26 Sept. 2023).

Restored, 'Why We Do what We Do' (2011) https://www.restored-uk.org/about/blog/why-we-do-what-we-do/ (accessed 10 Jul. 2024).

United Nations, 'Prof. Tomoya Obokata Special Rapporteur on Contemporary Forms of Slavery' (2020) https://www.ohchr.org/en/special-procedures/sr-slavery/prof-tomoya-obokata (accessed 15 Dec. 2023).

Washington Post, 'A Two-sided Descent into Full-scale War' (2008) https://www.washingtonpost.com/wp-dyn/content/article/2008/08/16/AR2008081600502_pf.html (accessed 5 Mar. 2024).

The White Post, 'NCJP Applauds Efforts to Combat Forced Marriages and Conversions' (2024) https://thewhiteposts.com/ncjp-applauds-efforts-to-combat-forced-marriages-and-conversions/ (accessed 12 Sept. 2024).

Zakaria, Rafia, *CNN Opinion*, 'It Will Take more than Laws to End Honor Killings in Pakistan' (2019) https://edition.cnn.com/2019/03/28/opinions/pakistan-honor-killings-afzal-kohistani-zakaria/index.html (accessed 23 Jul. 2023).

Podcasts

Musselman, Greg. 'Muslim Man Sentenced to 25 Years for Murdering Christian Woman', 3 Nov. 2023, *Closer to the Fire with Greg Musselman*, available on Spotify (accessed 1 Dec. 2023).

Musselman, Greg. 'Muslim Man Sentenced to 25 Years for Murdering Christian Woman (encore)', 24 Jun. 2024, *Closer to the Fire with Greg Musselman*, available on Spotify (accessed 25 Jun. 2024).

Petersen, Kristian. 'Rafia Zakaria, "Veil" (Bloomsbury Academic, 2017)', 13 Dec. 2017, *New Books in Religion*, available on Spotify (accessed 4 May 2023).

Sackur, Stephen. 'Jasvinder Sanghera: Abuse and the Church of England', 29 Jan. 2024, *HARDTalk*, available on BBC Sounds (accessed 31 Mar. 2024).

Films and Television

Blinded by the Light (2019) distributed by Entertainment One.
The Push: Murder on the Cliff (2024) distributed by Channel 4.
Stolen Lives: The Plight of Girls from Minority Religions Facing Forced Marriages and Conversions (2023) distributed by ADF International.

How to Help

Abduction and forced marriage of Christian women and girls in Pakistan

Cecil & Iris Chaudhry Foundation (CICF)

www.facebook.com/cicfpakistan
The Cecil & Iris Chaudhry Foundation is an independent, non-government, non-profit organization dedicated to eradicating injustice in society by advocating on behalf of the under-privileged, under-represented and marginalized groups in Pakistan.

Centre for Legal Aid, Assistance and Settlement (CLAAS)

www.claas.org.uk
A Christian organization committed to addressing ongoing religious persecution in Pakistan, with a particular focus on providing support for persecuted Christians and others from minority religious communities. Since its foundation in 1998, CLAAS staff, including lawyers and volunteers, have championed the cause of persecuted Christians and others, helping thousands of poverty-stricken and traumatized victims of religious persecution. Their ministry is based on the proclamation of Proverbs 31:8–9:

> Speak up for those who cannot speak for themselves,
> for the rights of all who are destitute.
> Speak up and judge fairly;
> defend the rights of the poor and needy.

Christian Solidarity Worldwide (CSW)

www.csw.org.uk

CSW's team of specialist advocates work in over twenty countries across Africa, Asia, Latin America and the Middle East to ensure that the right to freedom of religion or belief is upheld and protected. Their vision is a world free from religious persecution, where everyone can practise a religion or belief of their choice. As an organization, they are proud of their Christian heritage, identity and values: these are the foundations of all they do. This means that they believe in the power of prayer to transform situations, and they encourage their supporters to join them in praying for the cases and issues they work on.

Jubilee Campaign

https://www.jubileecampaign.co.uk in the UK; www.jubileecampaign.online in Europe; www.jubileecampaign.org in the USA

The Jubilee Campaign exists to give a voice to those suffering in silence. It promotes the human rights and religious liberty of ethnic and religious minorities around the world, works to restore the dignity of victims of human trafficking, and provides support to refugees in search of a peaceful tomorrow. This is the organization that supports Joseph in his work.

Open Doors International

www.opendoors.org
Open Doors is a global membership organization with twenty-five national bases. They share one mission: to support persecuted Christians worldwide and strengthen what remains. The World Watch List is Open Doors' annual ranking of the fifty countries where Christians face the most extreme persecution.

Teach The Children

www.teachthechildren.website
The Teach The Children Foundation is an initiative of the Jubilee Campaign Netherlands Foundation, a human rights organization that works on a political and legal level for persecuted Christians. When men and women are imprisoned for their religion, forced into slave labour or simply have a hard life due to discrimination and poverty, their children are the victims. By educating children, they help them grow up to be citizens who can make a positive contribution to society. In countries riven by conflict where minority groups face discrimination and persecution, the Teach The Children Foundation wants to use education as a means to break through persistent poverty and social exclusion and to counter terrorism, hatred and religious extremism.

Honour-based abuse and forced marriage in the UK

'Awareness of forced marriage' – free course

www.virtual-college.co.uk/resources/free-courses/awareness-of-forced-marriage
It is estimated that between approximately eight and ten thousand forced marriages of British citizens take place every year,

often resulting in devastating long-term consequences for the victims. This online course has been developed with the Forced Marriage Unit of the Foreign Office and aims to raise awareness, challenge perceptions and inform participants of the correct actions to take should they suspect someone is at risk.

Beauty for Ashes

www.beautyforashesrefuges.org
Beauty for Ashes Refuges envisions a world free from domestic abuse. They want to transform the lives of the most marginalized people by providing temporary accommodation in the form of refuge provision for migrant women with insecure immigration status and children with no recourse to public funds who are fleeing domestic abuse.

Evangelical Alliance South Asian Forum

www.eauk.org/what-They-do/networks/south-asian-forum
The South Asian Forum connects, unites and represents South Asians across the UK. Set up in 2010, it exists for two primary purposes: to connect and support the UK's growing South-Asian church, thereby enhancing its impact within the wider church, and to equip the church to engage with South Asians of different faiths and cultures confidently.

Karma Nirvana

www.karmanirvana.org.uk
In 1993, Karma Nirvana became the first specialist charity for victims and survivors of honour-based abuse in the UK. Since then, they have led the campaign against honour-based

abuse, supporting, empowering and educating those impacted so they can live a life free of abuse. They run the national Honour-Based Abuse Helpline, producing data on honour-based abuse, training front-line practitioners and professionals, and campaigning for change, working with parliamentarians and policy-makers.

Restored

www.restored-uk.org
Restored is a Christian charity working to raise awareness of domestic abuse, to support survivors and to equip the church to do the same. Since 2010, they've been speaking up about violence against women and equipping churches across the UK and beyond to respond to domestic abuse. Their Survivors' Network supports over six hundred female Christian survivors of domestic abuse, and their Survivor's Handbook has proved to be an invaluable resource to those navigating the challenges of leaving an abuser.

Migration and refugees

Canada: Group of Five

https://www.canada.ca/en/immigration-refugees-citizenship/services/refugees/sponsor-refugee/private-sponsorship-program/groups-five.html
A group of five (G5) is five or more Canadian citizens or permanent residents who have arranged to sponsor a refugee living abroad to come to Canada. G5s can sponsor only applicants who are recognized as refugees by either the United Nations

Refugee Agency (UNHCR) or the government of the country (foreign state) where the refugee lives. This is the sponsorship model that Emaan and her family will benefit from, but other sponsorship models are possible in Canada.

Freedom from Torture

www.freedomfromtorture.org
Freedom from Torture is dedicated to supporting survivors of torture to heal and feel safe and strong again. Many of the people they support are seeking sanctuary and have been placed in accommodation around the UK. To meet their needs, they have centres in Birmingham, Glasgow, London, Manchester and Newcastle.

Kathmandu International Christian Congregation (KICC) – Equipping Displaced Communities (EDC)

www.kiccnepal.org/service-programs
The EDC takes care of the refugee community in Kathmandu. Help be the hands and feet of Christ.

Safe Passage

www.safepassage.org.uk
They believe every person has the right to be safe to be with their family and safe to rebuild their lives. Their vision is a world where the people who need it have safe passage to a place of safety, family and justice. They champion the rights of refugees and displaced people as they flee persecution, using the law to help them access a safe route to a place of safety.

They work alongside refugees to campaign for change and build public support for safe passage for all. Their legal teams in France, Greece and the UK work to help child refugees reunite with their families through a safe route to a place where they can rebuild their lives.

Sponsor Refugees

www.sponsorrefugees.org
They work with community groups across the UK to welcome and resettle a refugee family to their local neighbourhood through community sponsorship, which allows ordinary people to take matters into their own hands and transform the lives of a refugee family. Anyone can get involved in community sponsorship: a group of friends or members of a faith institution. Sponsorship not only saves lives but also builds strong, resilient communities.

Notes

Introduction

1. I later discovered that 'quite' is used differently between British and American English. I use it in the British sense, which means 'fairly' or 'somewhat'. Americans use it to mean 'very'.
2. BBC, 'The Choir: Gareth's Best in Britain' (2016) https://www.bbc.co.uk/programmes/p04jqsjb (accessed 10 Nov. 2022).

1 Heir – Cecil

1. S. Rushdie, *Shame* (London: Jonathan Cape, 1983).
2. Rushdie, *Shame*.
3. *Express Tribune*, 'Obituary: War hero Cecil Chaudhry passes away' (2012) https://tribune.com.pk/story/364519/obituary-war-hero-During (accessed 30 Jan. 2023).
4. GreaterPakistan PK, 'Pakistan War Hero: Cecil Chaudhry – PAF Fighter Pilot' (2012) https://youtu.be/i29nSbpkTPE?si=_R8w4_po7IWupvmD (accessed 31 Jan. 2023).
5. I have written at length about the conditions at brick-kilns in Asia in my book *Come with Me to Kathmandu: Twelve Powerful Stories of Women's Courageous Faith in Nepal* (Bletchley: Authentic Media, 2023), ch. 11.
6. Center for Research and Security Studies, 'Blasphemy Cases in Pakistan: 1947–2021' (2022) https://crss.pk/blasphemy-cases-in-pakistan-1947-2021/ (accessed 8 Feb. 2023).
7. S. Inskeep, *Instant City: Life and Death in Karachi* (London: Penguin, 2011).

2 Brave – Abhita

1. Pakistan Press Foundation, 'Pressing Perils: Pakistani Journalists Navigate Challenges Reporting on Religious Minorities' (2019) https://www.pakistanpressfoundation.org/pressing-perils-pakistani-journalists-navigate-challenges-reporting-on-religious-minorities/ (accessed 13 Oct. 2023).

3 Lionheart – Joseph

1. The organization I run, Women Without Roofs, works with survivors of human-trafficking and I tell the story of a survivor's mother in my book *Come with Me to Kathmandu*.
2. Inskeep, *Instant City*.
3. A. Bibi and A. Tollet, *Free at Last: A Cup of Water, a Death Sentence, and an Inspiring Story of One Woman's Unwavering Faith* (Savage, MN: BroadStreet, 2020).
4. S. Tazeer, *Lost to the World: A Memoir of Faith, Family, and Five Years in Terrorist Captivity* (New York: Farrar, Straus & Giroux, 2022).
5. Bibi and Tollet, *Free at Last*.
6. Jubilee Campaign, 'Shagufta and Shafqat Prisoners of Conscience, Released' (2021) https://jubileecampaign.org/shagufta-and-shafqat/ (accessed 16 Feb. 2023).
7. Voice for Justice, 'Meeting with Mr. H.E. Mr. Suljuk Mustansar Tarar, Ambassador of Pakistan to Netherlands' (2021) http://voiceforjustice.eu/blog/meeting-with-mr-h-e-mr-suljuk-mustansar-tarar-ambassador-of-pakistan-to-netherlands/ (accessed 22 Mar. 2023).
8. The Fourcast, *Gender Violence in Pakistan: Women Fighting Back*, available on Spotify (accessed 12 Dec. 2022).
9. I have written at length about how Christians can be used by God to roar for justice in my book, *Destination Transformation: A Forty-day Journey to Change the World, Written for People with Baggage* (Scotts Valley, CA: CreateSpace, 2015).
10. Voice for Justice, 'Meeting' (2024) http://voiceforjustice.eu (accessed 25 Mar. 2025).

5 Girl Child – Nira

1. Barnabas Fund, Editorial: 'The Vital Importance of Christian Schools in Pakistan' (2023) https://www.barnabasaid.org/gb/news/editorial-the-vital-importance-of-christian-schools-in-pakistan/ (accessed 19 Dec. 2023).
2. Anna Townsend, 'When the Needs of the World are Overwhelming' (2023) https://www.bible.com/reading-plans/36328-when-the-needs-of-the-world-are-overwhelming (written Dec. 2022). This newsletter contains the painting, *The Good Samaritan* by Vincent van Gogh.
3. If you'd like to receive my emails, you can sign up here https://lp.constantcontactpages.com/su/oOAgYXH/OurSisters

6 Word Wielder – Marcela

1. The audio file of my interview with Hope FM is available on my website: https://dislocatedchristians.org/2023/09/06/my-story-my-song/
2. M. Szymanski, 'On the Misleading Use of the Terms "Forced Conversion" and "Forced Marriage" of Girls and Women' (Brussels, 2021: Working document, unpublished, available upon request).
3. P. Singer, *The Life You Can Save: How to Do Your Part to End World Poverty* (New York: Random, 2009).
4. Open Doors, 'World Watch List: Nigeria' (updated regularly) https://www.opendoors.org/en-US/persecution/countries/nigeria/ (accessed 6 Mar. 2024).
5. Congress, Government, House Resolution 82 (2024) https://www.congress.gov/bill/118th-congress/house-resolution/82?s=1&r=94 (accessed 6 Mar. 2024).
6. When a man explains to a woman something she already knows, or oversimplifies and talks condescendingly to a woman.

9 Tide Turner – Saima

1. The White Post, 'About Us' (2023) https://thewhiteposts.com/about-us/ (accessed 6 Mar. 2024).
2. The White Post, 'Remembering the Martyrs: 9th Anniversary of Youhanabad Church Bombings' (2024) https://thewhiteposts.com/remembering-the-martyrs-9th-anniversary-of-youhanabad-church-bombings/ (accessed 28 Mar. 2024).
3. Nicholas Sparks, *The Notebook: The Love Story to End All Love Stories* (London: Sphere, 2011).
4. The White Post, 'Lahore Joins Global Community in Observing World Water Day: Emphasis on Conservation and Awareness' (2024) https://thewhiteposts.com/lahore-joins-global-community-in-observing-world-water-day-emphasis-on-conservation-and-awareness/ (accessed 29 Mar. 2024).
5. S. Inayat and N. Sadiq, 'Empowerment or Subjugation? Women Through the Lens of Lollywood Films' (2019) *Sexuality & Culture* https://doi.org/10.1007/s12119-019-09664-w (accessed 25 Mar. 2024).
6. A. Khan, *Someone Like Her* (London: Orenda, 2023).

10 One of Us – Behien

1. Amnesty International, 'Pakistan Authorities Must Be Transparent about Covid 19 Cases in Prisons (2020) https://www.amnesty.org/en/latest/news/2020/05/pakistan-authorities-must-be-transparent-about-covid-19-cases-in-prisons/ (accessed 5 Dec. 2024).

11 Unexpected – Allam

1. Pontificio Istituto per le Missioni Estere, *Asia News*, 'Rashida's ordeal: ten years in chains in a forced marriage' (2024) https://www.asianews.it/news-en/Rashida's-ordeal:-ten-years-in-chains-in-a-forced-marriage-60326.html (accessed 30 Apr. 2024). The photo shows Rashida and the damage done to her nose.

2. *The Diplomat*, 'Jaranwala Church Attacks Another Example of the Misuse of Blasphemy Laws in Pakistan' (2023) https://thediplomat.com/2023/09/jaranwala-church-attacks-another-example-of-the-misuse-of-blasphemy-laws-in-pakistan/ (accessed 3 May 2024).
3. J. Goldingay, *Ignatian Approach* (Cambridge: Grove, 2002).
4. These photos and videos belong to Joseph. I have permission to show them at book talks, but I won't be posting them online. Please get in touch with me via the DislocatedChristians Facebook page if you'd like me to visit your church or small group.
5. Teach The Children (2019) https://www.teachthechildren.website/ (accessed 27 May 2024).

12 Apple of His Eye – Emaan

1. This idea is probably derived from 1 Thess. 2:9.
2. SAARC operates a little like the European Union and allows some movement between member states, similar to the Schengen zone. There are eight member countries: Afghanistan, Bangladesh, Bhutan, India, Maldives, Nepal, Pakistan and Sri Lanka.
3. Sponsor Refugees https://www.sponsorrefugees.org/ (accessed 10 Aug. 2024).

13 Seeker – Anna

1. J. Sanghera, *Shame* (London: Hodder & Stoughton, 2007); *Daughters of Shame* (London: Hodder & Stoughton, 2009); *Shame Travels* (London: Hodder & Stoughton, 2011).
2. Office for National Statistics, 'Suicides in England and Wales: 2021 Registrations' (2022) https://www.ons.gov.uk/peoplepopulationandcommunity/birthsdeathsandmarriages/deaths/bulletins/suicidesintheunitedkingdom/2021registrations (accessed 15 Jun. 2023).
3. Safelives, 'Ending Domestic Abuse' (2022) https://safelives.org.uk/ (accessed 15 Jun. 2023).
4. A. Rani, *The Right Sort of Girl* (London: Bonnier, 2021), p. 330.

14 Magnifier – Becky

1. Inspired . . . with Simon Guillebaud, *Living on a Prayer: Josh Green* (12 April 2024), available on Spotify (accessed 24 Apr. 2024).
2. E. Storkey, *Scars Across Humanity: Understanding and Overcoming Violence Against Women* (London: SPCK, 2015).
3. BBC, 'Almost Half of Family Courts to Allow Reporting in England and Wales (2024) https://www.bbc.com/news/uk-67940107 (accessed 16 Apr. 2024).
4. Domestic Abuse Commissioner (2022) https://domesticabusecommissioner.uk/ (accessed 25 Apr. 2024).

Conclusion

1. Church Leaders, 'Permanent Resettlement Not a Reality for 99 Percent of Refugees' (2020) https://churchleaders.com/outreach-missions/outreach-missions-articles/383949-permanent-resettlement-not-a-reality-for-99-percent-of-refugees.html (accessed 10 Sept. 2024).
2. Re-enchanting . . . *Comedy – Frank Skinner* (31 Oct. 2023), available on Spotify (accessed 18 Sept. 2024).
3. T. Kaushal, *Why Men Rape: An Indian Undercover Investigation* (Noida, UP: HarperCollins, 2020).
4. Statista, Pakistan, 'Average Age of the Population from 1950 to 2100' (2024) https://www.statista.com/statistics/383227/average-age-of-the-population-in-pakistan/ (accessed 19 Sept. 2024).
5. M. Hamid, *Discontent and its Civilizations: Dispatches from Lahore, New York and London* (New York: Riverhead, 2016), p. 130.
6. The term 'silent majority' in principle refers to a large block of voters who feel marginalized, silenced or underserved by the political system. It's commonly assumed that, if they voted en masse, this 'silent majority' would have an enormous ability to affect the outcome of any given election.

7 Pontificio Istituto per le Missioni Estere, *Asia News*, 'Church and Activists Praise Raising the Minimum Age for Christian Marriage' (2024) https://www.asianews.it/news-en/Church-and-activists-praise-raising-the-minimum-age-for-Christian-marriage-60258.html (accessed 12 Sept. 2024).
8 Inspired . . . with Simon Guillebaud, *Living Love in Living Hell: Dave Eubank* (6 Jun. 2024), available on Spotify (accessed 6 Jun. 2024).
9 *Free Burma Rangers* (2019) distributed by Deidox Films in partnership with Lifeway Films, available on Amazon Prime.

Authentic

We trust you enjoyed reading this book from Authentic. If you want to be informed of any new titles from this author and other releases you can sign up to the Authentic newsletter by scanning below:

Online:
authenticmedia.co.uk

Follow us:

www.ingramcontent.com/pod-product-compliance
Lightning Source LLC
Chambersburg PA
CBHW070726160426
43192CB00009B/1334